Ibsen in Practice

Relational Readings of Performance, Cultural Encounters and Power

Frode Helland

Series Editors
Enoch Brater and Mark Taylor-Batty

Bloomsbury Methuen Drama
An imprint of Bloomsbury Publishing Plc

B L O O M S B U R Y
LONDON · NEW DELHI · NEW YORK · SYDNEY

Bloomsbury Methuen Drama

An imprint of Bloomsbury Publishing Plc

Imprint previously known as Methuen Drama

50 Bedford Square	1385 Broadway
London	New York
WC1B 3DP	NY 10018
UK	USA

www.bloomsbury.com

BLOOMSBURY, METHUEN DRAMA and the Diana logo are trademarks of Bloomsbury Publishing Plc

First published 2015

© Frode Helland, 2015

Frode Helland has asserted his right under the Copyright, Designs and Patents Act, 1988, to be identified as author of this work.

British Library Cataloguing-in-Publication Data
A catalogue record for this book is available from the British Library.

ISBN:	HB:	978-1-4081-8497-4
	PB:	978-1-4725-1369-4
	ePDF:	978-1-4725-0500-2
	ePub:	978-1-4725-1496-7

Library of Congress Cataloging-in-Publication Data
A catalog record for this book is available from the Library of Congress.

Typeset by RefineCatch Limited, Bungay, Suffolk, UK
Printed and bound in Great Britain

To Thyra, Sigurd and Amund – my best and dearest.

Contents

Illustrations

Acknowledgements

Without the generous help of good colleagues and friends around the world, it would not have been possible to write a book like this one. Through conversations and discussions on five continents, they have helped me understand the world and the practice of Ibsen better. Through the whole process of writing and thinking about the materials presented in this book, Julie Holledge has been my primary intellectual sparring partner, helper, friend and critic. Without her enthusiasm, generosity and critical intelligence I would not have written this book. Our co-operation started with a research project called 'Ibsen Between Cultures', supported by the Norwegian Research Council (NRC). I would like to thank the NRC for the financial support that made it possible to put together a group of researchers from different parts of the world. This group of scholars have all contributed to the writing of the book through their insights from different locations around the world. He Chengzhou, Sun Jian and Xia Liyang from China; Kwok-kan Tam from Hong Kong; Kamaluddin Nilu, Sabiha Huq and Ahmed Ahsanuzzaman from Bangladesh; and Krishna Sen and Tapati Gupta from India, have all helped me understand many complexities better. Thanks also to Elisabeth Eide for sharing her knowledge of Ibsen in China and to Agnethe Haaland for sharing materials from her own archive and talking to me about her experiences of playing Nora in China.

I would also like to thank Thomas Ostermeier for his willingness to meet and to answer emails about his work. Thanks to Rebecca Berg at the Schaubühne in Berlin for her prompt answers and great help in finding the materials and figures I asked for. The work I have done on Chilean Ibsen productions would not have been possible without the assistance of Gabriela Espinosa, who helped set up all my interviews in Santiago and Valparaiso, and dig out reviews and other materials from archives in Chile. I would also like to thank the Chilean artists and theatre experts who generously took time to meet and share their knowledge and experience: Alejandro Castillo, Marcelo Alonso, Tamara Acosta, Alfredo Castro, Alexandra von Hummel, Maria de la Luz Hurtado, Matteo Iribarren, Ramon Lopez, Amparo Noguera, Hector Noguera, Alejandra Oviedo, Juan Andres Piña, Elsa Poblete, Rodrigo Ruiz and Sergio Zapata. I also owe thanks to Erika Fischer-Lichte and Rustom Bharucha for friendly, critical and enlightening discussions.

Without the help from a research assistant, this work would have taken much longer. Kaja S. Mollerin, Janicke S. Kaasa and Svein Henrik Nyhus have replaced each other in the job, and they have all contributed well beyond the call of duty. Randi Meyer, librarian at the Centre for Ibsen Studies, has been of valuable help in finding literature on the most diverse topics. William Dunstone and the copy editor at Methuen deserve great thanks for helping correct all the linguistic mistakes of a non-native speaker. My good colleague Ellen Rees has always been willing to engage in academic discussions, and to answer questions about details in the English language. Laila Y. Henriksen has helped in making administrative duties almost painless, and always efficient. Thanks also to my editors, Mark Taylor-Batty, Enoch Brater and Mark Dudgeon, for inviting me to publish the book in the Methuen Drama Engage series, for advice and critique, and for helping me keep on track. The responsibility for any mistakes and inaccuracies, however, is mine alone.

On a material level this work has been made possible through generous support from the Norwegian Writers' Association, who granted me a scholarship to do the basic research for the book. The Centre for Ibsen Studies at the University of Oslo has also given me good working conditions and a full year sabbatical to write the bulk of the text.

The author and publisher would like to thank the following for permission to reproduce copyright material: Schaubühne am Lehniner Platz and Arno Declair for Figures 1.2 and 1.3; Scanpix/Reuters for Figure 1.4; Alfredo Castro and Eduardo Cerón for Figure 2.1; Alfredo Castro and Ulises Nilo for Figure 2.2; Alexandra von Hummel and Rodrigo Ruiz for Figure 2.3; Le Hung and The Vietnam Youth Theatre for Figure 3.1; Dariush Mehrjui for Figures 3.2 and 3.3; Lin Zhaohua and Zhou Wei for Figure 3.4; Agnethe Haaland and the China National Contemporary Theatre for Figure 4.2; Robert McLaren, Chipawo and the New Horizon Theatre Company for Figure 5.1; and Scanpix/Reuters for Figure 5.2.

About the Author

Frode Helland is professor of Scandinavian Studies, and director of the Centre for Ibsen Studies at the University of Oslo, Norway. He has written extensively on Scandinavian literature, drama and theatre. He is the author of several books in Norwegian, and this is his first book in English.

Introduction

This book has been long in the making. I started collecting material for it in 2006, and it has been a great privilege to be able to see Ibsen performed on all continents during these years. The point of departure lies in quite a naïve wish to understand this conundrum: that the plays written by a nineteenth-century Norwegian with limited economic and cultural capital are still performed across the globe. Ibsen's dramatisation of the lies and sufferings of a Norwegian bourgeoisie living through a transitional phase of history still communicates across the greatest divides, in temporal, spatial, cultural, religious and political terms. Communication, then, undeniable communication, but not without friction, misunderstanding, distortion, feed-back, even conflict – hence the picture I will try to construct here will not be one of harmonious, seamless communication of the Great Artist's Work. This may have something to do with the nature of his plays, but more than anything with the contexts within which they are put to use. When a dramatic text moves from one culture to another, it does so because it can function in the new cultural context – it can 'speak' to a new audience, in a new and different situation. It is domesticated, becomes part of a local theatre tradition with its own norms, conflicts and needs. In practice it is not the same any more, but a classic like Ibsen has this almost protean quality, with the ability to change shape, to answer different needs, to be used in different contexts.

This book investigates the practice of Ibsen in this sense. The practical perspective leads, not surprisingly, to a major focus on Ibsen's plays as performed, above all in theatres. 'Practice' is a multivalent word, with a complex etymology. It is something done regularly, it is repeated; in order to get better we practise. It is also a trade – legal, medical, theatrical practise – a business of doing theatre with its own conventions, rules and material conditions. And it connotes truth and reality; in practice the theatre is by far the most important institution when it comes to the life of Ibsen's work. The Greek root of the word, praxis, points to the practical involvement with the world, with living, social reality. The life of dramatic literature is not up there in an ideal sphere, it is here and now, in specific practical circumstances, in unique theatrical performances, upheld by local theatre traditions, answering to local desires and needs, responding to new and old problems – not necessarily benign but as part of the world, at times part of the problems just as much as the solutions. Such is life, and as part of life art can be good or bad, but never transcends it. In practice Ibsen's plays are intertwined with the world, they are secular, worldly.

The following chapters analyse Ibsen productions on four continents, with a clear but not exclusive concentration on contemporary productions. One central finding in the book is how diverse and contradictory is the overall picture of Ibsen in practice. There are countless national, regional and local traditions of theatre, which will obviously influence the shape and function of the plays and playwrights performed. My goal has been to respect the uniqueness of these different traditions, and by no means to distil some kind of essential 'Ibsen'. Hence the title of this book could have been put in the plural; Ibsens in practice. There are many different Ibsens and Ibsen traditions in the world today, a point I have tried to clarify in each case through a fairly detailed analysis. The five chapters of the book are case studies, but not in the traditional sense of analysing a few unique productions that somehow stand out from the mass, nor are they chosen for geographical reasons, in the vain hope of 'covering' certain areas through the chosen cases. The cases are chosen because they can help make the big picture clearer. The goal of the book is to chart some of the relational factors that influence the practice in the performances analysed. This point may be posed in methodological terms. Where traditional studies of a playwright in performance tend to either treat a performance as a (quasi-)autonomous object to be interpreted in terms of internal structures and semiology, or as an example that can be explained through external factors, this book tries to investigate the relations between internal and external. It is, in other words, an attempt to escape the mutually exclusive alternatives of internal interpretation and external explanation.

Pierre Bourdieu has pointed to what he calls the 'ideology of the inexhaustible work of art' which masks 'the fact that the work of art is made not twice, but hundreds of times, thousands of times, by all those who have an interest in it'.[1] Following Bourdieu's critique of the ideological fetish-character of the inexhaustible 'work', I will emphasise the *social* and *political* production of 'Ibsen' as an ongoing process. The concept of 'interest' is indispensable in the argument of the book, as many of the cases will show how cultural, economic, ideological, political and social interests influence and motivate the practice of Ibsen. This is an important background for my choice of the term 'relational readings'. The objects of study are not primarily things, but relations between different things, systems and positions within systems. Such relations are many-faceted, and by no means one-sidedly oriented towards an 'original' or 'source'.

Each chapter will focus on some relations as being especially important for the understanding of the cases in question; not causality in a deterministic sense, but relational connections that contribute to the production of meaning and, in effect, to the production of 'Ibsen'. Hence the first chapter is the only one to focus on the work of a single director: Thomas Ostermeier. This is because he is the most influential Ibsen director today, which I will show not only through a discussion of his aesthetics and his politics, but also through an investigation of quantitative data on his Ibsen productions. The data will illustrate some of his influence, while also relating it to larger forces of economic and cultural power. Ostermeier's stagings of Ibsen seek to make him contemporary within a local cultural and political context that has

international relevance. The second chapter presents four versions of
A Doll's House from Chile. They are different from, but still not
without affinity to, some of the issues that come up in the discussion
of Ostermeier. The central relation in my investigation of the
Chilean productions is to a national trauma, the *coup d'état* in 1973
and the ensuing seventeen years of dictatorship. This shattering
upheaval, the event of the coup, has to be taken into account when
analysing the incredibly rich and diverse use of a writer like Henrik
Ibsen in the area of Chilean theatre. This may seem like a special case,
but alas, it is not.

In order to understand Ibsen in practice I have tried not to
investigate the primary practice of theatre and performance in
isolation, but to grasp how this practice is related to other practices.
It may come as a surprise to some that this has led me not so much to
the traditional practices of translating texts, making new editions,
publishing books, or transposing the plays into new media. Instead,
a central focus is on the far more important role that the state plays in
the transmitting and shaping of theatrical productions of Ibsen's plays
globally. On a very general level, the influence of the state can be seen
as working in two ways: as sponsorship or censorship. The two are not
opposites, as they often in paradoxical ways work in tandem. Obviously,
in countries that have explicit censorship of the theatre, what is performed
on stage will be influenced by this fact. In Chapter 3, I discuss this
influence through four highly different instances. The point lies not
only in the reality of repression but more importantly in how Ibsen
can pass under the radar of censorship in rich and challenging
productions where new meaning is produced through strategies of
deleting and supplementing. However, the state will often support
theatre; on the domestic level this goes without saying in countries as
different as Germany, Iran or Vietnam. Not so obvious is the role played
by a State like Norway through its support of Ibsen productions
performed abroad. One of the original claims in this book is that Ibsen
in practice is influenced by economic forces in this very literal sense. The
investigation into the financial background of a number of extremely

different productions originating in very different performance cultures will be an integral part of the book's argument. Norway is a small and insignificant country in the world, but it shares with other Western countries an increasingly strong emphasis on culture as a part of its soft diplomacy. The discussion of the many positive and negative aspects of the entanglement between culture and national politics is one part of the book with more general significance.

Because theatre is both a collective and a public art form, the claim is often made that it is also political. The more modest claim that theatre has political aspects or potential will find support in the following pages. In some cases the political aspects are evident in the content or form of the theatrical production itself, in other cases they will lie more in the relation between performance and context. For a theatre performance to succeed, the artists will have to be able to express and tap into living conflicts and contested topics, problems, feelings, needs and desires. A very basic goal in the following will be to try to understand how this is done in each case; that is, how the productions are addressing and transforming local needs, desires and conflicts within their culture of origin. Ibsen's first international, or European, breakthrough was made possible with plays that had strong political topicality – *Pillars of Society* (1877) and *A Doll's House* (1879) influenced the political debate in major European countries, and it is an interesting fact that these aspects are still strong in practice. Be it in Africa, Europe, the Americas or Asia, his plays are staged by artists who find them relevant here and now. This relevance and the concrete theatrical expression it leads to, however, can only be characterised as extremely diverse, in every aspect. The findings in this book contradict, then, the traditional view expressed by Knut Brynhildsvoll and Atle Kittang, then editors of the journal *Ibsen Studies,* when they reflected on 'the constant interest in' *A Doll's House* within the theatre and academy and claimed that:

> [O]ne can discern regionally varying accentuations [. . .] While in parts of the world where traditionally there is discrimination against women, people are first and foremost concerned with content and message [. . .] there seems in Western countries to be

Ibsen in Practice

an increasing tendency to focus attention on the aesthetic means and structural devices through which Ibsen communicates his content.[2]

The misconceptions contained in this sentence are legion. The argument, if one can call it that, rests on the presupposition that 'discrimination against women' only exists in certain parts of the world. The implied claim that this problem is solved in the West is too false to merit much arguing, let alone interest. And the living Western tradition of performing plays like *A Doll's House* or *Hedda Gabler* testifies to the fact that these problems are seen as highly topical by local theatre artists in the West. Brynhildsvoll and Kittang do, however, merit some attention because they give an unusually clear expression of the idea that there is a centre and a periphery, advanced and backward cultures. Written from within an unthematized position in the 'centre', they claim that the 'Western countries' have solved a number of problems that live on in 'the rest' of the world, and this 'rest' is simply denied equal value.[3] This is not only in terms of gender politics, but also, it would seem, when it comes to theatre and scholarship. The 'rest' of the world is still primarily interested in Ibsen's content, while the 'West' has moved on to a more advanced stage, where 'aesthetic means and structural devices' are in focus. There is no empirical evidence to support this view. The Western Ibsen is in no way more advanced in form or reflection, nor is it less political in content. In fact there is no essentially Western way of doing a theatre classic like Ibsen, as there is no characteristically Asian, African or Latin American practice of his plays. The main source of these ideological distortions of reality lies in the very distinction between an essentialised 'West' and the 'rest', and its implied notion that there is a (more advanced) 'centre'.

A further theoretical problem inherent in notions like these has to do with the position of the speaker, or the site of enunciation. To set forth propositions about world culture on such a level of generality presupposes a position outside of culture from which one can see the totality and make claims about all cultures, from above so to speak. This position does not exist; there is no position outside of culture. We are always within culture, and we are in countless ways products of our cultural background. The challenge is how to deal with this fact, both theoretically and analytically. Edward Said gave a good description of the complications and challenges at hand in his book *Culture and Imperialism*:

> there is no vantage outside the actuality of relationships among cultures, among unequal imperial and non-imperial powers, among us and others; no one has the epistemological privilege of somehow judging, evaluating and interpreting the world free from the encumbering interests and engagements of the ongoing relationships themselves.[4]

So, it is one thing to acknowledge that there is a Chinese or Bangladeshi Ibsen tradition, and that this testifies to the need to put Ibsen to work within a local context that will necessarily produce certain kinds of difference and deviation from what was the 'original'; it is quite another to recognise that this is a mechanism that works both ways, because no one has the epistemological privilege. In other words, if for example an Iranian film version of *A Doll's House* can be explained and interpreted through culture and difference, this also has to be the case for a Norwegian version of the same play. In this sense there is no original, no pure and uncontaminated source outside of culture. The awareness of the fact that there is a cross-cultural Ibsen, that Ibsen's dramas travel across borders of culture, religion and politics, should also be an awareness of the fact that there is no point outside of culture from where to discuss this fact. We are all *of* culture, and we cannot speak from outside of it. What I will say in this book is therefore said from within a certain cultural perspective and from a specific background, one that I constantly try to reflect on, critique and distance, but that has necessary biases intrinsic to it, from which I can never escape completely.

The work on this book has been a tremendously exciting and humbling process. Exciting because it has given me the opportunity to dig into many very different productions from very different theatre cultures and societies, humbling because it has inevitably been a series of strong encounters with my own ignorance. One person can never be an insider in many different cultures, and large parts of this book are by necessity written from an outsider's point of view. I have struggled to bridge the gap as best I could in every case, and hopefully with some success. But total communication across diverse cultures is impossible, and hence it has been important for me to point out the difference, and try not to assume too much. In many cases I have been an outsider also in the linguistic sense, which means that I have had to rely on translations of the scripts and have not been able to understand the dialogue as spoken on stage (in some cases made more easy through subtitles). Even though I know the texts well enough to understand what is going on at every stage, it makes my access more indirect. The solution has been to try to minimise the distance through reading all kinds of support in traces from the performances (scripts, images, reviews, recordings) and through interviews with artists involved in the productions. However, this can never solve the problem of not understanding the language in question. And my main strategy has been to be very careful not to jump to conclusions. I will analyse what I can understand from my point of view, and try to make it clear how far my findings go.

These difficulties would, in my view, have been insurmountable if the goal had been to analyse all the productions in their own right through the use of performance analysis. This is not the case. Chapter 4 discusses three different versions of *A Doll's House* performed in the People's Republic of China, the first in 1956 and the last in 2010. The main goal here is to understand how the already existing Chinese tradition of performing Ibsen was negotiated in different periods within the People's Republic of China. The examples show how the same text has been renegotiated and given new shape and meaning as a result of political, cultural and economic changes. Central to the discussion in this chapter is also the relation between Chinese culture and its foreign, Western 'other', and vice versa. Hence the argument in this chapter is not pursued through performance analysis, but through the investigation of traces of the productions – images, reviews, archive materials, political records, DVD recordings and interviews. The goal is to get a clearer understanding of the practice of this play through the use of reception studies, discourse analysis and culture studies in a broader sense. The same methods are used in the discussion of the Chilean cases in Chapter 2, but with quite different relations in the foreground.

A basic argument in the following is that the relations between 'culture' and 'empire' are much stronger than one usually takes into account – even today, after post-colonial theory, discourse analysis and different strands of critical theory and post-Marxism. The last chapter shows how the relations between empire and culture can be seen at work in the text of *Peer Gynt*: the text is by no means 'outside' of the conflicts dominating the political and economic struggles of its own social world, and neither was its creator, Henrik Ibsen. The main purpose of the chapter is, however, to examine two performances that took place in Africa in 2006. The first one, from Zimbabwe, directed by Robert McLaren (and Stephen Chifunese), used Ibsen's play as part of their project to empower youth, to build a strong civil sector in Southern Africa and to critique economic inequity and exploitation. The other one took place in Cairo, as the official conclusion of the Ibsen year 2006, and claimed to be an effort to build bridges between cultures and peoples, even to work for peace and brotherhood, and to be universal – but was unable to live up to these grandiose goals. The fact that one of these productions succeeded, while the other failed completely, can only be read from an analysis of the productions themselves, through an in-depth analysis of the relations between theatre performance and local culture, global economic forces, nationalism, soft diplomacy and political projects within, behind and outside the performance itself.

Against Capitalist Realism:
Thomas Ostermeier

This [dominant] aesthetic form, which we call capitalist realism, is affirmative, because it shows the individual as incapable of autonomous action. It suits those in power in this country when art withdraws completely.

Thomas Ostermeier[1]

Thomas Ostermeier was thirty-one years old when he took over as artistic director at the Schaubühne in 1999. Before that he had been in charge of the small Die Baracke (The Barracks) stage at the Volksbühne, where he had made a name for himself with productions of contemporary drama. To the far more established and mundane Schaubühne, he brought both his proclivity for new plays and many of the people he had worked with at Die Baracke. For the first season he and the other members of the artistic management wrote a short text called 'Der Auftrag', the mission, contract or assignment.[2] There they claimed that German theatre had lost its mission or purpose, and that they wanted to restore this through a theatre practice that was to establish the theatre as 're-politicised', a 'space for enlightenment' and 'consciousness-raising'. They wished for a theatre that once again would be able to connect the individual and existential to the social and economic conflicts in people's lives, and nothing less. It was surprising to some that this endeavour resulted not only in more contemporary drama, but also in a turn towards the classics. The critical emphasis on the effects of neoliberal globalisation is a common denominator for

Ostermeier's stagings of classics and contemporary drama alike. The most striking result is that he has become by far the most successful and influential director of Ibsen's plays today. Since the premier of his version of *A Doll's House*, called *Nora, oder ein Puppenheim* (*Nora* hereafter) in 2002, he has directed six of Ibsen's realistic dramas, four of them at the Schaubühne am Lehniner Platz in Berlin.[3] All have received very good reviews, drawn a lot of attention and attracted good audiences. One of the reasons that they continue to exert influence is that the Schaubühne is an active repertory theatre, which means that all four of Ostermeier's versions of Ibsen have been in the repertoire for years and have toured extensively.[4] In total, Ostermeier's Schaubühne Ibsens have been performed 644 times, to an estimated audience of 462,000 people.[5]

The Schaubühne caters to local audiences, but also to tourists through performances with subtitles in English and French. The genuinely international reach of the Schaubühne Ibsens, however, has been achieved through an astonishing number of international tours. *Nora* premiered in November 2002, and in the following year was invited first to other German venues and then to Amsterdam, Avignon, Zagreb, Belgrade, Prague and Toulouse. In the following years it went to Munich, London, Vienna, Istanbul, Oslo, Copenhagen, Zürich, Rennes, New York, Moscow, St Petersburg, Seoul, Tokyo, Nagano and Madrid, to mention only some of the thirty-eight destinations for the production. The other productions have not travelled as extensively, but the 2005 *Hedda Gabler* has been performed at twenty-four different locations, while *Volksfeind* (*An Enemy of the People*), first performed in 2012, has toured to twelve different destinations to date (May 2014). When plotted onto a world map by using the performance database on Ibsen productions, IbsenStage,[6] the image should prove that Ostermeier's Ibsen productions constitute a truly international theatrical success (Figure 1.1).

The map illustrates the extraordinary reach and influence of these productions. Some might object by claiming that reach and influence are not necessarily the same thing, which is true enough. But I do find it slightly problematic to claim that a director who is invited everywhere does not exert influence. Personally I am in no doubt that Ostermeier

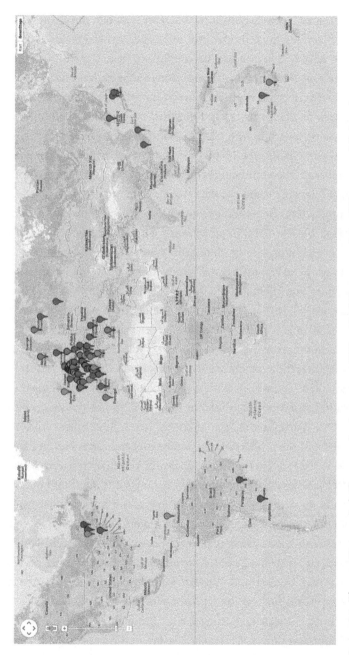

Figure 1.1 Thomas Ostermeier's Ibsen productions up until May 2014 (from www.https://ibsenstage.hf.uio.no).

has influenced Norwegian theatre,[7] but if we maintain the quantitative approach and try to go deeper into some geographical regions where we have reliable data, we will be able to see clear signs of a deeper influence. Due to the impressive work done on the national database on theatre and performance, AusStage, we have very good data on Australia. These show that Ostermeier has visited the country with three different Ibsen productions, first with *Nora* in 2006 and later with *Hedda Gabler* and *Volksfeind*. If we take 2006 as the point of departure and compare the number of Ibsen productions during the eight preceding years with the eight following years, the data will show that there were nineteen Ibsen productions in Australia from 1998 to 2005 and twenty-three in the period 2007 to 2014. In other words, a small increase. However, a closer investigation of the data will show that the first period is dominated by non-professional productions, often in educational institutions. From 1998 to 2005 there were only five professional Ibsen productions, while the corresponding number for the period between 2007 and 2014 is ten, and these were increasingly called 'adaptations', which meant that the director took a bigger role. This could be seen as indicating that the symbolic capital connected to Ibsen had increased substantially after the visits from the Schaubühne. A similar picture can be seen in Latin America, where the number of productions increased after 2006. Furthermore, the influence from Ostermeier can be discerned in Ibsen productions by prominent Latin American directors such as Alfredo Castro from Chile or Daniel Veronese from Argentina.

Before leaving the bigger picture of the map, it is important to note that while these productions have an impressive international reach they do not, strictly speaking, constitute a global phenomenon. When mapped like this, it is evident that what we see is a systematically skewed or biased, rather than a global, dissemination: these performances are spread across Central and Western Europe and other parts of the privileged world such as the United States, Australia, Canada, Japan, South Korea, Taiwan and Hong Kong. The only exceptions are the South American tours of *Hedda Gabler* to Caracas in 2006 and *Volksfeind* to Buenos Aires and São Paulo in 2014. The map displays the impressive trajectories of these productions, but it is equally a map of global centres of power and prestige. Not only do these Schaubühne Ibsens travel; they travel to important places and prominent festivals. From a materialist perspective, this would have to be explained in terms of the power of the German economy and the relatively generous funding of German theatre. Secure and generous funding is certainly an important factor, a *sine qua non* for the success of these performances.[8] Without strong financial support it would not be possible to make performances like those at the Schaubühne, nor would they be able to travel as extensively. Having said that, it is clear that many theatres and performances originating in the West receive similar levels of funding without achieving anything like the same kind of popular success or artistic quality. Hence the influence, success and importance of Ostermeier's Ibsen productions cannot be explained by funding or global power relations alone. Their indisputable artistic merit notwithstanding, they deserve attention because they represent highly ambitious attempts to make Ibsen our contemporary in political and social terms. Primarily focused on socio-economic, materialist aspects of the life of the modern individual, they are not deep psychological portraits, nor are they post-dramatic deconstructions of the plays; they are in many ways surprisingly traditional in their investigations of the theatrical and political potential of the texts for twenty-first century European social reality. In order to bring depth and detail to the discussion, I will focus on Ostermeier's productions of *Hedda Gabler* and *An Enemy of the People*, because each in some way represents an extreme in his approach to Ibsen, and each is still in the Schaubühne's repertoire of touring productions.

Hedda Gabler

The most significant of the artists Ostermeier took with him from Die Baracke, at least when it comes to Ibsen, was the stage designer Jan

Pappelbaum, who has designed the staging of all of Ostermeier's Ibsen productions at the Schaubühne. For *Nora* and *Hedda*, he built beautiful revolving podiums on a foundation, so that the actors stand not on the stage floor but on the floor of an architectural object erected on stage. In a conversation with the designer, Ostermeier commented that Pappelbaum does not 'create rooms' so much as 'objects'. Pappelbaum replied that he was not interested in the decorative aspect of architecture, but that he was indeed 'building rooms, too. They just do not have any outside walls.'[9] The revolving podium in *Hedda* measures 7.87 by 8.5 metres and is covered with dark stone tiles. Across the podium there is one long wall crossed three-quarters along its length by a shorter concrete wall. The main room is furnished with an oversized green sofa, and the wall consists of large sliding doors in glass. Above the podium there is a tilted mirror in the ceiling, which enables the spectator to see what is going on in parts of the stage that might otherwise be hidden from the audience (Figure 1.2). There is visual pleasure at play with multiple reflections here, as when the green of the sofa reflects in the

Figure 1.2 *Hedda Gabler*, Schaubühne am Lehniner Platz (2005), Katharina Schüttler as Hedda and Jörg Hartmann as Judge Brack (Photo: Arno Declair).

glass doors as a formal 'garden' outside. But the visual lure will soon enough become uncomfortable, a prison-like designer 'hell'.

The extensive revolving of the stage further enhances the transparency and three-dimensionality of the stage, letting the audience see things and actors from all angles. A count shows that the stage revolves at fifteen points during the performance; sometimes several full 360 degree turns at a time, sometimes less. Most of these turnings are accompanied by music and the longer ones are also combined with video or images projected onto the dark revolving stage. Three of these are of particular interest, because they can be said to structure the performance. The first takes place twenty-eight minutes into the performance, when the basic conflicts have been laid bare and Tesman has told Hedda that she has to live more modestly than they had originally planned. Hedda replies that she does have one thing to entertain herself with: her guns. The stage turns and we see images of Hedda driving through the city at night while the Beach Boys' 'God only knows (what I'd be without you)', from the album *Pet Sounds* (1966), is heard over the loudspeakers. As the song fades out, we see Hedda with her Walter PP 9#mm gun, which she carefully aims and fires, shattering the flower vases on stage. Then an hour into the performance, when Hedda has really set the conflicts in motion, we see Thea and Hedda going to sleep on the sofa, while images of a drunk and despairing Løvborg are projected on the set and the Beach Boys' 'Til I Die', from *Surf's Up* (1971), is played. Finally 'God only knows' is repeated during the closing scenes. The Beach Boys, it would be safe to say, contribute to the tone and feeling of the performance, a fact to which I will return.

Given the exquisite quality of everything on stage – real glass, real stone tiles, real concrete, a genuine designer sofa – the theatrical space reeks of modern bourgeois wealth. Pappelbaum has said that he strives for a theatrical space where everything is what he calls 'Spielmittel' (theatrical resources) (Dürrschmidt, 2006: 163). All objects and furniture on stage are used by the actors for the purposes of the performance, while at the same time they give an illusion of affluence, and hence of the social and economic heights from which one might fall. This 'aesthetic of affluence' (Dürrschmidt, 2006: 24) creates the illusion of contemporary bourgeois life, a picture of a living reality ornamented by a few objects chosen with exquisite taste, modelled after and by images from designer magazines. The effect is that the space in *Hedda* is both beautiful and uninhabitable or, in Pappelbaum's words, 'entmenscht', literally 'dehumanised', a world from which the human element is missing (Dürrschmidt, 2006: 25). What Pappelbaum and Ostermeier created in *Hedda* is an oversized display case, or panopticon, within which everything can be seen. The glass surface of the sliding doors makes the inner room completely transparent, so that the people inhabiting it are on display. Hedda's suffocating feeling that there is always 'someone there who'll … look at your legs' (*Oxford Ibsen*, Vol. VII, p. 208) is enhanced by the stage design. And as the panopticon is a technology of discipline – the ideal for a prison, and a metaphor for the discipline and surveillance of modern life[10] – the characters live their lives on stage under the regime of imagined surveillance and punishment by an external gaze that they have internalised. In the stage sculpture that Pappelbaum created for *Hedda* the façades are missing. But the performance is all about façade; façades that have turned inward, that are internalised.

This metaphor, embodied in the stage design, means at least three different things. First it points to the near-collapse of the distinction between private and public, such that the private sphere has the same basic characteristics as the public sphere, a place permeated by pretence and competition, where people have to take care of their appearance and in which they treat each other as a means to an end. Second, the individual has adapted to this regime of being on display in which the demand to maintain façade and status has been internalised as the norm. And third, Hedda has chosen to give up society as a public sphere and domain for action. In this sense, Ostermeier's *Hedda* points to a situation in which it has become almost impossible to imagine anything beyond or different from it, a space in which agency and change have been radically (and in part voluntarily) diminished almost to the point of elimination.

In the display case

In order to get an idea of how this critique of a society and a social class is put to work in practice, let us take a closer look at the opening scenes. In Ibsen's version, the action starts with a conversation between Aunt Julle and the maid Berte. Ostermeier's version has no maid and opens with the first conversation between Julle (Lore Stefanek) and Jørgen Tesman (Lars Eidinger). With a few exceptions, this is characteristic of the performance: it is almost surprisingly faithful to the text but cut down, modernised in terms of tone and slang, and speeded up. But there is an important shift of weight or nuance. In Ibsen, these two representatives of the 'Tesman world' seem genuinely fond of each other, they have time for each other, sharing warmth and feeling as they sit down to talk and reminisce. In Ostermeier's version, Tesman barely answers when Julle questions him. He is preoccupied with work, reading a manuscript and trying to write a little on the computer while talking to his admiring aunt. He is not really paying attention, and seems more interested in his computer and his paper than in her. Similarly, Julle is no longer the loveable, naïve and honest old lady: much more emphasis is put on her vanity and social ambition. She is happy that Tesman is home again, but she is fixed from the outset on the fact that he has married the 'beautiful Hedda Gabler, who had so many admirers'. The good aunt is, in other words, focused on appearance and social prestige. In Ibsen, Julle has bought a new hat so that Hedda would not be ashamed to be seen on the street with her. In Ostermeier's version, she has instead bought a sun visor (*Käppie*). The visor is completely out of place, a strange thing to wear inside the house, notwithstanding the fact that it is dark and raining outside (she has also brought an umbrella!). And where, in the Ibsen text, Tesman found the hat 'lovely', he finds the visor ridiculous: 'What's with the visor?' he asks, as he quite disrespectfully takes it from her head and puts it on his own. Even before Hedda has arrived, we witness a chilly world where there is little warmth and understanding: the characters pretend, they are self-absorbed, preoccupied with social standing and appearance.

In this way, we are better prepared for Hedda (Katharina Schüttler) in this performance than is often the case. Schüttler, however, has radicalised the manipulative and cold traits of the title character. Young at twenty-six years old, small and frail, Schüttler is often characterised as being a 'boyish' beauty. As she enters the stage she is in her sleepwear (*Schlafanzug*): low-slung grey tracksuit bottoms and a loose off-white, high-waisted sweater that leaves a lot of stomach on display to signify both her sexuality and the possible consequences of sexual activity. She is ever so cool and nonchalant as she enters but she still goes into battle immediately: when Julle greets her with a friendly 'Dear Hedda' she responds with a formal handshake, addressing Julle as 'Dear Mrs Tesman'. And Schüttler delivers the insult concerning Aunt Julle's new sun visor with malignant purpose: 'We will never get along with that cleaning lady . . . she has left her old sun visor.' It is meant as an insult, and is taken as one. Again, this slight shift of weight: there is no doubt that Hedda means to mock the old lady, and Tesman has already done the same, albeit in a milder, more friendly way. Once Julle has left they make it explicit; they both find the visor ridiculous and funny (*komisch*). Hence the naïve support that Tesman gives his aunt in Ibsen's text is nowhere to be found when Ostermeier's Hedda expresses disgust that such an item of clothing could enter her domain; it is 'totally embarrassing' (*total peinlich*). To be embarrassed is a deeply social feeling that borders on shame. It expresses Hedda's ingrained experience of being under surveillance, her perception of the disciplining effect of the other's gaze.

Almost as cold and hard as the stone, concrete and glass used in the set, Schüttler's Hedda was not loved but certainly admired by the reviewers.[11] Her Hedda is like the set in the sense that she is almost sheer surface: minimalist, transparent and yet opaque. She has chosen a life in which appearance is a deadly serious matter: not being able to master the codes of dress and looks on all levels amounts to being *déclassée*, to being cast out of the 'right' circles. This Hedda of the twenty-first century is a modern woman who craves a bourgeois status that will not require her to work. A woman of this class who works has, by definition, fallen in social status. Hedda has married Tesman because his status appears to match her social expectations. As Tesman says to Brack of the expenses and debt he has incurred: 'Hedda cannot be offered *petit bourgeois* (*kleinbürgerliche*) conditions.' Hence the possibility of social descent is present from the start in stage design, action and is expressed verbally. And it continues to be so, as when Hedda seeks Brack's reassurance that there is not anything 'really ridiculous' (*lächerlich*) about Tesman. To be comical, ridiculous – in any sense laughable – is the worst thing in this world of social anxiety and appearances.

Hyper-reflexive and ironical, however, Hedda knows that her situation is precarious, the result of a mixture of convenience and coincidence. As she tells Brack, she just happened to say to Tesman that she would like to live in this house, and one thing led to another: 'engagement . . . marriage . . . honeymoon . . . and everything', as she slowly enumerates the events while looking at Tesman who is standing outside with a pile of 'scholarly literature' in his hands. Hedda lets him stand there while finishing her sentence before she lets him in and they smile disdainfully at his naïve commitment to scholarly work. Their contempt and irony towards Tesman's academic work is not only because they find it boring, it is just as much an expression of class; the problem with Tesman from their point of view is that his work is *necessary*. He has to work, and getting the professorship is an economic necessity for him.[12] To be compelled by necessity is embarrassing. Complete economic freedom is best; second best, it seems, is to be under the spell of vaguely manipulated chance, provided the result can be met with disassociated, superior irony. Privilege combined with minimal autonomy is fine.

What makes Schüttler's Hedda special is the degree to which her cold and 'superior' character is hyper-reflexive and ironically modulated in and of itself. Accordingly, she concludes to Brack that 'the conditions' she has 'landed in' are 'pitiful', and that they amount to 'a ridiculous existence' (*ein lächerliches Dasein*). In order not to appear ridiculous, the safest strategy is to have an ironic attitude towards her own situation and label it as ridiculous. Another way of putting this is that Hedda has to claim not to believe in her own privileges in order to keep on believing in them in practice: by doing, living and enjoying them.

The point of Hedda's cynical, ironic logic of disavowal is to keep on practising what she does not 'really' believe in, so that it is futile even to attempt to think or act in opposition to the given. Ostermeier's Hedda, then, is a radicalised version of a typically Western postmodern form of ironic cynicism. By not 'really' believing in any kind of legitimacy, she can position herself on a 'higher' level of insight, thereby enjoying what she disclaims, with the added gain of being able to look down upon and ridicule those who are more naïve.[13] This form of ironic superiority bears the mark of its class-specific origin in the 'world-view' of the young and prosperous. This position of detachment and superiority comes with a toll to pay, because it threatens to empty out the self or person. There is no sin worse than being naïve or believing in 'authenticity', and Hedda takes very little, if anything seriously. When Hedda tells Brack that she was bored to death being 'always and for ever with the same person' during her honeymoon, Brack asks, 'Even when one loves that person?' Hedda's immediate reply is: 'Loves? Spare me the kitsch' (*Hören Sie mit dem Kitsch auf*). She has seen through everything, knows that her life is 'ridiculous', that there can be no 'real' feeling. Beyond the reflexive games of pretence, simulation, appearance and manipulation, there is only 'kitsch'.[14]

Ibsen's Hedda can be performed as a romantic heroine, hiding repressed greatness and grand ideas, as a victim of social or psychological ills, or as a deep, inexplicable evil. Schüttler's Hedda is none of these. She hurts others without remorse or empathy: in the most casual everyday manner she lies and manipulates; wrecks the relationship between Løvborg and Thea; tricks the reformed alcoholic Løvborg into drinking again; gives him a gun with which to kill himself; and destroys his unique manuscript by smashing his computer and burning the hard drive. But there is no tragic depth of the great personality to this Hedda's actions, only beautiful surface appearance. She does what she does, and Schüttler performs the role without any kind of 'grand personality' or 'un-measurable psychological depth' to it. Hedda has wished on herself a 'ridiculous' existence that precludes substantial change or action. She has chosen to lead a life of safety and idleness behind inner and outer façades that provide ample opportunities to be bored to death while exploring the smaller, malicious joys of manipulation and deceit.

Some reviewers have had difficulties in accepting that a modern Hedda would feel trapped or forced to stay in the 'display case'; she could just make a new choice, get a divorce and start over, seems to be the claim. To me this misses a central point in the performance, which is that the individuals depicted on stage exist within a context or social reality that radically constricts the individual's range of choice. What the programme leaflet calls 'the fear of social descent' is a fact. The journey from the affluent Charlottenburg, where the Schaubühne is located, to the misery of close-by Neuköln is short, both in the literal and metaphoric sense. Here, the possible fall in social standing – for a couple in which the husband fails to get a professorship or, worse, for a divorced mother without a job – will lead to a life on what is called 'Hartz IV' standard, the drastically reduced welfare benefit rates for unemployed Germans implemented on 1 January 2005. The austerity policies introduced by the Schröder government during the first years of the twenty-first century meant that a fall from the middle class could lead to very real poverty. These policies have continued under Angela Merkel's governments, further increasing inequality in Germany, and have subsequently led to the rise of a new group of 'working poor', who have jobs for which the payment is not enough to cover even modest daily expenses.[15] Hence the fear of social descent is based on material fact and is not to be understood as the whims of a spoilt General's daughter.

Growing social and economic inequality in itself leads to increased levels of insecurity and anxiety.[16] These sociological and psychological results of social and material change are to me the central aspects of this production. Hence it is extremely important to note how the cold, manipulative and alienated traits of the social world performed on stage are not at all exclusive to the main character. As we have already seen, the seemingly minor changes to the opening scenes make a significant difference; put bluntly, Tesman and Aunt Julle become more like Hedda than they seem to be in Ibsen's text. The majority of the reviews I have read point out that this Schaubühne Hedda is not a

sympathetic character and that Schüttler did not 'defend' her. According
to one critic, Schüttler's Hedda is 'not only a nasty piece of work, but a
dangerous one too', which to me is true only with the added reservation
that this goes for all the characters on stage.[17] This is the point of
Ostermeier's staging: it is a portrait of a generation and a social class,
not of a pathological woman. There cannot be much doubt, for instance,
that Tesman, seen by some reviewers as naïve and innocent in all his
bookish and boyish ways, is just as self-centred and cynical as Hedda.
In close private relations one would normally expect a certain degree of
personal solidarity. As we have seen, this quality is not strong in his
relationship with his aunt, and when it comes to his wife, he treats her
more than anything as a 'beautiful' trophy.

The actual nature of Tesman's relationship to Hedda, however,
becomes evident in the scene in which she tells him what she has done
to Løvborg's manuscript. When he understands that she has destroyed
the computer he first attacks her physically, throwing her around on the
sofa, but when she tells him that she has done it out of love for him, that
she could not bear to see him overshadowed by Løvborg, he kneels
down in front of her, embraces her and says that he did not know that
she was 'that much in love with' *him*. When she follows up by saying 'I
am pregnant', Tesman withdraws into himself and we can see the intense
emotional turmoil he is experiencing. Like an overheated boiler, he
fumes with emotional intensity, but the emotions are not directed
towards her. He moves away from his wife, rubs his face and tears his
hair before bursting out in a loud, shrill scream, startling his audience
on and off stage. After the first scream he jumps to his feet and runs
outside, where he roars and screams in ecstatic joy while jumping and
dancing around with his arms in the air. This would be a special and
vulnerable moment in any woman's life – and it is the only time in this
performance that Hedda seems psychologically naked – but here she is
literally left alone. Tesman does not relate to her, he does not see her,
and does not in any sense reach out to console or acknowledge her; he
only sees and feels his own joy, or victory even, which he celebrates on
his own, in private so to speak.

There is no sense of emotional support or solidarity, then, within the core of the Tesman family. Hedda certainly looks down upon Tesman and his aunt, but it is equally the case that they regard Hedda primarily as a beautiful, enviable trophy. These cold and alienated traits are even stronger when it comes to the remaining three characters on stage. Løvborg (Kay Bartholomäus Schulze) is pure contempt and arrogance, even before he falls into the abyss of his alcoholism. He blames Hedda for marrying Tesman, but only because it insults his pride. He wants to excel in his academic endeavours only in order to humiliate Tesman and show off. And he does not seem to care much about the truth of his research or his visions, nor for his 'true friend' Thea (Annedore Bauer), whom he wants as support but treats with little respect and almost no confidence. Thea, for her part, is deeply involved in Løvborg's writing and wants to support him, but she does not trust him. She certainly overcomes her grief at his death fast enough, when she sees the possibility of engaging herself in Tesman's work with the fragments of Løvborg's new book. Jörg Hartmann's Brack has even less emotional attachment and empathy than Hedda herself, only conspiring to force his way into her bed.

Violence to the end

Violence matters in Ostermeier's *Hedda Gabler*. The main character has obvious violent traits; she practises her aiming skills, shooting first one vase inside the room and then the one outside the open glass door, fires one of her pistols at Judge Brack and later gives it to Løvborg with the explicit wish that he use it on himself. Finally her violence becomes suicidal. She also commits a symbolic murder on stage, saying 'Now I kill your child, Thea' before smashing Løvborg's computer to pieces. Violence underlies every scene in Ostermeier's version of the play in the way in which the characters are on display, under surveillance. They are disciplined and they discipline and punish each other in every 'social' interaction, out to get an edge, seeking gain, and treating each other as a means to an end. The harsh coldly inhumane nature of these elegant and modern surroundings has its counterpart in the fact that almost every interpersonal relation on stage has elements of explicit violence. After Aunt Julle leaves at the beginning of the play, Tesman pulls his wife down on his lap and holds his arms around her. There is some fondness in his action but her response is to take his hand and bite it hard enough for him to scream in pain. They fight physically over Løvborg's briefcase and Tesman eventually throws her around, as he does again when she tells him what she has done to the computer. Hedda uses violent force to 'convince' Thea to stay with her after the men have left for Brack's party; a force to which Thea submits. Thea's stiff, nervous protective body language could connote – at least in the dramatic context of this performance – that she is a victim of domestic violence. The relation between Hedda and Løvborg displays an underlying reciprocal aggression, while Løvborg's violent tendencies are evident when he returns to Hedda after the party, torn, dirty and covered in blood from his fights with police and prostitutes. Brack clearly tries to rape Hedda when he drops in after the party. He gives up when Hedda puts up a fight, but he has more 'subtle' ways of forcing her.

Violence is a literal fact and it is symbolically omnipresent. The characters live under the symbolic violence of competition and manipulation in the private sphere, and of rigid social control and surveillance, coupled with the fear of economic disadvantage, even poverty, in the public sphere. However, the violence is gendered in Ostermeier's version of the play. Hedda is certainly not your average innocent victim but nor, as a woman, is she safe in her own home. All three men on stage covet her: Løvborg finds her choice of husband ridiculous and tells her so, while making quite direct advances himself; Brack progresses from 'subtle' proposals for a *ménage à trois* to attempted rape. This modern liberated woman is considered as nothing but a legitimate object or target for men's desire in her own home. And as we have seen, little protection is to be found from the man who is supposed to take care of her. Tesman does not recognise or respect Hedda and it is not beyond him to manhandle her if 'provoked'.

This underlying threat defines the social and political context of the climax of the play. This climax, like the rest of the performance, remains mostly faithful to the text but is finely tuned to its contemporary reality. Thus Hedda reacts to the news of Løvborg's death by saying that what she calls Ejlert's 'deed' (*Tat*) is a liberation (*eine Befreiung*) – not for him but for herself. The pathos of Hedda's romantic ideals of beauty and vine-leaves is toned down to the more modest expression that his deed had 'greatness' (*Größe*). As Hedda puts it, Løvborg had the courage to live life according to his own rules and the greatness to 'leave the party too early'. Brack then dispels Hedda's illusions, explains where and how Løvborg was shot, that the police have her pistol and that they will be interested to find its owner. He calls her 'Hedda *Gabler*' and makes it clear that she will be 'safe' only for as long as he keeps silent. Hedda concludes that she is in his 'power' (*Gewalt*), but the German term can also mean 'violence' or 'force'.[18] She is, then, subject to Brack's violence, a situation he claims he will not abuse, while adding drily that one does 'sooner or later, submit to the inevitable'. 'Maybe', Hedda replies as she goes inside. Brack follows her and closes the glass door: an accordion plays a sombre tune while we see the two of them in conversation inside. This is pantomime, silent action: Brack makes himself comfortable, takes off his jacket and shoes and lies down on the sofa. As a 'master' of the house he has her come to him, holds her hands and seems to be trying to pull her down on the sofa with him, but she frees herself and walks away. The music fades, and the stage turns so that we see Hedda walking into the next room, where Thea and Tesman are pasting the notes for Løvborg's book on the wall.

While Brack listens from the sofa, Tesman makes it clear that he, together with Thea, will put his energy into the reconstruction of Løvborg's manuscript, that this will take months and that Hedda's assistance is not wanted. He sends his wife back to Brack, who says that it will be his 'greatest pleasure' to keep her company. The effect of the action towards the end is, then, that the world closes in on Hedda: there is no way out, and she is pushed into Brack's *Gewalt* as Tesman and Thea plan to take their work out of the house. Tesman may or may not understand what this could mean for Hedda: the main point is that he does not seem to care. She has become even more invisible and insignificant to him. Hedda's last protest before shooting herself is to play loud music. In Ibsen she plays a 'wild dance tune' on the piano, but here she turns on the stereo and starts the song 'Rock Star' from the rap group N.E.R.D's album *In search of . . .* (2001). The opening lines are: 'Fuckin' posers! . . . For all you fuckin' posers, yeah/ It's almost over now, it's almost over now'. The music only lasts twenty-four seconds before Tesman runs in and turns it off, but it carries many layers of meaning, some obvious and some not so easy to see.

This music does not 'accompany' the performance in the manner of a soundtrack: Hedda herself puts it on within the action of the play and it should be read as an utterance made by her. Style of music, sheer volume and verbal content, all express her aggression. Hedda's choice of song implies to Tesman and Brack that their relationships with her are soon to be over, that she is about to leave them. At the same time, it is difficult not to recognise the meta-theatrical qualities of the music, that the play is 'almost over now', its end announced with a kind of romantic irony that can also mean that it may soon be over for this group of people, this class. This last interpretation is further supported by its reference to Ostermeier's production of *A Doll's House*, where the very same song was used by Nora to accompany her Lara Croft-inspired 'tarantella'. The music establishes a connection between the two productions, through scenes in which the female protagonists assert themselves and protest – in each case through violence. In *Nora* she will soon shoot her husband, and in *Hedda* she will turn the gun on herself. The basic point is, however, that both of these productions adapt Ibsen's plays to critique a specific class and a specific generation; an urban middle-class segment of 'successful' people in their thirties, 'poseurs' totally preoccupied with themselves.

Just how self-centred and hence isolated from each other these characters are is the central point at the ending of the performance. The stage revolves and we see Tesman and Thea sorting her notes for Løvborg's book in the living room, with Brack watching them from the sofa. Tesman suggests that they take their work to Aunt Julle's house, and Hedda shouts from her room off stage that Brack will now get what he dreamt of, to be 'the only cock in the yard'.[19] Then we hear a gunshot. Startled at first by the gun, the others go on with what they are doing. Tesman turns to the other two and says with a smile, 'Now she has shot herself', they laugh and he continues with his signature phrase, 'Think of that!' Brack replies with his signature phrase, 'For God's sake – people don't do such things'. But then of course they do (a fact proven by modern statistics) and as the stage revolves for the last time we see Hedda's corpse lying against the concrete wall, on which her blood and brains are splattered all over the notes posted there for Løvborg's manuscript.

Part of what makes this such a strong ending lies in the two contrasts played out on stage; the contrast between the three self-centred people in one room and the unnoticed corpse in the other. The fact that Hedda is not missed is reinforced or amplified in the long final scene. Just as important is the contrast between what we see on the slowly revolving stage and the music that accompanies the silent action. The Beach Boys' 'God only knows' is a musically complex song but its simple lyrics speak of a lasting romantic attachment, a love that will last as 'long as there are stars above you'. The song has only two stanzas: the first expresses the rock solid nature of the emotional attachment of the lyrical 'I', while the second puts the consequences of 'her' leaving him: 'Although life would still go on . . ./ The world could show nothing to me/ So what good would living do me'. The rest of the song consists of the title repeated more than twenty times as a refrain: 'God only knows what I'd be without you'. While the Beach Boys sing about an extremely strong personal commitment and lasting solidarity, what we see on stage is a complete lack of these same qualities; the (pregnant) young woman has killed herself and the corpse lies there without anyone noticing or even bothering to check what has happened. The use of this song from 1966 also sets up a historical contrast between a contemporary social reality – the cynicism of this twenty-first century generation – and the ideals of the corresponding social class at the beginning of social movements and reforms in the late 1960s and early 1970s. The fact that the song is repeated strengthens this effect. The first time it ends with the image of Hedda with her gun: her comment on the lyrics of the song is literally crushing. The second time emphasises the effects of a life without commitment between the 'I' and the 'you'. It is, with a twist on Marx's words, repeated 'first as farce, then as tragedy'.

This song can be interpreted in different ways. Hedda and her peers would only be able to listen to it with superb irony; should someone suggest that the lyrics be taken seriously, they would find it 'totally embarrassing' and 'ridiculous'. However, the song could be interpreted not as a celebration of the romantic ideal of everlasting love, but of lasting solidarity and commitment between people: what would 'I' be without a 'you'? And this contrast gives an edge to the performance: the song proclaims a wish to fulfil this kind of bond between people, but what we see acted out on stage is a world in which this kind of commitment and solidarity is no longer there, even as an ideal – it has become kitsch. Where alienation has become accepted, almost a strange kind of ideal, life is unbearable: even the suicide that is supposed to say 'no' to the world, to negate this way of living and express 'courage' and 'greatness', becomes insignificant, unnoticed, laughable. Ultimately then, it should be clear that a pivotal question in this version of *Hedda Gabler* has to do with agency, that is how the life world or world view performed on stage is one that has made human action and genuine change near impossible. Hedda is the only character on stage with some minimal wish for 'liberation', for another kind of life, but she has nowhere to take this wish or drive. Closed in by façade and economic necessity, she has no way out.

An Enemy of the People

Scholars of literature have often considered *An Enemy of the People* to be among Ibsen's weaker plays.[20] In theatrical practice, however, it has always been among his most popular. The performance history of the play can also testify to a central point in this book: that Ibsen in practice is a contextually over-determined phenomenon. Hence the play has undoubtedly been adapted to carry a critical, progressive message, but it has also been put to conservative and reactionary purposes. It was one of the most popular plays on German stages during the Third Reich. The ideological ambivalence that made the play suitable within Goebbels' propaganda system was also the reason that Arthur Miller felt the need to adapt the play when he made his version as a critique of the anti-communist hysteria of the McCarthy era in America. The general effect of Miller's changes to Ibsen's text was that the play became less ambiguous and the protagonist more positive. Miller above all found it necessary to cut and rewrite those parts of Dr Stockmann's public speech that, after World War II, could seem to imply a 'racist and fascist' ideology.[21] As we will see, this is also the point at which Ostermeier made the most radical changes to the text.

As with *Hedda Gabler*, Ostermeier transformed Ibsen's world into a twenty-first century German reality. The basic conflict is the same as in Ibsen: the small town has a relatively new bath and health spa, which it hopes will bring in tourists and secure the town's economic future. But the spa water is polluted, as the young spa doctor Thomas Stockmann (Stefan Stern) has discovered. No one contests the truth of his findings – the water *is* polluted – but his brother Peter (Ingo Hülsmann) and the town authorities want to suppress and rewrite the truth. Right is opposed to might, and the latter is stronger. In Ostermeier's version, the language is modernised to fit the urban young protagonists, and almost every line is shortened. The Stockmanns are in their early thirties and have only one child, an infant. By making the protagonists younger, Ostermeier could dispense with the three children. This contributes to shortening the performance and it gives Ms Katharina Stockmann (Eva Meckbach) a stronger and more independent voice: she is given many of the lines spoken by the grown-up daughter Petra in Ibsen. In addition, Ostermeier has cut the character of Captain Horster, the only one with the guts to support the good doctor when the going gets tough. One obvious effect of these changes is that the young couple become even more isolated in the ending scenes.

Katharina works as a teacher, they share the housework and struggle to pay their bills. In their spare time, they play in a rock band together with Hovstad (Christoph Gawenda) and Billing (Moritz Gottwald). The performance opens with Billing seated at the dinner table playing the guitar and singing Gnarls Barkley's 'Crazy' from 2006, while Katharina is setting the table and about to serve spaghetti. The conflict between Thomas and his brother Peter and the discovery of the pollution are introduced as they eat, drink and have a band rehearsal, interrupted at times by the crying baby. During the first part they rehearse different versions of David Bowie's 'Changes' from the album *Hunky Dory* (1971), another song that acquires meaning (although not unequivocal) within the performance. Music is an important element in Ostermeier's stagings of Ibsen, and even more so here due to the performative quality it adds when the music is performed live on stage by the actors. In terms of social and economic capital, we are one step down from the milieu of *Hedda*. The characters are well educated, newly established, with a baby and a mortgage and they both work (Katharina in a part-time position). Hence they are not (yet) proper Bobos. All band members voice liberal left-wing anti-establishment opinions, and they still nurture a slightly bohemian lifestyle, while their material aspirations are as middle class or bourgeois as can be. Their aspirations are illustrated on stage by chalk drawings on the walls of things they do not yet possess: a TV set with a Play Station, a Charles Eames lounge chair and a Le Corbusier recliner.

Jan Pappelbaum has observed that they took the stage design of *Hedda Gabler* as far as it could go 'in that direction' (Dürrschmitt, 2006: 22). In their version of *An Enemy of the People* (hereafter called *Volksfeind*), he certainly took it in a very different direction. The stage design here consists not of a revolving podium but of walls constructing rooms using the full width of the stage floor. The walls are blackboards with chalk drawings and slogans on them. First we are in Stockmann's apartment, a trendy loft or warehouse flat with an old sofa, coffee table and chair to the left, and a dinner table centre stage in an opening that leads to a room at the rear in which we see a mountainscape drawn on the back wall (Figure 1.3). To the left is a door leading to the kitchen, and another door to the right leads to the bedroom. The front room is 5.43 metres deep, and the back room 4.38 metres. 'Stockmann' is written in capital letters on the arch above the door centre stage. The shifts in time or place are performed on stage: with Ostermeier's near-perfect sense of timing and rhythm, the actors move furniture and redecorate the stage, often accompanied by music. The first shift is done simply by lowering a semi-transparent curtain on stage as Hovstad writes 'The next day' on the wall and Billing plays the guitar and sings 'Survivor' by Destiny's Child. When the action is transferred to the newspaper editor's office, the actors move some furniture and climb a ladder to erase 'Stockmann' and replace it with the word '*Redaktion*' (newsroom), while they do a rudimentary repainting of the room in white before the public meeting. The performing of music on stage, the use of chalk writing and drawing on the walls and the redecorating of the stage by the actors during the performance are not in any way shocking or new on stage, but they are of interest here because they contribute to a specific reduction of the distance between stage and auditorium, between audience and performance. On the one hand there is perfect illusion with exquisite

Figure 1.3 *Volksfeind*, Schaubühne am Lehniner Platz (2012). From left to right: Moritz Gottwald as Billing, Stefan Stern as Dr Stockmann, Eva Meckbach as Katharina Stockmann and Christoph Gawenda as Hovstad (Photo: Arno Declair).

realist acting, while on the other hand meta-theatrical reflection negates the illusion, forcing the spectator to reflect on the fact that this is theatre. The spectator is absorbed in the realistic illusion, while simultaneously having to reflect on the relation between the performance and the world outside it. This specific movement back and forth between the two is typical of Ostermeier's Ibsen productions.

The performance raises a wide variety of topical issues – pollution, corruption in politics and business, the decay of critical journalism, the increasing influence of money in all areas of life, public or private – but they all relate to central conflicts between truth and money, democracy and capitalism, and the question concerning the individual's possibility to take action, to change his or her world. This agenda is announced at the beginning of the performance: as the audience take their seats at Schaubühne to watch this production of *An Enemy of the People*, they see a small text projected on a semi-transparent curtain hanging in front of the stage. It says:

> 'I AM WHAT I AM,' the slogan of an American producer of running shoes, is not simply a lie, a simple advertising campaign, but a *military* campaign, a war cry directed against everything that exists *between* beings, against everything that circulates indistinctly, everything that invisibly links them, everything that prevents complete desolation, against everything that makes us *exist*, and ensures that the whole world doesn't everywhere have the look and feel of a highway, an amusement park or a new town: pure boredom, passionless but well-ordered, empty, frozen space, where nothing moves apart from registered bodies, molecular automobiles, and ideal commodities.

Those who know their fringe leftist literature will recognise that it is a quotation from *The Coming Insurrection*, a book by the anonymous French collective called 'The Invisible Committee', first published online in 2007.[22] Spectators who have read the programme booklet before the performance will also recognise it as the third paragraph of a seven-page extract from the book reprinted there.[23] This quotation opens the performance and introduces one of its central topics: that the individual at its core is under pressure from commercial forces that are transforming every relation into a relation between things – the result being an overwhelming alienation. The reason for the prominence given this quotation at the beginning of the performance lies above all in its proleptic function in relation to Dr Stockmann's speech at the public meeting, in the simple sense that the bulk of his speech consists of the same extracts from *The Coming Insurrection* that we find in the programme. For the audience, the projection of this paragraph on stage, initially and once during the performance itself, functions as a prolegomena to the topics and style of Stockmann's speech while pointing beyond it, so to speak. The doctor's speech at the public meeting has a reference beyond the performance, to another text with its own force and agenda. This will necessarily influence the performance more for those who know the text in question.[24] Briefly put, the 'Invisible Committee' prophesises a coming insurrection against what they see as the totally destructive forces of capitalism. They give advice on how to resist and survive ('Form communes', 'Flee visibility', 'Organise self-defence', etc.), but the main part of the book consists of an analysis of the current situation organised in seven 'circles' – the allusion to Dante's nine 'circles' of Hell is no accident. Stockmann's speech consists of extracts from five of the circles, but above all from the first one, called 'I AM WHAT I AM'. The principal claim here is that modern capitalism colonises the self and moulds it in the form of an isolated entity, alienated, and without binding attachments to the world or to other people, becoming a pure, and empty, tautology: I am I. Stockmann's speech is coherent, but he certainly jumps from one topic to the next, saying that what we have today is 'a clinically dead civilisation' (Invisible Committee, 2009: 92), and continuing with attacks on the family, the petit bourgeoisie, the use of Ritalin to control active children, environmentalism and the political economy: 'the economy is not "in" crisis, the economy is itself the crisis' (Invisible Committee, 2009: 63).

More important than the specific content of the speech and its relation to *The Coming Insurrection* however, is the performative context, that is the form of presentation within the performance. While the actors move the furniture and repaint the room, we hear a cover version of The Clash's 'Guns of Brixton' by Daniel Freitag.[25] The lyrics call for anti-authoritarian insurrection, asking the listener to stand up and fight back. Equally important is what we see enacted on stage during the song: people working together, participating without words in doing a job. This, together with the co-operation in the band rehearsals, represents an optimism performed on stage. Participation is central to Stockmann's lecture. He takes the podium and asks for the lights to be turned on: they are and we, the spectators, are his audience, participating in the public meeting. The direction that the performance takes during the meeting will depend on the response from the audience; when I have seen it the audience was always active from the start,[26] shouting and booing at Peter Stockmann as he tried to influence the meeting before his younger brother was allowed to speak. Once Thomas is given the floor, he delivers a nine-minute speech from *The Coming Insurrection*. It is performed in a rambling and hesitant way that gives us the impression that he is in part thinking aloud, but it is a verbatim rendering with one important exception: he concludes this part of his speech by saying that 'It's even become a contemporary strategy to critique this society – *often also in the theatre* – in the vain hope of saving the civilisation' (Invisible Committee, 2009: 94). The reference to the theatre (not there in the original) gives the speech a meta-theatrical twist that opens the performance to a wider reflection on what it is trying to do, and questions its own agenda and the relation to the world outside the auditorium. The literal meaning of this punch line is that this whole civilisation must go, and that the most ludicrous belief of all is that it can be critiqued, corrected or saved from within. More significant within the performance, however, is the explicit mentioning of the theatre as a futile arena or agent for change. The punch line functions as a meta-theatrical antidote to any naïve belief in the transformative power of the performance itself. This reminder is important, but it is not cynical; it does not mean that nothing matters, or that Stockmann withdraws the substance of what he has just said. Stockmann insists on the truth of what he is saying, while a meta-dramatic performative irony points to the fact that his claim is made *in the theatre*, an arena where anything can be said without any direct effect on the world outside.

When I saw the play, the audience laughed and applauded Stockmann at this point. He took a pause, drank some water and returned to Ibsen's text by saying that the authorities in the town are like 'goats in a young forest' damaging growth and that they should be 'exterminated'.[27] The word extermination (*Ausrottung*) has specific connotations in the German context and it is no surprise that Aslaksen (David Ruland) immediately jumps up and accuses Stockmann of being a fascist. Equally specific to the local situation is Stockmann's instant reply: 'Here come the Nazi accusations.'[28] He continues by attacking the 'damn liberal majority' and claims that 'the majority is *never* right'. Aslaksen walks up onto the stage, repeating that Stockmann's opinions are tantamount to fascism, something he is certain that the majority 'in our democratic society' will never support. He then asks the audience what they think about the doctor's views. This is the decisive moment in the performance. The reviews from the performances in different parts of the world support Thomas Ostermeier's claim that audiences everywhere respond strongly at this point in the performance.[29] There are certainly differences, from ordinary political debates to fierce struggles and even physical fighting, and when I saw it the audience was somewhere in the middle of this scale. They were eager to participate, and the support for Dr Stockmann and the attacks on Peter Stockmann, Aslaksen and Hovstad were so strong that the actors had some difficulty in reining in the performance. Members of the audience got the microphone and emphatically stated that Stockmann was one hundred per cent right in everything he had said, that the authorities were lying, that 'our' democracy was in shambles, that one could not negotiate or make deals about poisonous water or people's health, and so on. The feeling in the audience was one of energy and enthusiasm, excitement at a shared sense of rebellion. The meeting is, of course, predestined to end with the public denunciation of Dr Stockmann, and this was made difficult at one point because the participants in the public meeting were strongly in support of the doctor. Even the most rebellious audience member will not normally break the rules of the performance, and there was no protest – naturally no one got up to defend Stockmann physically – as Hovstad and Billing (i.e. the press) started throwing water balloons filled with coloured water at him.[30] Stockmann hid behind the rostrum, yelling that this 'society deserves to perish' while they bombarded him.

What makes this *Volksfeind* not just great theatre but a truly intriguing and challenging performance can be summed up in three points, each of them related in some sense to the introductory text from *The Coming Insurrection*. First of all, it must be rather surprising that the majority of the audience of which I was a part accepted and supported the radical content of Stockmann's speech, at least in the moment of the performance. Second, it is also surprising that this well-tried device of involving the audience directly in the performance, almost like forum theatre à la Boal, could work so well today. To me it was an immensely important aspect of the performance that the audience actually experienced a sense of euphoria, of happy revolt, no matter how 'staged', unreal and meta-theatrical, in being given the opportunity to tell the authorities that they are corrupt liars, that they manipulate the truth, control the media and destroy the environment. The third point, of equal importance, is that the audience shared the experience of oppression: we were told that, after all, we do live in a democratic society, that we were invited to participate, we had our say, even voted and won, but to no avail. The importance of the participatory aspect of the performance lies not only in the momentary feeling of 'insurrection' it aroused, but in the shared experience of being manipulated, tricked and forced into submission. And here, in effect, lies the main difference between *Volksfeind* and the political theatre of the 1970s. Consciousness raising, empowerment and action were the central goals of the use of this participatory device then, but while this may still be part of the audience's experience today, it is consciously constructed as transitory and illusory. The wished-for effect seems not to have been a desire to act on an understanding provoked in us by the performance, but rather that we should recognise the cynical mechanism itself, acknowledge that we are manipulated and coerced, but do nothing aside from this cynical knowing. It is this experience that the audience is intended to share in the physical manner that only theatre can offer.

At this point in a staging of *An Enemy of the People*, the audience will usually know what to expect, but in this version multiple directions are kept open. Stockmann could be depicted as the martyr of truth, as a fanatic or a comic figure. This openness is a key aspect of the performance, and it continues in what follows. As Thomas is sitting on stage alone after the meeting, trying to sort out what has just happened, his father-in-law Morten Kiil (Thomas Bading) enters. Kiil has been peripheral up to this point, dropping in only a couple of times, always accompanied by his large Schafer dog. Bading gives Kiil a sinister, menacing air; without ever raising his voice he brings an underlying threat to his words. Well-dressed but shabbily unshaven and constantly smoking, Kiil remains alert while looking like a man who has been drinking. The Schafer strengthens the feeling that the man is dangerous, without scruples. In a low-key lingering voice he asks Stockmann about his findings: will he publish them in the national or regional media; is his own factory among the polluters? When Stockmann answers in the affirmative Kiil looks at the dog and then at Stockmann, as if to indicate that the dog might be told to attack him, points at him with two fingers like a gun and sneers 'Watch out, Stockmann!' as he leaves.

The remaining twenty-five minutes of the performance follow the main line of Ibsen's fifth act, with a focus on the economic aspect. Katharina returns home, telling Thomas that she has been fired, he tells her that they have been given notice from the landlord, then Peter comes to tell Thomas that he has been fired from the spa. When Thomas maintains his uncompromising position, Peter tells him that he knows about Thomas' schemes with his father-in-law. Thomas and Katharina are shocked when he tells them that Morten Kiil has been buying stocks in the spa at very low prices, but Peter is not impressed and suspects that this has been their plan from the beginning. A doctor uses his position to discredit the firm for which he works, even making scandalous claims at a public meeting; the following morning he has his father-in-law buy up all the stocks now that their value has plummeted. Peter tells him that the case will go to court, and that he will have to face punishment for having used his position for personal gains. When Peter leaves, telling his younger brother that everything is over between them, Kiil re-enters. In his cold, languid voice Kiil tells them that he has bought the stocks at a good price and that he has used their money, the sum that Katharina and their son were to inherit from him. Kiil gives them the shares and says that he wants to see if Stockmann is as mad as everyone says he is, or whether he can make something worthwhile out it. Maybe he could re-examine the water, and besides, were not the guests sick before they came to the spa? Why else would they go there? Or could it be something they had eaten that made them sick? As a scientist he has to admit that there are different possibilities, there can be no absolute certainty. Maybe he can install something that would disinfect the water, kill the germs if there are any: 'everything can be killed', Kiil says, 'that's science.'

This mixture of sinister, threatening manipulation and underlying comic elements is sustained when Hovstad and Aslaksen arrive with their proposal to support Stockmann with a campaign to show that he acted as a scientist out of concern for the public good when he bought the shares in the spa; they can use the newspaper to spin public opinion in his favour, but they make it very clear that they can also do the opposite. They would of course need a piece of the action, not for their personal profit but to save the newspaper! As in Ibsen, Stockmann is furious; he throws them out but is left in a void. The remaining two-and-a-half minutes of the performance pass in silent action. Thomas and Katharina sit down, pick up the portfolio containing the shares in the spa, look at the document, take a sip of their beer in sync, look at the document again, look at each other and – lights out. An extremely open ending, without any declamations about 'the strongest man in the world' being the 'man who stands most alone' (Ibsen, 1960: 126). In Ibsen, Stockmann simply sends a note to Kiil saying a three-fold 'no' to his offer, but economic coercion seems to be stronger here. The couple are left alone to consider their options. Thomas and Katharina could be free of all economic worries if they were willing to compromise, play the game and spin the truth a little at the risk of other people's health. On the one hand, truth, opposition, radical ideals – and economic misery. On the other hand, lies, conformity, compromise – and true wealth. Not an easy choice, but a familiar one for large sections of most societies today: there is a limit, an invisible point of no return from which most of us would flinch. There are bills to be paid, children to provide for, mortgages to be paid, reputations and careers to be protected. In a performance that engages directly with the spectator in so many ways, the openness of the ending poses a set of questions for the audience to consider: What would you do? Would you be able to act? Can change take place? Are there ways out? Do you believe in this democracy?'

Excursus: Between cultures (Istanbul, May 2014)

The fact that these productions tour large parts of the world poses some questions. They are on the one hand very local and definitely from Schaubühne am Lehniner Platz in Berlin's Charlottenburg. But they are also able to engage and be experienced as highly topical by audiences in very different social, cultural and political contexts. This can in part be explained by the fact that many of the issues addressed in these productions are global. Thomas Ostermeier himself has pointed to this by saying that 'Globalisation is not only economic but also means that the effect and suffering of globalisation is globalised.' In other words, global problems given a local expression strong enough to communicate with people across cultures. In addition, it seems reasonable to presume that social class plays a role; a specific segment of the middle class dominates the theatre-going public, often a segment versed in foreign languages and part of international networks. Equally important is probably the fact that Ibsen's plays to a large extent are about the middle class and its conflicts, a fact that Ostermeier himself has pointed out a number of times.[31]

It would, however, be indicative of a poor understanding of the world to believe that the international success of these productions means that they function in the same way everywhere. They do not glide seamlessly into new cultural contexts where they can mean 'the same' or be translated without alterations, distortions and renewals. This is a phenomenon that is difficult to investigate, but the interactive character of the public meeting allows access to a material where one can study the audience's response more directly.[32] The reviews indicate that the meeting does cause a lively debate among audiences everywhere, but the reviewers have not felt the same about this part of the performance. In spite of, or perhaps because of the lively response by the audience, some reviewers have opined that the production is too political and too leftist. After having seen it at the Brooklyn Academy of Music, the reviewer in the *New York Times* claimed that the performance derailed during the public meeting, and that it could be seen as 'good fun, if you happen to like attending wildly disorganised meetings of left-leaning activist organizations', but that it was surely a 'downer' for everyone else.[33] A few reviewers seem to have found it problematic that the performance could engage the audience to this degree, but even more so that they could come to support the view presented by the doctor. In some cases the audience has crossed the line and broken the rules of the theatre by trying to interfere physically in the performance. This participatory aspect got out of control during the performance in Buenos Aires, when some members of the audience attempted physically to prevent Hovstad and Billing from throwing paintballs at Stockmann. Here the discussions among members of the audience (or participants in the public meeting) even escalated into physical fighting.[34]

Seeing the show in Istanbul gave me new insights into other aspects of the Schaubühne tours. When the play is performed for what the Schaubühne calls their 'international audience' in Berlin, the performance will have subtitles, and during the public meeting the audience can give their comments and questions in German, French and English, and replies are given in the same languages. In Istanbul, however, the subtitles were of course in Turkish, but Aslaksen had to open the meeting by saying that he unfortunately could not speak Turkish, and that translators had been hired to take care of this difficulty. The discussion between stage and auditorium was mediated by a translator in both directions; from audience to actors, mostly Aslaksen and Peter Stockmann, and back again. In spite of the delay, or buffer, that is created when a translator mediates like this, it became a very lively debate, with strong statements being made from audience members who claimed that Aslaksen's accusing Stockmann of fascism was ludicrous in light of the Turkish situation, because, as he said, 'here we live with a clear, latent fascism every day ... Tomorrow there will be demonstrations at Taksim Square; come along and you will see real fascism!' Another participant asked Aslaksen if he 'knew what happened to the Armenians in this country, and not least what would happen to us if we talk about it in public!' When the meeting takes place in new cultures, it also brings forth new possibilities; new contexts give occasion for new, local meanings. Hence the travels of this production also bring out an aspect of the relative autonomy of art not always seen, namely how extremely important context is in creating meaning.

New meanings are necessarily produced by the new context, but the performance in Istanbul also made it clear that Ostermeier and the Schaubühne make conscious efforts to relate to new contexts when they travel. In Istanbul they had made some minor but important changes to the production. In Berlin the relationship between the brothers was tense from the beginning, as it is in Ibsen, and the two almost started to fight twice during the performance. In Istanbul, however, this was taken further as the brothers started fighting for real. After a short while Peter got the upper hand; he threw Thomas down on the floor and started kicking him. When he had kicked him a few times, however, he seemed to hurt his foot. So he jumped around on one foot while holding the other and making exaggerated, theatrical gestures indicating pain. The audience's response was immediate and strong; they laughed out loud, cheered and interrupted the performance with applause. The background for this response can be seen in Figure 1.4.

The photo catches Yusuf Yerkel, aide to the Turkish Prime Minister, kicking a protester who was already being restrained on the ground by

Figure 1.4 Yusuf Yerkel, aide to the Turkish Prime Minister, kicking a protester on 14 May 2014 (Source: Scanpix/Reuters).

two policemen on 14 May 2014. This incident took place during Prime Minister Erdogan's visit to Soma after the tragic mining accident there on 13 May. When the image reached the media, Yerkel apologised for having lost his temper, but the scandal was a fact, and was seen as indicative of the government's botched handling of the mining accident. It did not help that Yerkel himself had suffered soft tissue trauma in the leg used to kick and was granted sick leave. He was fired a few days later. What makes this image interesting in connection to *Volksfeind*, however, is how elegantly it was invoked in the performance through this small gesture. The poor guy hurts his foot, and the audience automatically sees the connection to the photo, and a cluster of topical issues becomes part of the performance; the exploitation of the miners, the lack of work security, politicians who only care about possibilities for 'economic' growth and advancement for the few, the violent police crackdown on the protesters, corruption, the role of the press (and probably other issues undetected by me) became part of what happened on stage during the performance of Ibsen's play from 1882. It represented an extremely successful connection to a local reality across linguistic and cultural borders. The link was still alive in the audience's minds, made explicit when a young woman got up and asked Peter sarcastically if his foot still hurt.

The relation to capitalism

Ostermeier's Ibsen productions clearly question today's capitalism, on many levels. And in spite of their many meta-dramatic devices and playful turnings toward the spectator, they are not just shedding the possibility of answers through impossible questions, or opening up fields of inquiry with unending complexity as the given conclusion. They have a clear tendency. What used to be called socialist realism in the eastern bloc was an affirmative theatre, designed to support the system of actually existing socialism, and what Ostermeier calls 'capitalist realism' is equally affirmative in his view. Major strands of what is known as post-dramatic or postmodern theatre are, according to this view, affirmative in supporting the contemporary system of globalised, neoliberal capitalism through an aesthetic that presupposes:

> That dramatic action is no longer contemporary and relevant; that human beings can no longer be understood as subjects with agency, ability to act; that there are exactly as many truths in the auditorium as there are spectators present, but no representable truth, valid for all, underlying the actions on stage; that our experience of reality is completely fragmented, and that the point is to present this experience of reality on stage.[35]

Whether this is a fair description of major parts of European theatre today is something I will leave for others to discuss; the point here is that it clarifies some important aspects of Ostermeier's version of Ibsen. He believes in and tries to bring forth the narrative in the plays; he certainly cuts and modernises but the basic threads of the plot are retained. They are seen as relevant to our social reality of today, not least because they highlight basic sociological problems or facts that are still pressing, maybe more so today than in Ibsen's time. He sees 'theatre as a sociological laboratory that examines the behaviour of human beings'.[36] In this laboratory the presupposition is that agency is possible (but not given), and that there may be access to a representable set of truths about the world. If this truth was to be summed up in one word, it would in my view have to be 'capitalism'. The basic truth of the world performed on stage is that it is a (neoliberal) capitalist world, where all relations are in some sense touched by the mechanism of this economic system. In *Hedda Gabler* this is explored with a consistent focus on the individual. The people on stage and their interpersonal relations are deeply marked by a capitalist system that commodifies and alienates the individuals, to the extent that it is hard to see possible ways out. If Ostermeier's *Hedda* represents the destructive influence on the individual, his *Enemy of the People* focuses on the inherent contradiction between capitalism and democracy. As Germany and the rest of Europe become more and more marred by austerity plans, crises, unemployment and growing inequality, it becomes clearer that 'democratic capitalism' is fundamentally 'ruled by an endemic conflict between capitalist markets and democratic politics'.[37] We may be entering into a phase where only money counts, a complete 'Dollarocracy'.[38] There can be no democracy without individuals who are more than consuming machines, who can stand outside the economic necessity and the anxieties of falling socio-economic standards.

This is not to say that these productions are anywhere close to agit-prop. They do not hammer in these connections, nor do they take a clear stand, but there is nonetheless a clear and conscious tendency in them. With this tendency one can disagree or not; a spectator can be for or against, but never indifferent. The invitations to think beyond the stories presented on stage, to a world outside where the audience lives and tries to act, is often made through meta-dramatic devices, breaks with the realistic illusions of the performances. These dramatic techniques, however, at the same time emphasise the relevance of the dramatic action for our own social world. And the accusations of being too political or leftist are in my view unjustified in light of the way the productions end – often even more open and pessimistic than Ibsen's own.

A *Doll's House* in Chile:
Dictatorship and its Aftermath

All art is at once surface and symbol. Those who go beneath the surface do so at their peril.

Oscar Wilde: *The Picture of Dorian Gray*

On 11 September 1973, the Chilean military, backed by the Central Intelligence Agency (CIA) and other United States agencies, overthrew the democratically elected government of Chile's socialist president Salvador Allende.[1] The violent *coup d'état* was led by General Augusto Pinochet, soon to become the dictator of the previously peaceful and democratic country. His rule was to last sixteen years, during which time Chile became known for the massive human rights violations perpetrated by the regime. Current figures show that more than 3,100 people were killed or 'disappeared', more than 30,000 were severely tortured and more than 200,000 were forced into exile during the dictatorship. Because Allende's goal was to achieve socialism through democratic means, he had not sought to arm his supporters. As a consequence, the military easily crushed their civilian opponents. Pinochet and his army saw the coup as the first battle in a war in which the goal was to root out all traces of Marxism and leftist politics that had 'contaminated' the Chilean social body. 'In the six weeks following the coup', according to a CIA report, 'the military had massacred approximately 1,500 civilians and tortured thousands more.'[2]

Pinochet's objectives were to take out as many as possible of those most liable to resist and to terrorise any bystanders who might consider future political opposition. Through the organised terror of killings, disappearances, torture and forced exile, the population was scared into submission. In the words of Chilean psychiatrist and dramatist Marco Antonio de la Parra, the result of the coup was that people were 'confused and anguished, docile and waiting to take orders [...] people regressed; they became more dependent and fearful.'[3] As would soon become clear, the coup was not about political repression alone; it was also (and equally, according to some) about economic repression and redistribution from the poor to the rich. In the words of André Gunder Frank, the coup constituted an act of 'economic genocide'.[4]

The shocking regime of repression and violence hit the cultural and artistic sphere hard. The preceding period of cultural richness, vigour and vitality was immediately replaced by what has often been labelled a 'cultural blackout'.[5] Not only were many theatre artists arrested, tortured, blacklisted, exiled or killed: according to Grinor Rojo, 'the military dealt the *final* blow to the historical structure within which Chilean theatrical practice had operated since the 1940s and 50s'.[6] Historically, the two main pillars of theatre in Chile were the university theatres and the popular theatre. Professional theatre in Chile had been organised from the outset in and through the universities. The popular theatre, a political theatre for and by the people, had seen immense growth in the years before the coup. Political theatre was immediately crushed, as the military regime set about cleansing anything connected to Marxism and popular resistance from the social body. The universities were politically and economically restructured to the same end. Courses seen to have any connection with left wing political ideas or grass roots movements were closed, academic staff were fired and students expelled.

By 1976, the only two university theatres left in the country were those at the University of Chile and the Catholic University respectively, both in Santiago.[7] However, the theatre regained strength and grew to be an important artistic arena in the following years. This revival was due to the fact that the regime considered theatre to be less of a potential threat to its repressive policies than books, films or television.

A memorandum from the head of the secret police, *la Dirección de Inteligencia Nacional* (DINA), is supposed to have read:

> As long as the theatre groups working in the shanty towns remain in the shanty towns, and the groups working in the downtown theatres stay in the downtown theatres, they can do us little harm, whilst giving their followers an illusion of power. To persecute them would harm our image and stir them up to cause bigger trouble. I recommend making occasional low helicopter flights over the first and levying a heavy tax on the second.[8]

Both measures were taken, and while a new tax on theatres hampered their activities they were not as strongly censored as other media. Even so, an extreme culture of fear was created through arrests and torture, with the result that the established theatres turned to the classics, creating what the critic Juan Andrés Piña has called a 'boom de los clásicos'.[9]

In silence: *A Doll's House* at the Catholic University (1980)

The Pinochet regime considered theatre classics from the European canon to be too removed from everyday Chilean reality to be of local political consequence. Furthermore, because the authorities regarded the canon to be of unquestioned universal cultural value, they permitted, even encouraged, the staging of the classics. Performances of the classics gave direction and meaning to theatrical practice, so that the choice of plays in this extraordinarily repressive situation was by no means gratuitous. These years of political repression saw many performances of dramas from the golden age of Spanish drama: notably, plays by Calderon de la Barca, Lope de Vega and Cervantes. Calderon's *La vida es sueno* (*Life is a Dream*) was a clear favourite due to its investigation of power, repression and truth. Shakespeare's *Hamlet* was also staged several times, with no little emphasis on 'The Mousetrap' and its local implications for the illegitimate usurpation of power through murder and violence. These performances afforded actors and audiences a shared space in which the enforced silence about all contentious issues concerning the dictatorship could be broken without anything being said directly.

This was the context in which *A Doll's House* was produced at the Catholic University theatre in 1980.[10] Set and costumes were designed as for a period piece, and great effort went into the construction of a *mise en scène* that looked as authentically nineteenth-century European as possible. The production testified to the wealth of resources that the Catholic University had at its disposal: a large cast accounted for all the roles in the text (including the children), with customised period sets, properties and costumes designed and tailored for the occasion. The play was performed in the Catholic University's large auditorium theatre, which at the time had a capacity of 1,200 seats. *A Doll's House* drew full houses throughout the season and was chosen for inclusion in a national festival that showcased the best theatre performances of that year.

Chile's theatres at that time sought to produce plays that dealt in some way with oppression. Accordingly, the Catholic University production of *A Doll's House* was interpreted as Nora's revolt against a system of repression represented in this instance by Helmer. Even though the original script was not adapted or altered, the majority of the audience interpreted the play as the story of a woman who had the courage to take a stand against overwhelming systematic repression.[11] In this respect, the play implied a strong belief in, and a call for, individual agency. According to one source, many spectators regarded Nora as an allegorical representation of 'the entire Chilean people'.[12] The double significance of what took place in the auditorium was reflected in reviews of the play. Critics wrote of Ibsen's belief 'in equality of human beings, with no gender or social class differences', and argued that although the play is about a marriage, it 'at the same time gives an account of a wider social order'.[13] With a similar double meaning, critic Wilfredo Mayorga found reason in his review to quote Lona Hessel's statement from *Pillars of Society* that 'the true pillars of society are liberty and truth', and to conclude that Ibsen's plays were part of a 'fight for the rights and freedom of human beings'.

DINA, the Chilean secret police, were right of course to assess this kind of theatre as a forum for the few that could not in any way threaten security. But the importance of this theatre was that it provided one of the very few arenas in which people who shared an opposition to the regime could experience solidarity in corporeal (but silent) acknowledgement of the play's connection with dire realities outside the theatre. However, while hinting at the general political significance of *A Doll's House*, many reviewers explicitly denied the play's feminist aspects; Ibsen's importance was to be found in broader claims for freedom and liberation. This paradoxical view corresponds with Elsa Poblete's observation that the audience's overwhelming support for her performance of Nora carried her through the final scenes of the play. Nevertheless, many of the speakers and audience who participated in the Forum on Women's Position that took place in connection with the performance did not support Nora's decision to leave her family.[14] It is not overly surprising that the discussions at the forum were a disappointment to Poblete, given that the panel of speakers consisted of women from the Chilean middle class: a lawyer, a nun, a professor, a psychologist and a journalist, in addition to Poblete and fellow actor Gloria Munchmeyer. Furthermore, the forum was an official event, in all likelihood set up to support the regime's highly traditional patriarchal gender politics. Any attempt to voice a radically feminist reading of the play would have been considered highly 'anti-Pinochet', because the coup itself had promoted the traditional gender roles of men and women in the family, in opposition to the Allende Marxist government's alleged attacks on this 'natural' order. Indeed, many women, especially those of the middle class, supported the coup for much the same reason.[15]

While it seems clear that the clandestine discourse of resistance to the regime was the main issue for many, this does not imply that gender politics were effaced completely from this production of *A Doll's House*. Based on reviews of the production and my interviews with participants in the performance, it seems accurate to say that gender politics intersected with resistance to the dictatorship in this performance. Political and economic repression during the dictatorship had changed the situation for Chilean women in significant ways. With so many men killed, incarcerated or simply unemployed, women were forced to take part in public life in new ways, as breadwinners and as protesters. This participation led to a new consciousness of the nature of oppression in which authoritarianism was linked not to the military regime alone, but to the patriarchy. The dictatorship's pervasive politicisation of daily life also led to new insights into the connections between overarching political mechanisms and the private sphere of the family. Chilean sociologist Julieta Kirkwood has observed that, when 'confronted by [military] authoritarianism, women, in a certain sense, are faced with a phenomenon well known to them: authoritarianism in their daily experiences.'[16]

The reason that this highly traditional 1980 production of *A Doll's House* remains important and strong in the memory of Chilean theatre is that it manages to address several acute problems of life under the dictatorship. The play's durability as an allegorical reflection of political issues seems to have derived from this production. *A Doll's House* could be interpreted in this regard as an interrogation of the intimate connection between large-scale economic and political repression under the dictatorship and, conversely, the manner in which oppression under the dictatorship was reproduced within the family. This staging of a nineteenth-century European classic afforded its audience a sophisticated expression of the slogan that 'the personal is political', not least because Nora's plight spoke to a Chilean reality in which married women could not control their economic means or obtain a legal divorce.[17] This slogan from second-wave international feminism was given extra local significance by Pinochet's strict ideological division between the private and public spheres: a distinction that gave rise to what has been labelled an 'unholy alliance' between patriarchy, militarism, authoritarianism and capitalism, and one that fortuitously reinforced the gender terms central to Ibsen's play.[18] Another issue in *A Doll's House* that resonated with the Chilean audience was the centrality of economic and financial relations to the plot of the play. In some ways the complete restructuring of Chile's economy, an important aspect of Pinochet's 'therapy', had more far-reaching consequences for ordinary Chileans than did the coup itself. Pinochet's extreme neoliberal policies had come far by 1980, when this production took place, so that Nora's and Krogstad's stories of debt and the suffocating experience of economic entrapment resonated well with a declining Chilean middle-class audience. This economic factor, as we will see, has been a recurrent focus of the staging of A *Doll's House* in Chile from 1980 onwards. It is especially interesting that, in those productions with an economic emphasis, Krogstad's role seems to have acquired an added importance and impact *vis á vis* local audiences living within enforced economic constraints.

Nora under the (continuing) neoliberal regime

In their 1995 article about theatre in Chile and Argentina 'after the dictatorships', Ian Watson and Susana Epstein interviewed Héctor Noguera and his daughter Amparo Noguera.[19] Father and daughter are among the leading theatre artists in Chile, and of special interest to this discussion for their involvement in major productions of A *Doll's House* in Santiago: Héctor as Helmer in 1980 and Amparo as Nora in 2006 and 2011. During the interview they stressed the 'huge' differences that occurred in the theatre after the end of Pinochet's rule.[20] This renewed freedom of expression, when people no longer feared being reported to the DINA for their opinions, gave rise to a new wealth of artistic expression. It also led to a renewed focus on the personal; once everything was no longer related to the regime, artists felt free to explore individual experience in fresh ways. At the same time, however, the Nogueras lamented a certain loss of urgency and purpose and were disappointed with the democracy that was now in place. In Amparo Noguera's words, 'we all expected something radically different. There have not been any spectacular changes in Chile.'[21]

It is no surprise that the end of sixteen years of stark repression and revolting human rights abuses should raise expectations of radical change. But it is equally obvious that the chances for structural change were slim, given the fact that General Pinochet was still in charge of the military, a force not to be provoked. When Patricio Aylwin assumed office as the democratically elected President of Chile in 1990, he took over a country in which the radical left and the trade unions had been effectively crushed and a neoliberal state had been installed – with some success, be it said – on its own terms and with disregard for the price paid by its victims. Inflation was down and the country experienced economic growth from year to year. The downside of the macro-economic success was that Chile had gone from being a relatively egalitarian society with strong workers' rights to one of the most inequitable societies in the region, with virtually no protection to prevent workers being fired or their jobs out-sourced. Along with the creation of a 'flexible' job market through deregulation, Pinochet's regime had privatised substantial parts of society. Pensions, education, culture and health were privatised together with manufacturing, agriculture and banking, leaving the ordinary citizen in a position of dependency on market solutions in almost every area of life. The 'trick' of privatisation and deregulation is, of course, that in addition to creating an arena of profit for some, it is a process that is extremely difficult to reverse. This form of 'accumulation by dispossession' will represent a gain for some, while for others it is a constant threat of loss.[22]

Based solely on macro-economic parameters such as growth in the Gross Domestic Product (GDP) and levels of inflation, Chile is an ongoing success story, but judged in terms of equity, poverty rates or social security, the picture is more negative. Duncan Green quotes *El Mercurio* newspaper's report of a World Health Organization (WHO) survey showing that 'over half of all visits to Chile's public health system involve psychological ailments, mainly depression.'[23] This does not mean that life in Chile is worse than in other places. The difference is that the Chilean population has had to face the double challenge of living in the shadow of an especially brutal dictatorship, and in the cold laboratory light of the neoliberal experiment, at one and the same time.[24] Quoting José Joaquín Brunner, the Chilean cultural critic Nelly Richard has characterised the changes in Chilean society as:

> a reasoned substitution of the dictatorial model consisting of 'market, repression, and television' [...] by means of a new model of market, consensus, and television with which the political Transition realised its economic path of adaptation-integration to the modernising pact of neoliberalism.[25]

It was Alfredo Castro's explicit goal to address these changes in Chilean society through his stagings of *A Doll's House* in 2006 and 2011.

Teatro Nacional: Alfredo Castro (2006)

Alfredo Castro is one of Chile's leading directors and actors in theatre, film and television. At his own Teatro la Memoria, Castro has interrogated the experience of dictatorship in complex productions based on real life testimonials in the 1990s.[26] His decision to direct *A Doll's House* at Chile's Teatro Nacional in 2006 was surprising to many, because he had not previously staged a classical play or, for that matter, a performance based on a realistic text. Castro felt that *A Doll's House* could be adapted to make a strong statement about his own Chilean reality, although on a more prosaic level the production was presented as part of the Ibsen centenary in 2006 with financial assistance from the Royal Norwegian Embassy, Santiago. The production was highly successful in terms of reviews and audience turnout, and was selected as one of the three best theatre performances in Chile that year.[27]

Although broadly faithful to the text, the performance was cut down to 1 hour and 50 minutes. The set consisted of a small rhomboid box set, opening out towards the audience from a narrow back wall (Figure 2.1). The lightweight material from which this box was built gave the impression that the Helmers' home was fragile, a confined space within a larger stage. The raked floor and diagonal walls resulted

Figure 2.1 Amparo Noguera as Nora in *A Doll's House*, Teatro Nacional, Santiago, Chile (2006), directed by Alfredo Castro (Photo: Eduardo Cerón).

in an exaggerated perspective, creating an optical illusion which made every person entering the room seem enormous: an effect that was especially striking in the case of Bástian Bodenhöfer as Helmer and Marcelo Alonso as Krogstad, each actor being relatively tall in any case. The pink walls and ceiling could be said to give the set a feminine character, though not in the sense that the woman inhabiting this space was 'at home'.

Nora, played by Amparo Noguera, was constantly on display, with nowhere to hide in this confined space. There being only two small benches to sit on, Nora moved erratically from one corner to the other. Like a caged animal, she would pace up and down, sit, get up, lie down, kneel, wave her feet in the air.[28] In spite of Nora's almost exalted mood, her body spoke of suffering from the beginning of the performance. The confined space of this 'doll's house' was 'modestly' but in no way 'tastefully' furnished: it gave absolutely no feeling of Ibsen's cosy, 'pleasant' middle-class home.[29] The set offered no respite or sanctuary for the woman inhabiting the space, who was set up to be seen and perceived as desirable at all times. Constantly taking care of her appearance, showing her legs, fixing her hair, Amparo Noguera's Nora was conscious that, as a woman, it was her vocation in life to be looked at. Performing the role of the 'attractive woman' had become second nature to her, but this trait was emphasised to such a degree that its hyperbolic nature became disturbing to see. Her repertoire of postures derived from the world of advertising and fashion, all intended to emphasise legs, hips and hair, certainly had charm but (in-)tended to alienate the audience as the performance went on.

Ibsen's *A Doll's House* has proved to be as universal as a play can be, even though its realist text targets the conflicts and problems of a specific social class at a precise historical moment. Castro's 2006 version strongly emphasised and updated the class-specific aspect of the play to make a pointed critique of Chile's bourgeois middle class. This segment of the Chilean population had seen extraordinary economic growth under the dictatorship and in the years after its dissolution. Castro's production portrayed this class as consumers for whom material wealth, and the display of the signs of that wealth, is everything. In this production, Nora arrives onstage burdened with gifts that she has bought for her children; paper wrappings scattered about the floor the day after signify a culture of consumption and waste. Nora throws the miniature Christmas tree into a corner, where it lies with its lights blinking for the rest of the performance, emphasising a complete lack of respect for the value of objects. Nora is a privileged woman who lives in affluence but has no purpose in life. In this sense she seems to be on a par with the objects she consumes. Nora 'belongs' to her husband, is his property. For his part, Helmer does not seem much interested in his attractive wife. For the most part he is cold, aloof and treats Nora like a naughty child. It is only in the scene after the party, when Helmer is drunk, that he shows any desire towards his wife: a vulgar, exploitative desire, unwanted and unanswered by her.

The centrality of Elena the nanny/maid, played by Mireya Moreno in this production, also exposed the mechanisms of a specific capitalist class-based society. Castro had cut the length of the play and given it a faster pace but the scenes with Elena were prolonged, with moments of genuine tenderness as she and Nora consoled each other. But the same scenes showed how submissive Elena has learnt to be, and how badly she is treated, even by Nora: ordered around, yelled at and disregarded when other things are considered more important. Because these scenes are often cut in practice, they stand out in such an economical, high-tempo performance as this. According to Castro, it was impossible to cut the scenes because the presence of a maid is of such importance to the middle-class Chilean world. My informants stress that two other aspects of Ibsen's play had special local resonance: these were the constant underlying presence of secrets from the past and the burden of debt. Two phrases, 'a culture of fear' and 'a culture of enemies', recur as characteristics of Chilean society during the dictatorship.[30] It can be no surprise that Chile is still plagued by memories of human rights abuses. The question of guilt for past deeds arises in many contexts, not least because forgetting had virtually become 'official policy' during the transition to democracy.[31] Bastián Bodenhöfer's Helmer most exemplified this past; ruthless, cold, aloof and buttoned up, but boiling with suppressed brutality and rage, he clearly invoked the figure of the (ex-)torturer.

That Chile has suffered debt crises on national and individual levels is well known. Increased consumerism has also given rise to new forms of debt – credit card debt as well as mortgages. Nora embodies both these aspects in the production, yet Krogstad is the character at the centre of these problems in all the Chilean versions of *A Doll's House*. Marcelo Alonso shaped a Krogstad whose outer appearance and personality was that of a marked man. Wearing an inelegant greenish-brown suit and overcoat, with a badly knotted tie and worn shoes, he appeared to be a man with a troubled past. His past also marked him in the sense that he was played as a man with brutal traits, physically threatening and even violent towards Nora. The sympathy that Krogstad aroused in the audience can be interpreted as an acknowledgement that circumstance has forced him to act as he did. Krogstad embodied a fate to which many members of the audience could relate; threatened with a fall in social status, the decent man had become less than he really was.

Trapped in this narrow confined space, her secrets from the past having returned to haunt her and under attack from Krogstad, Nora becomes more and more frantic. Towards the end of the performance Nora's desperation causes her to transgress the bounds of morality and decency. Upon entering to see Nora, Rank, played by Mateo Iribarren, pours himself two straight drinks and gulps them down while standing. Once he is seated, Nora gives him a third glass, dims the lights and stages a virtual striptease. In this version of the 'stocking scene', Nora waves the thigh-length black silk stockings in the air, removes her 'flesh-coloured' tights and ever so slowly puts on the black stockings, all the while showing more of her legs than Rank wishes to see. In one final movement, she lies on the bench, her legs wide open to him in an unequivocal invitation to sex. Rank, still in his jacket, tie and overcoat, stands up in embarrassment before her. When he confesses his feelings towards Nora, she calms down, walks over to him and slaps him in the face. Feelings and commitment have no place in this world.

By the time of the 'tarantella' scene, Nora's desperation has driven her to lose most of her social inhibitions. She first dances gracefully to the music but soon lapses into a vulgar erotic dance. Her dance is wild and erratic, switching haphazardly from one style to the other, but its main thrust is erotic, even aggressively sexual. Nora performs a virtual lap dance for Rank, who raises his hands in the air to signal that he will not touch her in spite of her invitations. Helmer yells in anger as Nora's hip-thrusts become more and more explicit. When the men change roles, with Rank at the 'piano' and Helmer directing, Nora becomes even wilder, virtually bouncing off the walls and making sexually explicit movements. Helmer's response is to scream at her like a madman, while Kristine and Elena look on with shocked expressions.

The 'tarantella' and 'stocking' scenes are pivotal moments in Ibsen's play and they remain so in Castro's version. But Castro's direction of these scenes differs from many other versions, in the sense that they give a highly ambiguous picture of Nora. To some spectators, the sexual elements in Nora's behaviour might show her to be a spoilt bourgeois woman of low morals, whereas others might interpret them as part of a significant discussion about the perceived lack of sexual intimacy and reciprocity in Nora's world. What is striking in Amparo Noguera's version of these scenes, however, is that she depicts a Nora without interiority, as a person who is difficult to understand, one with whom it is hard to connect or empathise. In all her helpless desperation, what comes across is a woman reduced to her body, projecting a series of sexually charged bodily movements that are typical of a commercial, exploitative culture. This Nora is a privileged woman, but at the same time she is depicted as a person with very few resources. Her good looks and sexuality certainly give her some power in daily life within the 'doll's house' but, when crisis threatens, this is in fact all she has to rely on. The corresponding scenes in Ibsen's play often foreshadow signs of autonomy and assertiveness in Nora, but in Castro's version Nora's decline into the bodily gestures of pornography and prostitution point, more than anything, to her subaltern position. Castro's re-interpretation of these scenes makes it clear that Nora's room to manoeuvre is extremely restricted. As Nora's actions become more and more sexually explicit she increasingly resembles an automaton, with the saddening confirmation that this woman has only her body to negotiate with.

The central thrust of Castro's version of the play is that a woman of Nora's social class is objectified; her body is an item of exchange, a field of transactions between men. This point becomes even clearer as they return quite drunk from the party: Nora lies down facing the wall on the bench to the right, while Helmer presses himself down next to her. As he starts making advances she kicks him onto the floor. Her rejection enrages him: he jumps up, pulls her to her feet and starts kissing her on the mouth while clutching her head in a violent grip. Thus Rank's arrival seems to interrupt the early stages of a marital rape. Dressed as a clown, Rank is even drunker than the others. At this point both men show their desire for Nora's body in the other's presence, and when Helmer passes out for a moment Rank and Nora kiss. Having said goodbye to

Nora, Rank kicks Helmer's leg to wake him up and the men stagger across the floor, bidding each other farewell. Rank's death note, however, has a sobering effect on Helmer and he exits to read his correspondence.

Although Castro's version addressed contemporary class-specific problems within the realistically localised setting of present-day Santiago, it kept faithfully to Ibsen's text up to this point in the performance. However, the most controversial aspect of the performance was the literal interpretation of the soliloquy in which Nora speaks of never seeing her family again and mentions 'the black, icy water' in which she has previously fantasised about ending her life.[32] These imaginings materialise in Castro's version. Nora takes a pair of scissors and tries to slit her wrists. She sits, with blood running from both wrists, as Helmer re-enters with Krogstad's letter in his hand. Helmer then has to cool down and show some concern, calming Nora and tying a scarf around her wrists before he reproaches and accuses her. Nora sits paralysed in shock. Not all reviewers approved of this interpretation of the text. It is problematic in that it victimises Nora as an hysteric beyond rational control; in so doing, it denies Nora's agency only minutes before the actress is required to show Nora's self-control and capacity for rational action.

The audience's laughter makes it clear that Nora retains their sympathy when, after she has left the room on the arrival of Krogstad's second letter, Helmer declares that he is saved and that he will now protect and shelter her as his dearest property. When Nora re-enters, wearing only her shoes and a brief slip, she takes control of the stage. Helmer remains seated while Nora has her say, puts on an overcoat and walks out of the door. Almost naked under her coat, and with no other possessions, Nora walks out into the real world, wiggling her hips with the exaggerated movement of a model on a catwalk or a prostitute in the street. The manner of Nora's exit emphasises her vulnerability. It injects further doubt and ambiguity into the play's ending and bodes ill for Nora's future. A few seconds after Nora has left we hear the door slam, not once but five times, at intervals of five to ten seconds. The performance symbolically hammers home the message that this ending is final – this class and this social reality must end.

Teatro la Memoria (2011)

In spite of the immense success of Castro's 2006 version of *A Doll's House*, he felt that there was more to the play than he and his actors had been able to elicit. He therefore decided to stage a new interpretation of *A Doll's House* in 2011. Funding from the Norwegian Embassy in Santiago had made it possible to build a new set and design costumes and props for the 2006 production. However, Castro's Teatro la Memoria received no external funding for the 2011 performance. In hindsight, Castro came to see this financial situation as an advantage, because the 2011 production of necessity delivered an even starker, more naked version of the play. Parts of the 2006 set, including the optical illusions of the box set and raked stage, were reused, but there were fewer properties: a sofa on the left and five old chairs on the right, a record player on the wall to the left and a set of (ominous) Japanese swords to the right. Teatro la Memoria could not afford costumes, so the actors wore their own clothes. Although the production kept to the main plot line, it offered a fresh staging and re-contextualisation of the play. Castro and several of the actors felt that it was more successful in artistic terms, but it attracted smaller audiences than the 2006 version had done, and did not fare as well with the reviewers.

The most significant changes to the 2011 production centred on the casting: Luis Gnecco replaced Bodenhöfer as Helmer, while Claudia de Girolamo replaced Court as Ms Linde, and Rodrigo Pérez replaced Iribarren as Rank. While the cast contributed collectively to the interpretation of the 2011 production, the bodily presence of Gnecco's Helmer exerted a radical influence. Whereas Bodenhöfer's Helmer had come across as a tall, stern well-dressed man of the world, Gnecco's Helmer was small, bald, overweight and inelegantly dressed. The main difference, however, was that Gnecco's Helmer was explicitly violent. During their first conversation (1 minute and 40 seconds into the 2011 performance) Helmer crossed to the seated Nora and twisted her nose between his thumb and index finger while he reprimanded her for spending too much money. The casual manner with which Helmer inflicted physical pain on his wife, and her submissive acceptance of it, established from the outset that physical violence permeates this relationship.

This violence reshaped the relationship between Helmer and Nora and significantly altered the actors' interpretations of these roles. Amparo Noguera's Nora in 2006 was as frustrated as she was hyperactive, stressed and oversexed. In 2011, she played a more subdued, controlled and rational Nora. Whereas Noguera's 2006 Nora had virtual freedom of the theatrical space, her 2011 Nora's capacity to move about the performance space was radically constrained. When Gnecco's Helmer raised his voice or yelled at Nora, as he frequently did, she would sit still and lower her head or turn her face away, as if to deflect a blow that might follow. Although no strong domestic violence was acted out, almost every scene showed a woman living in fear of an escalation that might lead to physical assault. The question of domestic violence – whether Helmer is a wife-beater – often arises during rehearsals of *A Doll's House*. The difficulty for Castro was that a focus on physical domestic violence had the potential to be reductive: the broader political problem of the patriarchal system, which is at stake, might be reduced to the monstrous behaviour of an individual man. Nora's problems, and those of women in society, are not to be solved simply by men not hitting them. Having said that, it is my opinion that Castro's 2011 production of the play demonstrates that this choice can succeed in the theatre, when its effects reverberate as strongly with local historical and political circumstance as they did in his version.

Castro stressed that there were many reasons for foregrounding violence in the performance.[33] Most obvious was the recognition that domestic violence constituted a serious, widespread but hidden problem in Chilean society, especially among the bourgeoisie. Symbolically, however, the violence in the private sphere was part of a reflection on the cultural inheritance from the dictatorship, an interrogation of memories of violent political repression and their lived presence. There was a class-specific aspect to this heritage of repression. The production reflected the fact that the privileges enjoyed by the middle class are a direct effect of violence and repression and that violence and repression have, in turn, permeated the fabric of the bourgeoisie's private and interpersonal relationships. The social, cultural and psychological effects of violence were variously manifested in performance: in Nora's body, in the silence of those witnessing the violence, and in the character of the maid Elena, whose arm in a cast prompted the unspoken question of how it came to be broken. The effects of a different but no less relevant form of social violence were reflected in Marcello Alonso's revised performance as Krogstad. Whereas Alonso's 2006 Krogstad had not been without its positive aspects, his 2011 version stood out as the only estimable character in an otherwise bleak world. Alonso gave a low-key performance as Krogstad but endowed the role with moral standing. His Krogstad did not intend to hurt anyone. He acts for the well-being of his family, and his misfortune is of an economic nature rather than the result of moral failure. In fact, the lines in which Krogstad speaks of his past crimes were cut. Shabbily dressed, with holes in his worn-out shoes, he pleads to be given a chance to prove himself. Like so many members of Chile's lower middle class, he is ruined by debt and economic misfortunes but struggles to retain his dignity. Hence the calm, almost serene character of the scene in which Krogstad and Ms Linde speak and reunite stands out in a performance that has so many sordid elements.

Amparo Noguera's Nora displayed her sexuality in vulgar, helplessly desperate ways in the 2006 production, but her more calculating 2011 version of Nora played the sexual cards more calmly and deliberately. This Nora turns the lights down for the 'stocking scene' and dances seductively in front of Rank before removing her panties and holding them up to the good doctor's nose. When Rank confesses his feelings for her, Nora is infuriated, slaps him in the face, walks halfway into the dining room and puts her underwear back on. The image of her standing in front of him, holding her underwear up to his face, presents a double vulnerability: hers and his. The sex with which she tries to lure him is not what he desires. Nora knows that her body is exchange value. Her sexuality is all barter and calculation, a means to an end that inevitably excludes emotional involvement. In the same cold, calculating way, she makes sexual advances towards both Helmer and Krogstad in order to manipulate them. This Nora is conscious that her body is what she has to bargain with: a subaltern position from which it is extremely difficult to speak.

A similar point is made when Helmer directs Nora like a drill sergeant in the 'tarantella' scene, yelling, barking orders at her and actually performing the dance in order to show how it is done. Not without grace, the small, slightly obese man dances the 'erotic dance' he wants his wife to perform: a prostitute's dance that ends with Helmer leaning his body backwards on the sofa, as if offering his hips suggestively to his onstage audience. Nora's response is not to dance but to break down. She goes down on all fours, waving her head violently, rolls over onto her back and shakes in uncontrolled, spasm-like movements on the floor. Helmer is infuriated and yells at her constantly.

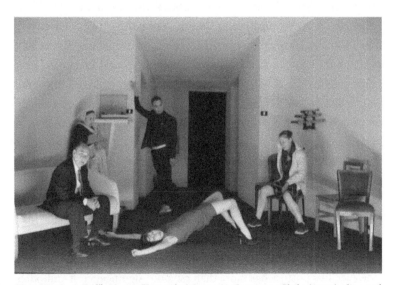

Figure 2.2 *A Doll's House*, Teatro la Memoria, Santiago, Chile (2011), directed by Alfredo Castro. From left to right: Helmer (Luis Gnecco), Elena (Mireya Moreno), Rank (Rodrigo Pérez), Ms Linde (Claudia de Girolamo) and Nora (Amparo Noguera) on the floor (Photo: Ulises Nilo).

As Nora gets up, she dances different dance forms in fits and spasms. In this way, Nora's ability to communicate with the audience in the auditorium through her body is reduced to a 'no' that is implicit in the breakdown of bodily movement and grace. Castro's version of the 'tarantella scene', in which the husband instructs his wife how to dance out his fantasy of her as a prostitute, elicits some of the darker, more perverse elements of Ibsen's text. The inherent violence of this fantasy becomes explicit when Nora begs Helmer to leave her in peace as they return from the party: 'No, Torvaldo. No. Por favor!' Even in the presence of Ms Linde, Helmer gropes his wife, making it clear that he demands her services. When Rank arrives a few minutes later, dressed in drag, he interrupts a marital rape.[34]

Several reviewers found Nora's suicide attempt in the 2006 production to be 'problematic'. I would contend that the 2011 version of her attempted suicide was far more successful due to its explicit departure from realism. In this latter version, a row of light bulbs faced the audience from the walls of the Helmers' box-like apartment. When switched on at the beginning of this scene these lights effectively transform the stage from a 'realistic' room to something like a box containing pictures or tableaux that one might view in passing at a sideshow. This effect is further enhanced by the repeated blinking of the light bulbs on and off, as if to underscore a departure from realistic action towards a symbolic or allegorical content. Nora's slow, operatic movement creates a similar effect as she lifts a pair of scissors high in the air and lets them descend ever so slowly to her wrist. Although Nora moans in physical agony as she cuts herself, she seems to be trying to excise a part of her psychology that has prevailed until now, rather than take her life as such. As Torvaldo enters, she sits on the sofa, both wrists bloodied although she has cut only one. She holds her arms out loosely from her sides, as if alluding to Christ on the cross. However, this posture has more than religious significance; it embodies the recognition that a clean break with the past is necessary if one is to liberate oneself. Nora's attempt at suicide symbolically enacts a transformation of her status from object to subject. In order to liberate herself, to bring about a genuine change, Nora must 'kill' parts of her being that have prevailed to that point. The material fact of her bleeding is scarcely emphasised; Torvaldo simply ties a scarf around her wrists and continues his verbal abuse. But Nora now seems changed as, sitting erect and unflinching, head unbowed, she listens to Torvaldo.

Having read the second letter, Helmer says that he is 'saved', that he 'forgives' Nora and wants to continue their life together. But Nora exits through the door to the living quarters. When, later, Helmer calls for her through the same door, Nora reappears below the stage, in front of the raised box set, looking into it from the audience's point of view. Hence, when Nora tells Helmer to sit down and listen to what she has to say, she speaks from a position that is literally and metaphorically outside the 'doll's house'. This staging suggests that liberation presupposes an outside of the oppressive mechanisms. In order to understand that something is seriously wrong, and that one can break out of an oppressive situation, one has to see it as such, and this is only possible if one can, to some degree, take an external position from which other possibilities become conceivable. That this position is difficult to achieve, and may be only temporarily held, is reflected in performance by Nora's re-entry to the stage space during their discussion. She jumps back into the set again and talks back, with strength. As in 2006, this Nora is dressed only in a brief slip but she stands her ground, and Helmer seems to accept that physical violence will not change anything. It is significant that in this latter production Nora does not exit with the exaggerated bodily movements of the prostitute or the model, as in 2006. She simply puts on a coat, walks through the main door of the box set, and reappears at the front of the stage to speak her final words and depart. There is no reason to slam the door repeatedly in this production.

Large sections of the audience at the 1980 Catholic University production of *A Doll's House* identified Nora with 'the Chilean people', and a similar identification can be read in Castro's 2011 version. In contrast, the tone of the 2006 production was bleaker; it was almost an aggressive attack on a social class, the bourgeoisie. However, the explicit violence of the 2011 production at Teatro la Memoria paradoxically endowed Nora with more empathy and stronger autonomy. The audience was willing to believe in and emotionally support the protagonist, and therefore to construe the ending as more than a judgement on a specific class. This same version of *A Doll's House* also invited a clearer meta-dramatic reading along broader symbolic and political lines. Due to its stronger emphasis on violence and the symbolic character of the *mise en scène*, it is possible to interpret the Teatro la Memoria production of the play as, at one and the same time, a woman's struggle to free herself from oppression and a people's struggle for political freedom. Interpreted along these lines, the performance thematises the severe difficulties of breaking out of a situation of oppressive violence, not least because of the subterranean ways in which this violence persists and lives on through its effects and memories.

In pursuit of Nora Helmer (2012)

Under the leadership of actors Alexandra von Hummel and Alexis Moreno, Santiago's Teatro la Maria, founded in 1999, has become 'one of the leading theatrical groups in Chile'.[35] The company focuses on collective work within an avant-garde postmodern aesthetic that critically addresses contemporary issues in an open-ended, multi-faceted manner. In 2012 von Hummel directed the company's adaptation of *A Doll's House*, called *Persiguendo a Nora Helmer* (*In pursuit of Nora Helmer*). As the title indicates, this adaptation centred on the role of Nora from her perspective as the one targeted, in the double sense of being pursued and investigated meta-theatrically.

According to von Hummel, the performance was developed largely through improvisation.[36] This is most obvious with regard to the first part of the performance, an improvised induction as it were, not to be found in Ibsen's play. The performance opens with the stage in complete darkness. To a simple, brief melody on a flute, just enough cross-lighting comes up to show the legs of five actors in skirts and high heels.

Gradually the actors begin to move: four of them take seats in chairs lined horizontally at centre stage, while the fifth moves to the left, where we hear her knock on a door. When there is no response she returns to the remaining chair. As the lighting gradually increases the audience sees that some of these 'women' have quite a lot of facial hair. The performance starts by blurring the gender boundaries, leading the audience to misinterpret the visual information (skirts, bare legs, high heels) as specifically feminine. The opening sequence sets up the audience to experience its own misattribution of secondary sexual characteristics and gender identities to the actors, three of whom are in fact males. Thus, during the first twenty minutes of the performance there are five 'women' on stage, three of them performed by male actors dressed as women, with wigs, false breasts and make-up. The set, a rectangular room with bare walls and several doors, is designed to suggest a waiting-room. Exactly what the 'women' are waiting for is never clarified; no one is served, even though the 'women' repeatedly knock on the door to the left. It is the day before Christmas and they are desperate to be attended to, because the office will be closed the day after. The most active woman juggles a lot of shopping bags, another talks on her cell phone, one smokes a cigarette in spite of it being forbidden, one cries – and they all quarrel. It is difficult to align these five figures with Ibsen's characters during this sequence, although one might suspect that the woman with the shopping bags is (or is to become) Nora. Indeed, she says that her husband has placed her on a diet, forbids her to eat sweets and is about to take up a well-paid job.

Much of the dialogue during this first part of the performance centres on money, consumer goods and debt. The five characters on stage seem to be middle-class women struggling to make ends meet. Most striking, however, is their complete lack of solidarity or empathy for each other. No one bothers in the least when one of them (who later plays Krogstad) starts crying. The others abuse the Nora figure with crude sexist taunts, as she becomes the centre of their attention, calling her a 'cunt' and telling her that what she needs is 'a good fuck'. She should ask Santa Claus for a 'piece of dick', someone 'to fuck [her] hard, from every single hole [her] body has.'[37] This 2012 performance presented Nora as a hunted figure, with no women's solidarity to back her up. The actors later claimed in interviews that this misogynist sexism was 'realistic'; women in Chile could, and would, address each other in this way.[38]

The cross-dressing in the opening sequence certainly served to blur gender boundaries but at the same time it had a more specific bearing on how male chauvinist rhetoric has invaded, even taken over, discourse between women. These women, it would seem, have no recourse to a space free from the verbal violence of patriarchy. The sinister waiting-room sequence does away with any redeeming belief in a more positive, gentle, humane 'feminine'. The quotation marks are apt here; it matters that three of these 'women' are clearly men. In other words, while the fiction in the opening sequence is that all five figures are 'women', it would also be obvious to an audience that three of them are cross-dressed males. For this reason, it seems to me that the performance oscillates between the fiction that all five figures are 'women' and an awareness that three are transvestites. Unstable, unresolvable double meanings are central to the performance.

Richard points out the extent to which 'Artistic imagery invoking the figure of the transvestite (art, photography, video, literature, theatre) exploded under the dictatorship'.[39] She argues that, under Pinochet's regime, the figure of the transvestite functioned as a critical trope to destabilise patriarchal repression in the name of 'family values'. Cross-dressing is of double local significance in this production. It points up the situation of women here and now in post-dictatorial Chile, where the majority of politicians promote 'traditional' gender roles with the assertion: 'that what is essential for women is being a mother.'[40] At the same time, it points back in history to the Pinochet era, during which women were 'pursued', although not in the same sense and manner. Ultimately, this improvised, self-referential cross-dressing situates *Persiguendo a Nora Helmer* within a larger, global context in which theatre classics are re-interpreted so as to diffuse and denaturalise traditional gender roles. Transvestism releases the gender politics of the production from any anchoring in biological or sexual essence.

On a more formal level, a primary function of this opening sequence
is to frame the performance of Ibsen's play in a disjunctive post-
dramatic mode that offers very little in the way of psychological
development or unilinear action. The opening sequence is also post-
dramatic in that the actors switch roles as the performance shifts from
'five women in a waiting-room' to Henrik Ibsen's *A Doll's House*. The
switch itself is initiated in an ostentatious way when Nora addresses
each of the 'women' as an Ibsen character. Thus, when Nora refers to one
of the verbally abusive women as 'Helmer', the latter instantly switches
to the Ibsen character of that name. After a short exchange, this newly
constituted but still cross-dressed Helmer leaves through the door to
the left, but when Nora tries to follow him the door is locked. The same
pattern recurs, as she activates the roles of Krogstad, Linde and Rank.
The latter two exit through the door to the right, while dancing joyfully
to music with their arms in the air.[41] Once again, Nora finds the door
locked. She remains isolated, trapped.

When Krogstad re-enters to ask Nora to help him keep his job, and
threatens her with the forged signature on the mortgage, he has lost
some of his female attributes – the false breasts and wig – but still wears
his short grey skirt, white blouse and ladies' shoes. Having talked to
Ms Linde about his predicament and the prospect of losing his job,
Krogstad sits on a high chair facing the audience, spreads his legs and
exposes his naked genitals under the short skirt. So while Krogstad
recapitulates how Nora came to him to borrow money, with the proviso
that her father should sign the mortgage as security, he himself is, so to
speak, fully exposed. The contradictory meanings of this scene and this
image sum up much of the production. Krogstad seems vulnerable and
feminine as he takes out a lipstick to fix his make-up while talking to
Nora. His nakedness adds to his vulnerability, but at the same time it
makes him (or her) phallic.[42] His casually exposed genitals emphasise
his masculinity while simultaneously evoking the image of the phallic
woman – often perceived as threatening. Hence the scene and its central
image oscillate between opposing meanings that leave its interpretation
open-ended and contradictory.

The performance continues after an intermission, with all five characters seated around a table to the left of the stage 'as if they have just finished Christmas dinner' (von Hummel: 22). All remain on stage, listening attentively and responding non-verbally to Nora's 'private' duologues with each of them. Rank smiles, even laughs, as Nora describes him to Kristine as her daily companion and a friend of the family; Krogstad leaves the table, as if he cannot bear to hear what Helmer says about him; and Ms Linde leans forward, shaking her head and knocking it on the table, as Nora walks round the table to show Rank the flesh-coloured stockings she is (not in fact) wearing, lifting her short skirt to show more thigh. Nora is the only one to speak into a microphone during these conversations, her voice amplified and emphatic, although the microphone gives her no real authority. Several such V-effects serve at this point to counteract and undermine the psychological realism and other mimetic aspects of the play. But that does not mean that this

Figure 2.3 *In Pursuit of Nora Helmer*, Teatro la Maria, Santiago, Chile (2012), directed by Alexandra von Hummel. From left to right: Nora (Tamara Acosta), Krogstad (Alexis Moreno), Ms Linde (Alejandra Oviedo), Helmer (Elvis Fuentes) and Rank (Rodrigo Soto) (Photo: Courtesy of Alexandra von Hummel).

version of the play is unequivocally deconstructed or anti-theatrical. Several scenes, notably Nora's conversations with Rank and Krogstad, are played with emotional intensity, but as episodes rather than as part of a genuine psychological development. The production focuses on Nora's perspective as the one being pursued.

All dramatic transitions linking the scenes to each other in realistic sequence have been cut, and Nora goes directly from one episode with a single character to the next. In the same vein, the 'tarantella' scene begins as Nora simply picks up a plastic bag that contains her costume, which she quickly slips on. This is made possible by the simplicity of the costume, which consists only of a golden cape, articulated so that it takes differing shapes as Nora swirls it behind her. Her dance lacks elegance and rhythm, her rigid body and clumsy movements are not those of a dancer. This interpretation of the dance is one of the few elements that von Hummel's version shares with Castro's two versions of the play; all three renditions of the tarantella register Nora as subaltern. This effect is heightened as Helmer, seated on a barstool, a drink in his hand, laughs his head off at his wife's inept dance. Nor does Nora evince sympathy from Rank, who slouches sneeringly around the floor. Kristine simply giggles.

This post-dramatic adaptation of *A Doll's House* focuses on episodes of intensity with little regard for psychological depth and development. However, there is one kind of development hard to overlook – one that works in tandem with the basic sequence of the text itself (which is largely intact in von Hummel's version) – and that is the development in terms of dress and gender. As noted above, the male characters shed certain of their 'feminine' attributes during the course of the action until, in the final scene following the party, Helmer and Krogstad, who passes silently through the room to deliver his last letter, are dressed unequivocally as men, with no gender ambivalence. Schematically speaking, *Persiguondo a Nora Helmer* opens with five 'women' figures and progresses, by diminishing degrees of transvestism, towards clear traditional boundaries. In the manner of a conceptualist work of art, von Hummel's adaptation of *A Doll's House* invites reflection on the meaning of the concepts of power, gender and sex as invoked by its visual signs.

Although the production offers no clear-cut answer to the question of what is socially constructed with regard to gender and what is not, it is of vital importance to identify who or what it is that Nora leaves at the end of this performance. In fact, she leaves Thorvald who has reappeared as a traditional man. In the scenes in which Helmer is at his 'worst', those in which he is, for the first time, constructed as a traditional man, Nora comes to see that she has been living through a repressive swindle. This construction of the masculine – the transvestism underscores its constructedness – is identified as the problem itself. The socially constructed gender roles may be impossible to escape or discard with any finality, but they still have to be broken down; which is why Nora leaves. It is worth noting that in order for the performance to make its point it has to go beyond the semiotics of transvestism, while the unresolved ambiguities of male cross-dressing reverberate through to the ending.

According to the Chilean artist Ernesto Muñoz, when 'you work with transvestites in art, you are not offering correct information. This creates difficulties for the spectator'.[43] In my view, these 'difficulties' of interpretation and understanding were central to Teatro la Maria's version of *A Doll's House*. Certain reviewers perceived them as a deplorable 'lack of clarity', but the 'lack' was in any case consciously constructed.[44] The open-ended, contradictory meanings of parts of the dramatic sign system were intentionally constructed to prevent the performance from being readily assimilated, reduced to a simple meaning or 'natural' narrative flow. As I see it, this aspect of the performance is rooted in the contradictions of the post-dictatorial Chilean situation, in which so little about the past and the future is clear, reconciled and uncontested.

The future is definitely at stake in *A Doll's House*. However open the future might be, it has to be dealt with in any staging of the play. In von Hummel's version, future prospects are minimised. The omission of lines that reflect on what life will be like when Nora leaves, and what it would take for there to be a future for the two of them together, stress the past and the urgent need to break with it.[45] As Nora 'exits through the only door that wasn't used during the play' she laments the fact that she has been living for eight years with a strange man, adding that 'thousands of women [...] every day' sacrifice 'their honour' for a man (von Hummel: 46). She leaves a hostile world of pursuit and, it would seem, a wasted past; the one door that she has not yet tried turns out to be the one that opens for her. The situation at the conclusion of the play remains open-ended. There is little for Nora to rely on once she leaves. Even so, Tamara Acosta's Nora is calm and resolute at the end; unlike Amparo Noguera's versions of Nora, Acosta's Nora clearly has the strength and ability to act. The spectator can believe that this woman is able take care of herself, even as the 'pursuit' goes on.

The Chilean way

Salvador Allende's Chilean way to socialism through democracy was blocked by violence, repression and dictatorship. The same cannot be said of Chilean theatre. The four differing versions of *A Doll's House* discussed in this chapter testify to the artistic strength, resilience and social relevance of Chilean theatre. These four productions are of interest for the distinctive ways in which each brings a precise Chilean topicality to broader global issues in Ibsen's play. Each version invites its own double-layered realistic and allegorical, or symbolic, reading of the play in a contemporary Chilean context. The Pinochet regime's repressive violence endowed everything on stage in Castillo's 1980 version with double-layered meaning. The same violence was everywhere implied in adaptations by Castro in 2006 and von Hummel in 2012, and was once more explicit in Castro's 2011 revision of the play. Violence, however, is never simply violence. This is especially so in these Chilean versions of *A Doll's House*, which never focus on domestic violence alone but address systemic violence that derives equally from political and economic conditions, and gender discrimination. The scope widens to include the past violence of the dictatorship, and the violence subsequently done to the memory of that past.

Memory is rarely neutral and uncontested. What a person or a society remembers will vary, as will the interpretation and colouring of remembered 'facts'. The past that Thorvald remembers as good, harmonious and normal is a remembered past of repression, misdirection and patriarchal heteronomy to Nora. The notion that liberation presupposes a reckoning with the past informs the ways in which Amparo Noguera and Tamara Acosta each shaped the role of Nora. As interpreted by director Alfredo Castro, this means that Nora must find a space that is beyond the pressure placed on her as an object of desire, and beyond the flimsy flashes of intensity and enjoyment that capitalist hyper-consumption offers. These systemic pressures and gratifications afford no space for real memory, and hence no space for agency. To escape the forgetfulness of consumerism – or indeed, the destruction of memory through torture – presupposes memory as coherence, direction and continuity in the individual, and in the political sense.

There can be no doubt that the Chilean context of these performances informs their global significance. Castro's and von Hummel's versions of *A Doll's House* are examples of how Ibsen can be staged in practice with complete topicality and, at the same time, address broader complexities ranging from questions of class and gender to the precariousness of individual life under globalising capitalism. An understanding of these Chilean productions requires knowledge of the local, but they cannot be reduced to their local context; the intriguing thickness of the sign systems performed make these productions transcend their immediate context. It is no accident that Dr Rank, as played by Rodrigo Pérez in 2011, returns from the party in women's clothes; his cross-dressing establishes a fresh set of signs, a space of interpretation beyond the violence that permeates the fictional world of the production. Rank's dress is a marginal sign, but one that points towards an alternative space that is external to the claustrophobic cage Castro creates on stage. I am very conscious that I am interpreting these four Chilean productions of

A Doll's House from traces: recordings, photos, reviews, scripts and interviews from performances I have not seen. But judging from these traces, it is clear that when, for instance, the transvestite figure appears on Castro's stage, it questions gender constructions performed on (and off) stage, and the relations of power inherent in them. This questioning is perhaps the central strategy of these post-dictatorship productions; to make the signs 'insubordinate', as Nelly Richard puts it.[46] This strategy is taken several steps further in Teatro la Maria's version, which brings together post-dramatic and queer elements in a production that, like those before it, cannot be summed up in a formulaic way. And I have no wish to do so. While these productions differ radically in their approach to theatrical semiotics, form and content, each addresses vital issues concerning symbolic and real violence, identity politics and the politics of material distribution, with critical rigour and playful humour.

Ibsen under the Radar: Censorship and Artistic Expression

Censorship represents one of the most difficult and complex issues within the field of criticism and aesthetics. The analytic and theoretical difficulties are multiple: many stem from the fact that censorship influences the artistic process and end result in ways that remain necessarily hidden, subterranean. We may safely infer that as a film or theatre performance passes through some kind of censorship body or office, it will be marked by the presence of the censoring body. What these marks or traces look like, how they can be discerned, decoded and analysed are, however, far more difficult questions.

Ibsen's plays were subject to censorship in one form or another in many European countries from the outset. However, I do not intend to give this history: my focus here is on a selection of prominent theatre and film adaptations of Ibsen's plays that have been chosen as strong and interesting artistic works in their own right. It is important to stress that these instances are chosen not because they illustrate overt censorship in 'other' cultures (which they do), but because they radically transcend the fact that they originate in systems that exercise state censorship. Part of what makes this issue so complex and intriguing is that there is no simple equation when it comes to aesthetic richness (or the lack thereof) and censorship. It is important to stress that the question of censorship is not a-cultural; it cannot be addressed from a trans-cultural or meta-cultural vantage point. The all too common Western assumption that censorship is only to be found in 'other' cultures is quite simply false.[1] Censorship in some sense is everywhere, not only in societies that the West regards as unenlightened or undemocratic. The right to free speech, like all human rights, carries with it obligations, and all societies have rules governing what can be expressed, how, when and by whom. Even if a society does not have explicit censorship laws, it will have laws and regulations concerning morality, decency, libel and national security.

This granted, it remains the case that what may be taken for censorship is, in many cases, merely a matter of perfectly legitimate cultural differences: the way that nudity can be displayed on stage in the West is manifestly unacceptable in many parts of Asia, without that being a case of censorship in the strict sense. What concerns me here, then, is not so much the moral or cultural differences that render some types of expression illegal or impossible in certain cultures, but rather what we could term political or ideological state censorship. The borders between culture practice and political censorship are at times difficult to draw, a point that the early censorship of Ibsen illustrates. *A Doll's House* and *Ghosts*, for example, were censored in Europe not only for reasons of moral offence, but (more probably) because they were seen as attacks on the authority of family, church and state.[2] The crucial point is that what ruling powers claim to be their concern for morality is in fact very often an ideological strategy to hide or protect what is in reality an amoral, repressive and inhumane state of affairs.[3] The (mis)use of public morality to justify attempts to censor and suppress unwanted political or ideological utterances is surely still with us in most countries. The besetting difficulty is to discern between these ideological strategies and the more legitimate cases that are grounded in respect for cultural difference. It may not be possible to draw a clear dividing line between the two, and I will not attempt to do so here.

In my view, it is fair to say that censorship within the arts in Western capitalist societies is to a large extent managed through a combination of public sponsorship agencies and what we call the market. But self-censorship is, after all, the most efficient form of censorship, and there is every reason to believe that this mechanism currently works well in Western societies.[4] It is important, however, to stress that there are different kinds and degrees of censorship, and that a central distinction can be made between those societies that have explicit, law-enforced, bureaucratic systems of censorship, and those that do not.[5] How, and to what extent, censorship exists in the latter is not part of the present discussion. What interests me is how systems of censorship affect the staging of Ibsen in a few well-documented cases. How is artistic expression influenced by state censorship? What happens when Ibsen passes under the radar of state censors? And can we say that artists adapt Ibsen for specific purposes within cultures or countries that exercise official censorship?

In his reflection on censorship, J. M. Coetzee critiques the notion, frequently advanced, that censorship is there to protect the public from 'undesirable' utterances or expressions.[6] But clearly they are desire-able, there *is* a desire for them, or there would be no need for the censor. However, that which the censor seeks to suppress is not so much the single utterance itself but the general desire for a specific kind of utterance. The ultimate goal of censorship is that the desire for these utterances should disappear, such that the need for official censorship disappears as censorship itself becomes a sub-conscious or pre-conscious process. This is why self-censorship is the most efficient form of censorship, and the true goal of all censors. However, self-censorship is already practised to some degree by everyone everywhere, a fact that poses extreme difficulties for any analysis. The problem is exacerbated when a cultural outsider carries out the analysis. To be precise, my analyses of adaptations of Ibsen that originate in cultures of which I have only a secondary knowledge pose cultural, political and ethical challenges to my own subject position. For this reason I have tried to be modest and tentative in my conclusions.

Prelude: Double dolls in Hanoi

When we say that part of a play or film has been censored, what we usually mean is that it has been suppressed. Where a performance text of a theatre classic is concerned, this would usually mean that certain scenes or lines have had to be rewritten or removed in order for the performance to pass the censors. This, then, is the most obvious point of departure when analysing a performance under systems of state censorship; that is to say, to look for absences or alterations that can be explained or interpreted as the effects of censorship. The complementary, more difficult but no less interesting, process is constituted by additions and supplements.

The incorporation of dolls and marionettes into the *mise en scène* of Le Hung's highly successful 2006 production of *A Doll's House* in Hanoi can illustrate the intricacies involved when a practitioner adds elements to a source text.[7] As a prologue to the Hanoi production, a small elderly man wearing a long, dark unbuttoned overcoat enters through the stage curtain. He stands in the spotlight for a short while before he lifts an arm and points upward, first to his left and then to his right, where puppets are being lowered from the stage loft. The puppets to his right are male and those to the left are female, each puppet hanging from a clearly visible string. Once the puppets have descended to floor level, the old man, like a seller of counterfeit watches, opens his overcoat to show that the inside is lined with small puppets, miniatures of those hanging about him. He then exits through the stage curtain, having led us into the performance through visual signs and gestures.

When the actor playing Nora, Lê Khanh, enters she walks about with an expression of mild surprise, looking at and touching the puppets hanging down to the stage around her. The actor's entry onstage may be seen as a further sign both of the relevance of the 'puppetness' of the depicted world, and of the distance of the performance from any naïve realism. It precludes any contract of simple realistic identification, and invites the spectator to think in terms of an added, more open play of signifiers. The audience is, in this sense, invited to infer, to interpret, even to allegorise what they see on stage. This invitation to semiosis is hard to limit, and can take many directions, depending on the intellectual and emotional sensibility of the individual spectator.

These four puppets, two male and two female, remain present on stage throughout the performance, sometimes hanging down in front of one of the windows, sometimes seated on the window sill (Figure 3.1). Later Nora is accompanied in the tarantella scene by marionettes, and by humans acting as puppets. The juxtaposition of actual marionettes with human actors performing the stiff mechanical movements of puppets has the disturbing effect of blurring the boundaries between human and doll: the doll-like character of human relations becomes pervasive. These 'puppet-characters' are also on stage at the ending of the performance. After Nora has left, the spotlight falls on Helmer sitting in his chair, surrounded by puppets both actual and human. The 'puppetness' of human life in this stage world is emphasised from beginning to end, and Nora chooses to leave a situation where she is constricted and manipulated by the strings of power. In other words, this ending shows a woman breaking out of a world in which the boundaries between humans and marionettes are blurred. A naïve

Figure 3.1 *A Doll's House*, Hanoi, Vitenam (2006), directed by Le Hung. From left to right: Nora (Lê Khanh) and Ms Linde (Hoa Thuý) (Photo: Courtesy of Vietnam Youth Theatre).

interpretation would be that this added, symbolic element in the performance simply emphasises what the title of the play implies: that this social world is a home for dolls, a space in which doll-like relations prevail. This device might be seen as an overly simplistic induction to the play, so to speak, through an external, almost naïve symbolism. But to me as a spectator, it introduced new and sinister dimensions of an overtly political nature to the play. A puppet on a string implies that an agent is pulling the strings: that greater forces offstage are manipulating the action onstage. The question arises: who, then, is pulling the strings?

Because the puppets are of both sexes, the answer to this question cannot be men alone, even though the central point of the production, as of the source text, is that women suffer the effects of patriarchy. This initial framing device permeates the production and seems to signify that invisible hands govern these puppets with a repressive, manipulative force that is stifling and hard to identify or understand. But while this puppetry can be read in terms of political oppression, it does not necessarily have to be interpreted as regime-critical, which would surely be the Western reading. The strings could be construed in the local ideological context as the economic effects of global capitalism. Alternatively, they could point to the generic function of ideology itself; that is to say, how we are governed by ways of speaking and thinking that we ourselves do not master. My intention is not to determine a 'correct' reading, but simply to illustrate the difficulties posed by a performance carried out under censorship. When something is added in this way it inevitably opens a different space for interpretation, a space of the supplement that can be read in almost diametrically opposite ways, speaking in one way to 'deaf' ears, but in another to those that 'hear'.

Iran: *A Doll's House* and *The Wild Duck*

With this in mind, let us turn to The Islamic Republic of Iran and its well-documented, long-standing Ibsen tradition.[8] Whether as print texts, in the theatre, on the radio, or on television, Ibsen's plays have a strong presence in Iran. Farindokht Zahedi has shown that Ibsen's influence on Iranian elites – more precisely, on writers, intellectuals and artists well versed in foreign languages – goes back to the nineteenth century. Zahedi identifies thirty-four different Farsi translations of Ibsen texts, ranging from *The Vikings of Helgeland* to *Brand, Ghosts* and *The Master Builder* that have appeared since the first synoptic Farsi translation of *Peer Gynt* in 1955 (Zahedi, 2006: 214–15). Not surprisingly, the plays most frequently translated are *An Enemy of the People* and *A Doll's House*. The fact that each of these two plays has been translated into Farsi five times demonstrates their capacity to address needs and problems in Iranian society and its theatre culture. Probably due to the Pahlavi regime's politics of 'Westernisation', the first staging of *A Doll's House* in Iran in 1958 did not provoke any buzz or strong discussion. However, the Marxist director and playwright Said Soltanpour's staging of *An Enemy of the People* in 1969 drew a fierce reaction from the Shah's secret police. Soltanpour had altered several scenes to the fourth and fifth acts of Ibsen's play, and introduced some Brechtian techniques in an appeal for a public uprising, for the proletariat to take things into its own hands. As Nasser Rahmani Nejad observes, the group responsible for the performance had 'tricked' the authorities by changing:

> the plot into a family quarrel between the two brothers and submitted it to the authorities to get permission to have it staged. After obtaining the permission, we staged Ibsen's play with the changes we had made in it, not with the one we had given to the censorship department. We staged the play in the Iran-America Institute because it was 'safe' (Zahedi, 2006: 170).

'Safe' it was not: several of those involved in the production were eventually arrested, among them Nejad himself, who had played the role of Dr Stockman.[9] Said Soltanpour's fate illustrates the plight of not a few Iranian artists and intellectuals: having been censored and persecuted under the Shah's regime, he was subsequently arrested and executed by the new Islamic leadership of Iran in 1981. The success of

Soltanpour's *Enemy of the People* made it difficult to obtain permission to do Ibsen on Iranian stages for some time. Ibsen's place in Iranian theatre, however, was secured by a number of popular, and deliberately non-political, stagings of his plays during the 1960s and 1970s. Zahedi records that radio play adaptations of seven of Ibsen's plays went to air on Iranian radio in 1999 and 2000 alone (Zahedi, 2006: 218). These figures indicate that Ibsen the playwright remains as popular within the Islamic Republic as he was in the Shah's Iran.

Dariush Mehrjui's *Sara*

Best known outside Iran, and readily accessible, is *Sara*, Dariush Mehrjui's 1993 film version of *A Doll's House*. The film, which bears the eponymous character's name, may claim to be the most powerful film version of an Ibsen drama. Born in 1939, Mehrjui is one of the great masters of Iranian cinema. His 1969 'masterpiece' *Gav* (*The Cow*) is often credited as 'the first serious' high-quality Iranian movie, the beginning of the country's New Wave cinema.[10] This film and his 1990 *Hamoun* often figure as strong nominees for the honour of being awarded the best Iranian film ever.

   Gav is based on a story by Gholamhossein Sa'edi, and tells the story of Mash Hassan, a farmer who owns the only cow in the village of Bail.[11] This sole cow is extremely important not only to Mash Hassan but to the village, which relies on the cow as a source of income and food. Hassan cares for the cow with tenderness and jealous feelings of fear and threat. The menacing but distant presence of a group of men from a neighbouring village makes him shake with anxiety; we get the impression that they want to steal or harm the cow. When Hassan leaves on a short visit to the city, the cow dies during the night, either at the hands of the strangers from outside or by natural causes. The villagers dare not tell Mash Hassan the brutal truth; after some deliberation they decide to bury the cow in the village square and tell Hassan that the cow has run away. Hassan breaks down at this news and gradually undergoes a psychological metamorphosis into the animal itself. The film ends with his fellow villagers trying to drag Hassan, tied like a cow, to a doctor in the city. On the way Hassan breaks free and plunges down a gorge, dying the death of a stampeding cow.

Gav foreshadows some defining traits of what was to become the Iranian New Wave cinema: an innovative juxtaposition of strict, almost documentary realism with non-realistic, almost surrealistic elements, and what must be considered as formal ways to subvert censorship. Most commentators have observed a parallel between the villagers' reliance on the cow and Iran's vulnerable dependency on oil. In addition to being a touching and alarmingly strange story, *Gav* invites allegorical and metaphorical readings of layered political meaning. The stark poverty of the village, the menacing atmosphere of threat and uncertainty, the barren and ugly surroundings, the passivity and superstitious nature of the villagers, and the sad fate of the man turning into an animal all carry surplus meaning and invite further interpretation. Mehrjui's breakthrough as a director represents the beginning of Iranian New Wave cinema's remarkable power of indirect communication. As Richard Tapper puts it, '*The Cow* in particular started a genre of allegorical "protest" films'.[12]

Iranian cinema has been subjected to elaborate forms of censorship from its inception. During the Pahlavi regime the rules of censorship varied and were seen as unpredictable, but in 1965 they were strengthened and detailed in a law that included twenty-seven articles and two footnotes.[13] As we have seen in the case of Mehrjui, this law seems to have impelled directors towards indirect modes of communication. But what distinguishes the Islamic Republic from the Pahlavi regime is the former's determined will to promote cinema and the domestic production of what it sees as high-quality Islamic films. Given Islam's hostility towards visual representation, and the Islamic Revolution's strong anti-Western position, the regime's willingness to promote a domestic film industry may seem surprising.[14] However, it is a fact that, along with what has been called 'the most advanced and complicated methods of film censorship ever seen', the new rulers of

Iran installed a system that promotes cinema.[15] There is no reason to romanticise censorship, but it seems obvious that state censorship itself is one of the reasons for Iranian cinema's originality and strength, especially since the Islamic Revolution. Iranian New Wave Cinema cannot be understood without considering the combined effects that state sponsorship and strong, systematic censorship have had on it in the years after the Revolution.

While censorship seeks to limit the possibilities of expression, it has the paradoxical effect of opening the range of interpretation: very few meanings if any can be considered pure and simple, to be read literally in a society governed by explicit censorship. This semantic indirection poses new and difficult challenges to a cultural outsider, not least when it arises from self-censorship. This may account for another defining trait of Iranian cinema, namely the many ways in which it reflects on itself and on film as a medium. This meta-filmic aspect is central to many of Mehrjui's films, although not foregrounded as such in *Sara*.

Dariush Mehrjui, like Soltanpour and many other artists, has had the distinction of being banned by the censors under the Shah and the Islamic Republic alike. His latest movie *Santouri*, made in 2007, was subsequently banned. *Sara*, however, was not banned and proved to be immensely popular in Iran's cinemas. It is, like many of Mehrjui's films, an adaptation; based on *A Doll's House*, but without the source play being explicitly identified in the film.[16] In other words, it is possible to see the film without detecting any reference to a European playwright. *Sara* is one of several films by Mehrjui that focus on the situation of women living in the Islamic Republic.[17] To choose Ibsen's classic as a source for adaptation is to signal coded meanings. Although *A Doll's House* is not a feminist classic, it is taken by many women to be a play with a clear feminist resonance. *Sara* largely follows the action of Ibsen's text, but the setting is relocated to contemporary Teheran. In the words of Gönül Dönmez-Colin (2004: 122), *Sara* is a realistic Iranian film that portrays 'contemporary women trapped between tradition and modernity'.

The fragmented female

The first ten minutes of *Sara* are devoted to an exposition of past events that, in Ibsen, are narrated by Nora. This departure from Ibsen's text reinforces the necessity of the main character's actions: Sara's husband Hessam, played by Amin Tarokh, is fatally ill with a rare form of bone marrow cancer, but the doctor says he can be cured if Sara, performed by Niki Karimi, can get him to a hospital in Germany or Switzerland, where the required medical expertise is to be found. At the hospital, Sara meets Goshtasb, one of her husband's colleagues and the film's 'Krogstad' figure, played by Khosro Shakibai. Ghohtasb knows about Hessam's diagnosis and offers to help. This establishes a further reassurance, not offered by Ibsen, that Sara has done nothing improper to obtain the loan; it is offered to her out of friendship and concern.

The film then jumps three years forward to the present, to a scene in which Sara is having her eyes tested. While we hear the examining physician express surprise at how rapidly her sight is deteriorating, we have a frontal view of Sara sitting before an old-fashioned phoropter that measures the strength of spectacle lenses (Figure 3.2). This shot

Figure 3.2 *Sara*, directed by Dariush Mehrjui (1993), Sara (Niki Karimi) at the ophthalmologist.

implies, from the outset, that Sara is under an unspecified influence that is weakening her sight. The image is striking: all we see are her head and shoulders and the phoropter which, despite its small size, holds her as in a vice. As constructed, the eye-test image has overtones of torture. We see almost nothing of the actual Sara, hidden as she is on one side by her traditional headwear, the hijab, and on the other by the measuring instrument. Sara appears by virtue of this image to be a woman under pressure from two directions: from tradition (the hijab), and from modernity (the phoropter). This genuinely ambiguous image sums up a theme that is central to the film and source play alike. Positive meaning does not reside in either of these cultural forces alone; each involves suffering and loss.

Sara opens with the main character at home, standing at a window and smoking a cigarette while looking out through the curtains. When after a short while an elderly aunt comes calling, and Sara tries half-heartedly and unsuccessfully to conceal that she has been smoking. The aunt's first words are reproachful: 'Have you been smoking?' The cigarette in the film is analogous to the macaroons that serve in Ibsen's text as an emblem of Nora's will and ability to disregard Helmer's commandments. Sara's smoking is represented as a minor transgression that reveals her to be a person who does not submit to every order. But it is Sara's aunt and not her husband who disapproves of smoking, and for reasons of health, whereas Ibsen's Helmer refers to Nora's figure and teeth when justifying his interrogation of her. Another significant distinction is that while Ibsen's Nora will readily tell a lie, Sara will not. The image of a woman smoking a cigarette also connotes modernity and independence, even a form of feminine emancipation. But any implied emancipation is limited. As the sharp distinction between interior and exterior spaces demonstrates, the main character is shut in with her despair, she stares at the outside world through a thin curtain that can be read symbolically as another version of the veil. The mode of presentation is highly significant: the film is constructed by means of montage; fragments and small segments of the world fill the screen from its opening moments. The film's first shot is a close-up of a woman's hand dangling a lit cigarette. This visualised fragmentation is maintained fairly consistently throughout the film: with skill and intention, Mehrjui lets the camera eye linger over fragments of life, objects and people.

The subsequent scene in which Sara dresses to go out employs the same technique: the camera focuses on the coat-stand, as we watch Sara's hands hanging up the grey cape she has been wearing over her shoulders and taking down a full-length black chador. We next see first one hand then the other emerging from the black cloth of the sleeve, after which we zoom out a little to see the torso of a black figure, the chador covering the face. The figure remains black for a moment until the cloth draws back a little to show Sara's face. The shot focuses on the clothes, showing how they restrict the woman's body and conceal it from view. At the same time, Sara's beautiful face lights up in contrast with the depersonalising black.

This use of the fragmented image in which the part is cut out, isolated from the whole female body to which it belongs, is emphasised in an ostentatious way in the opening scenes, and it is central in several other sequences of the film. In the scene in which Sara visits Hessam at the hospital, the camera focuses not on the woman as she walks up the steps, but on her hand as it follows the staircase railing; we see Sara's hands picking up fruit and vegetables when she is shopping; we watch her hands at work when she is preparing food, or tidying things and washing up after the party. This kind of fragmentation would normally be understood as a meta-fictional effect that points to the film as artifice, as a product of cutting, camera-angle and direction. But this fragmentation acquires a gender-specific coding in *Sara*: it does not apply to the male roles. Within this fictional world women, unlike men, are not figured as wholly and fully embodied human beings. In other words, when camera work and cinematic technique are accentuated in this way, they reflect on the filmic medium's relation to gender discourse, gesturing towards an external world of prohibitions and regulations beyond, and not restricted to, the film industry itself. This technique of fragmentation is significantly modified in the concluding scenes of the film. When Sara has her reckoning with Hessam and speaks her mind, insisting that she is a human being just as he is, she is seen in full, not as a montage of fragmented bodily parts.

The politics of clothing

As the opening shot in which Sara dresses to go out suggests, garments and dress play a significant part in the film's plot structure and symbolism. It is important that any adaptation of the plot structure of *A Doll's House* should give a credible account of how Nora is able to repay the loan to Krogstad without Helmer knowing about it, and in Mehrjui's version Sara pays off the loan with the help of money she earns as a seamstress. While the way in which Sara earns her extra money is completely realistic, it also opens possibilities for further symbolic communication. Sara's workplace itself has discursive significance in that the darkness of the cellar room in which she 'hides' with her embroidery damages her eyesight. That Sara injures her eyes in her efforts to 'save' her husband is made clear at the ending of the film, but it is also communicated indirectly through earlier shots of Sara at her sewing. The images of garments, cloth, pearls and beads enhance the sensual appeal and beauty of these scenes, not least when we see the exhausted Sara asleep on the exclusive silk of an unfinished wedding dress. The moment at which Sara accidentally pricks her finger and a finely delineated drop of her blood stains the white silk, hints at her own suffering and that of brides to come. At the same time, Sara's career as a seamstress delivering her products to the shop in the bazaar affirms her as a figure of feminine enterprise and efficiency. When in response to Goshtasb's threats Sara attempts to sell her grandmother's old wedding shawl at a shop in the bazaar, the woman shopkeeper refuses it as worthless. Nevertheless, and without asking questions, the shopkeeper volunteers to loan Sara the money she needs without security or signatures. The loan affirms the existence of an underlying network of female companionship and solidarity from which Sara (and other women) can take strength.

The figural significance of the dress code is evident in the sequence in which Sara goes to Hessam's office late at night to convince him to come home in spite of the information in Goshtasb's letter. Sara manages to convince Helmer to return home with her and as they walk the streets of Tehran together he lectures her on the disasters she has brought upon him, more or less as in Ibsen.[18] Their passage through the dark streets is a visual metaphor of gendered power relations: Hessam wears a white shirt, his jacket over his arm, while Sara walks behind him in her black chador, almost invisible in the dark. His shirt glows and collects the light, whereas she is reduced to a walking shadow.

That clothing is emphasised and politicised in *Sara* is not to be wondered at in an Iranian context, for there are few places other than Iran where clothes and dress have been so politicised. Under Reza Shah Pahlavi, the so-called 'Unveiling Act' of 1936 banned the wearing of women's traditional clothing with face veils in public places. The Act was enforced by the Shah's soldiers, who could turn women wearing chadors away from main streets or simply tear their veils from them. As a result, many women who experienced this as a gross violation absented themselves from public space.[19] The Act was ideologically ambiguous in that it linked gender equality and feminism to what many Iranians perceived as 'un-Islamic', 'immoral' and repressive forces. Paradoxically enough, radical women who took part in demonstrations against the Shah in the lead up to the Islamic Revolution wore the veil as a symbol of revolt. Strict enforcement of Sharia laws under the Revolutionary regime saw the re-introduction of the obligatory chador. Women and their male sympathisers took to the streets to demonstrate against the resolution, but the demonstrations were brutally beaten down by the Revolutionary Guard.

The politicising of dress is readily recognisable in present-day Iran. Policing of the dress code can be interpreted as hostility to women in Iranian society in the sense that enforcement of the Act restricts women's freedom of movement, subjects them to surveillance and constructs the feminine as 'foreign' in the reality of the modern Iranian metropolis. Indeed, this is how the film is often interpreted in the West,[20] but it has to be acknowledged that Iranian women can, after all, move freely in the public arena provided they conform to dress regulations. Hence *Sara* could be read as arguing that women can and should take part in public life on an equal footing with men, and that this equality is in fact made possible by the hijab.[21] This is an important aspect of the scenes showing Sara's travels around the city and those that show Sima, the Ms Linde figure played by Yasman Malek-Nasr, as a professional career woman living on her own and working in the bank for Hessam in a position she has won in competition with Goshtasb. It is important that an analysis of *Sara* should acknowledge this layered vision that at one and the same time critiques a repressive regime of clothing while affirming that the regime is a means to attain women's right to freedom of movement and self-fulfilment. An immediate commonsense Western reading of the film could be a little simplistic where this is concerned. Perhaps it is we scholars and onlookers from the West who attribute excessive, even mistaken significance to headwear and shawls.[22]

This ambivalence in the film should caution against an all too easy reading that attributes an unequivocally negative meaning to the chador. Such a reading of the chador or hijab could imply that the liberation of women in other cultures can only be achieved by following an example from the outside, through an imitative 'catching up' with the West. The implication here is that there can be no genuine freedom or agency within the hijab, obviously a mistake that *Sara* critiques. This stance also fails to acknowledge that the ideological otherness of non-Western women has played a central role in Western colonial and post-colonial exploitation and suppression of other cultures. The discourse on clothing in *Sara* should not be interpreted to mean that Iranian culture is necessarily and intrinsically repressive in this regard, or that Iranian women's liberation can only be achieved through the abolition of norms affecting their dress in favour of ideals imported from a supposedly more advanced or progressive society.[23]

A further point to be made about the politics of clothing in *Sara*, and in Iranian cinema in general, is that the film's dress code is a direct and obvious result of censorship. Sharia law applies specifically to women's dress in public: in practice, few Iranian women would dress in accordance with the law in the home. That the women in *Sara* dress according to Sharia law even when alone at home is, to that extent, a visual construction, and not a realistic one. Female characters in contemporary Iranian film are thereby portrayed through a distorted double image; their everyday lives and dress are adapted to the demands of censorship. The outcome is realism with an inbuilt meta-filmic twist. Sara's dress when at home could in this way be said to mark the presence of the censors.[24] The distinctly non-realistic artifice of the film's dress code contributes a meta-fictional dimension to *Sara* as a film that at every point, so to speak, testifies to the conditions of film-making under this specific regime.

Decency and identification

To put this another way, Iran's elaborate system of film censorship gives rise to a complicated enunciation: a film always addresses the audience in the cinema, but at the same time, and in a primary sense, it addresses the censor. As we have seen, it also gives rise to a constitutive double communication in which implicit meanings will be deciphered in accord with levels of audience sophistication. Many scenes in *Sara* lend themselves to this kind of symbolic or allegorical reading. I will mention two here, one rather obvious and one more ambiguous. When Sara goes out to shop for Hessam's promotion party, her search for the right vegetables is crosscut with close-ups of two canaries in a cage that hangs from the ceiling of the shop. It is difficult to avoid the inference that Sara and Sima, who meet in this scene, are as it were similarly caged, forced as women into a jail-like existence. A more complex visualisation occurs in the following scene, in which the two women walk back towards Sara's home, happily engaged in conversation. As they pause on either side of a narrow alley and burst out laughing, a car accelerates between them, splashing puddle water over them. Given that the laughter of two young women in the street could, in fact, be interpreted as frivolous, the scene can be read as an instance of how a modern system of violent repression, for which the speeding car is metonymic, controls and 'censors' the daily lives of Iranian women. The menace of this scene at first startles and silences the women, yet in a split second their community or solidarity wins through and they laugh wholeheartedly at the whole business. The sequence of actions in this scene is not so overtly symbolic as the crosscuts to the caged birds, but given the film's overall thrust it is hard to miss their implications.[25]

It is clear that a great many scenes in *Sara* can be read at multiple levels, as is the case with so many Iranian films. Comparison with *A Doll's House*, from which *Sara* is adapted, reveals levels of cultural and ideological negotiation that are embedded in the film. *A Doll's House* lends itself to intercultural studies not simply because it is performed across so many cultures, but because certain of its scenes serve as cultural 'litmus tests'. Three scenes in particular give an indication of the cultural boundaries that *A Doll's House* challenges: these are the scenes in which Nora shows Rank her stockings; the tarantella dance; and, of course, the ending.

A number of scenes in Ibsen's play touch directly on sexuality, in particular on Helmer's male desire and how Nora plays up to it. These elements have all been excised from Mehrjui's film. *Sara* has no 'stocking scene'; indeed, Rank's character does not appear in the film. The main reason for this is that it would be problematic in Iran's strict Islamic culture for a married woman to engage in any kind of emotional intimacy, however platonic, with a man other than her husband. Not to mention the suggestive conversation in which Ibsen's Nora tempts Rank with her 'lovely . . . flesh-coloured' silk stockings and Rank alludes, somewhat equivocally, to his hereditary syphilis. The absence of this suggestiveness from *Sara* shows how the production is adapted to local culture and tradition. If Ibsen's play is to be read as a feminist drama in which women are unjustly and unreasonably treated, it must be possible for the audience to invest emotionally in the protagonist. A psychological and intellectual space needs to be established in which spectators can identify with the character. Such an identity space would have been closed if Sara had appeared immoral.[26] Having said that, we should remind ourselves that the film would not have seen the light of day had it failed to satisfy its other implied readers in absolute need of 'identity space', the censors.

Tarantella

The tarantella dance is sometimes deleted from adaptations of *A Doll's House*, or substituted with a poetry-reading or local dance.[27] In Iran's Muslim culture, strict prohibitions and prejudices against exposure and display of the female body make the tarantella unthinkable. Rather than take out the tarantella altogether, Mehrjui chose to have the male characters dance. Mehrjui thus retains the original situation in which Sara fears that Hessam will read Goshtasb's revealing letter. Sara knows that the letter has been sent to Hessam's office and, while anxiously awaiting Hessam's reaction, she arranges a big party to celebrate his

Figure 3.3 Dancing the 'tarantella', from *Sara*, directed by Dariush Mehrjui (1993). Hessam (Amin Tarokh), dancer second from the right.

promotion. The film shows Sara and her guests awaiting the guest of honour's arrival at the party. Music begins to play as Hessam arrives, and Hessam hardly has time to take off his shoes before he is swept up into a row of dancing men.

The tarantella is among the most frequently discussed scenes in the whole of Ibsen. In it, Nora gives physical and unspoken expression to her torment and suffering, while the men see her only as a desirable female body. The male gaze is central to the scene, as is Nora's ability to communicate her anguish beyond her onstage spectators, Rank and Helmer, to her spectators in the auditorium. The film medium enables Mehrjui to emphasise these disparate subject positions: as Hessam dances, Sara shows her anxiety in close-up, as she wonders in a 'voice-over' at her husband's good mood.

In *Sara*, then, the close attention to the men's desiring gazes has been deferred, but the actual contrast between the sexes remains very much in place. The men's dance, of course, differentiates between the gendered spaces allocated to the sexes where social activity is concerned. That the party is given in Hessam's honour likewise gives a clear indication that he is the dominant personality in his own life and in Sara's. As in *A Doll's House*, the fundamental point is made that Hessam, like Helmer, lacks the ability to see and hear the woman he lives with. These scenes significantly anticipate Sara's (and Nora's) retort in the closing scene that she has been living with a 'stranger'. The primary significance of the dance lies in its demonstration of gender difference and the contrast it draws between Sara and Hessam: that women work while men dance is an eloquent image. The film devotes a good deal of time to displaying Sara's anxiety and self-sacrifice as she works hard to prepare a successful party for her husband. Even so, the question remains: why was the dance not deleted altogether? The replacement of Nora's tarantella with the men's dance highlights the difference between the film and Ibsen's text in a way other than if the dance had simply been cut. For the spectator who knows Ibsen's version, the men's dance is all the more effective, because it activates Mehrjui's and Ibsen's versions at the same time.

This could be said to be an intercultural aspect of the film, in the sense that meaning is produced through interactions between Iranian film and culture on the one hand, and Norwegian play text and culture on the other. A more specifically intracultural significance lies in the music to which the men dance, a point that I owe to an Iranian colleague, and that is hard to grasp unless one is familiar with the local context.[28] This music is a traditional Kurdish *gaz levah*, often performed at weddings and larger social events. In its local cultural context, this music is accompanied with a dance in which both men and women dance in a circle while holding hands. This suggests that the exclusion of women from the dance in *Sara* will be conspicuous in its intracultural Iranian context. The lack of female participation in the dance is therefore doubly significant, from intercultural and intracultural positions.

In the local Iranian context, the relation of the men's dance to the corresponding scene in *A Doll's House* is, of course, of secondary importance, and even then only to an informed audience. But the relation will at any rate be activated for *some* spectators. And this may entail more than a mere doubling of meaning for those who recognise both versions: it may be that Mehrjui's version of the dance also critiques those Western film versions of *A Doll's House* that give prominence to the tarantella, with the camera directing its voyeuristic gaze at the dancing Nora.[29] Moreover, it is possible that Mehrjui's version of the dance critiques not only Western film culture but the sexual politics of Ibsen's play. The experience of identifying with Helmer's gaze at Nora may render this scene distressing to a (male) spectator. It may, in other words, be a critical point that the audience experiences its own gaze fixed on this female body: it is precisely while Nora is dancing her suffering, as if her life depends on it, that one may find oneself admiring her figure and feeling a touch of Helmer's desire. Some of this duality is built into Ibsen's play, perhaps necessarily, although the fundamental critical point lies in his presentation of a male gaze that sees one thing and is blind to another. At times, however, this point is missed, both in the theatre and on film. Some Western film versions simply reproduce Helmer's gaze, a practice that Mehrjui's film may be thought to critique.[30]

It is precisely by virtue of its intercultural nature that this film activates new layers of meaning as it positions itself in the tension between the cultures. And it may happen to tell us something about cultural difference at this point: can we be sure that anything would have been better if Mehrjui's Sara had danced? Is it precisely through this gender reversal that Mehrjui expresses a criticism of Western society's unremitting (and commercial) exploitation of the female body?

Hence this scene can illustrate a more theoretical point about censorship. When a central element of a classic is changed, it will be obvious to some segment of the audience, probably, in the case of *Sara*, to a substantial part. This in itself points towards the workings of censorship. Like a ventriloquist, the censored work of art speaks without seeming to: something is said in and through silence or alteration. To put it in psychoanalytical terms, the repressed speaks through the symptom, and the symptom here is the specific change made in the name of censorship. Last but not least, this is true even if the alterations were in fact done, consciously and willingly, for reasons other than those of the censor. Symptomatic behaviour will point towards the repressed trauma, even if – or perhaps especially if – the behaviour is done for 'rational' and completely sound reasons. Correspondingly, because a system of explicit censorship opens up a subterranean world of double meanings, any overt major changes in a classic may evoke precisely what the censorship system is designed to repress.

The question of agency

There is hardly a play in world literature that has had such radically altered versions of its ending as *A Doll's House*. Ever since it first appeared, *A Doll's House* has provoked a variety of revisions and adaptations. In Ibsen's time it was, of course, sufficiently offensive for a wife to leave home, but given the divorce rates in all Western countries today this is no longer the case. What remains provocative, or at least highly unusual, is for a woman to leave her children without demanding the right to care for them. Such matters are viewed somewhat differently in a Muslim culture, because according to Islam, marriage is a contractual relation, not a sacrament. The Muslim marriage contract is binding, and it is far more difficult for the wife to obtain a divorce than it is for the husband, but the contract has built-in provisos that can trigger a woman's right to break the contract. It is therefore not necessarily of great moment for a Muslim woman to obtain a divorce, or for her to remarry. However, matters are radically different where custody of children is concerned. According to Islam, and under Iranian law, the children belong to the husband and his family. Hence if a woman leaves, she has to leave her children. What is provocative in Mehrjui's film is that Sara, in contrast with Nora, takes her daughter with her when she leaves. As in Ibsen, this is an optimistic ending in the sense that it constitutes a utopian gesture, emphasising that a radical break, a significant action, is possible. But it may also be the case that this ending is even more open than Ibsen's, because Sara takes a taxi home to her father. She does not slam the gate behind her, only the car door. Hessam is also presented more sympathetically in the final scene, because he is sick and bed-ridden (but getting better). When Sara leaves he follows her into the street; wrapped in a sheet, he is left standing on the pavement, looking helpless.

A vital over-riding point in *A Doll's House* is that Nora is not a passive victim. She (like Kristine Linde) is an inquiring woman who takes action. This reading of Nora is germane to intracultural as well as intercultural readings of *Sara*. Indeed, Sara's strength and her ability to act are qualities that run counter to orientalist figurations of Iranian women as backward, passive victims, hidden and kept in ignorance behind veils and chadors. An intercultural reading of *Sara* suggests the film's dual testimony to the suppression of women in Iran, and to the fact that Iranian women are more and other than passive victims of oppression. The film's duality is a corrective to self-congratulatory Eurocentric misconceptions that Muslim women are suppressed: that 'things are not like that in the West'. The film's global significance is precisely that it shows, at one and the same time, that while Ibsen's plays appeal to artists and audiences across the widest cultural frontiers, intercultural understanding has its limits, blind spots, and areas of conflict.

Mehrjui's film, then, derives its intracultural significance from Sara's will to liberate herself within her own society while, from an intercultural perspective, her agency acts as a kind of ideological antidote to orientalist Western prejudice. The film may be seen in this way as a double critique of women's situation in Iran and, conversely, of Western stereotypes of Iranian women. The stereotype of the Muslim woman functions as a kind of ideological master trope in the West, partly as conservative self-congratulation that 'things are a lot better' at home, and in the last instance as part of an institutionalised misogyny that legitimises violence and military force abroad. In my view, it is hard to underestimate the importance of this last point, at least in Europe where the post-9/11 revenge motive can no longer be mobilised to justify attacks on other countries. As a consequence, such wars are now configured in Gayatri Chakravorty Spivak's words as 'white men saving brown women from brown men'.[31] I argue that *Sara* delivers a similar critique.

Life-lies in the theatre: *My Wild Duck*

Theatre in the widest sense of 'dramatic performance' has existed in Iran 'throughout history'.[32] Iran's rich contemporary theatre has its roots in a mix of the country's ancient performance heritage with influences of Western theatre from the nineteenth century on. Like most contemporary theatre, Iran's has been from the outset an effect of cultural exchange and blending traditions. In addition, the development of contemporary Iranian theatre, as with Iranian culture in general, has been strongly influenced by the country's political turmoil. As we have already seen, Iran's theatre has had to live under the keen eye of its official censors from the days of the Pahlavi regime to the present. Theatre suffered severely during the first years of the Islamic Republic, and for several years it was not possible to stage anything but performances that promoted the revolution. A common view holds that the situation improved decisively only after the end of the Iran–Iraq war in 1988, 'when the country could focus once again on living rather than dying' (Floor, 2005: 298). Since then, the Islamic Republic has seen the value of supporting a vibrant, high-quality but tightly monitored and controlled theatre scene. The system of theatre censorship in Iran is designed to control the entire creative process from scripting to casting, rehearsals, previews and into the live performance itself, much like the system for film-censorship.[33] The current regime has made sure that it will not repeat the kind of 'mistake' that the Shah's regime made with Soltanpour's performance of *An Enemy of the People*: so should someone be seen to cross the invisible lines of morality or 'Islamic values', the show will be closed and the artists face prosecution.[34] A staging of *Hedda Gabler* was closed down after a few nights' run in January 2011 because the prosecutor's office held it to be, as Fars News Agency put it, 'based on nihilistic and hedonistic ideas' and 'performed in a very vulgar and inappropriate way for the public'.[35]

Yet in spite of strict censorship, and the self-censorship that goes with it, the 'current theatre scene in Iran is [...] a vibrant one'.[36] And interestingly enough, what Floor calls a 'theatre boom' in contemporary Iran is to a large extent an outcome of the Government's support.[37] It might also be the case that under 'boom' conditions such as these, the creative energy of the artists will find ways to encode officially 'undesirable' views for the audience. As Floor puts it:

> Theatre performers try to push the limits of censorship and both playwrights and actors are very inventive. [...] Iranian actors use kerchiefs, gestures and other props to symbolise bodily relationships. This demands much refined acting from the actors and actresses and a public of connoisseurs. (Floor, 2005: 300)

The volatile combination of censorship, government support and an audience of 'connoisseurs' defines the general background for an understanding of Iranian theatre. And even although these background parameters might define a situation in which the difficulties of understanding may seem insurmountable to an outside spectator, the Moaser Theatre Group's adaptation of *The Wild Duck* made a strong impression when I saw it played to an auditorium of foreigners in Dhaka in 2009.[38] Despite the fact that only a few of the spectators were Iranians (namely, staff from the Iranian Embassy in Dhaka), the performance came across strongly and immediately to an enthusiastic audience.

The director, Nader Borhany Marand, had made several major adjustments to the plot and its presentation. The title of Ibsen's play was changed to *My Wild Duck*, and the play was given a narrative frame. In this framing narrative we see the middle-aged Hedvig Ekdal, very much alive, sitting at her desk with a play she has written called *My Wild Duck*. Hedvig is about to leave with Molvik to meet with the famous dramatist 'Henrik Ibsen', to whom she wishes to show her manuscript. Before leaving, however, she hesitates and starts leafing through the manuscript, which is about her own life and which is then enacted as if 'in her mind' before the audience. The matter of suicide apart, Hedvig's 'play within the play' about her own life follows Ibsen's text. In addition to these two layers, the frame and play within the play, we hear two letters addressed to Hedvig: one from her mother, Gina, and one from Gregers Werle. Both letters are suicide notes.

The framing device has several interesting aspects. By definition it distances the play-within-the-play, placing it in the past and 'fictionalising' it as Hedvig's creation, albeit based on her own life. This meta-theatricality necessarily diminishes the topicality and realism of Hedvig's play. However, this postmodern meta-fictional turn of the performance is counteracted by the acting itself, in the sense that the actors never abandon their finely tuned naturalistic approach to character. The profound duality of the performance can also be seen in the *mise en scène*, which opens with an abstract postmodern stage design that counteracts the actors' naturalistic nineteenth-century costumes. The costumes themselves are double in the sense that they are Western, with the small but marked exception of the women's scarf-like hijabs.[39] The performance is thus in many ways positioned between realism and meta-theatre, modernism and postmodernism, but also between West and East, modernity and tradition, and (perhaps) domesticating and foreignising. The contrast between Borhany Marand's multiple strategies to distance *The Wild Duck* from the Iranian reality of 2009 and Mehrjui's immersion of *A Doll's House* in contemporary Tehran in 1993 could indicate a change in the practice of censorship.

This *mise en scène*, then, would seem to be intended in part to distance difficult aspects of the story: the framing device, the Western costumes and the letters all contribute to this effect. The major changes to the plot create a similar distance; the survivor Hedvig retells a melancholy tale of loss and failure through her manuscript, her letters and stories. Apart from the fact that Hedvig is alive, the major changes in Borhany Marand's version of the story are that Gina has committed suicide quite soon after the end of Ibsen's plot, and that Gregers has taken his life some ten years after that. These two 'new' suicides are connected in different ways. In Ibsen's version, Gina claims that she does not know who is Hedvig's biological father, so that part of the tragedy of the source play lies in Hjalmar's lack of confidence in his own position as a parent. In Borhany Marand's version, Gina has been 'seduced' (in whatever sense this word may be interpreted) by Werle, but in her letter she claims to know for certain that Hjalmar, and not Werle, is Hedvig's father. She has made Werle believe that he was the father in order to secure her daughter's future and to get even with the man who 'seduced' her:

> Gina: I didn't want to let your father understand I was hiding a secret. I confess that it was a big sin. I deceived the old man. Werle thought you were his child all his life. It was just a lie. A lie which let me take revenge on Werle and guarantee your future.[40]

Gina cannot tell Werle the truth, and it becomes existentially impossible for her to be open with Hjalmar when he accuses her and devalues their life together as husband, wife and parents. She simply says that she has 'forgotten the past' and that she 'deserves forgiveness'. But more important than these changes to interpersonal and psychological aspects is the way in which this Iranian version strengthens the discourse of class within the play. There is quite a lot of talk about poverty and its effects in Borhany Marand's adaptation and economic exploitation accounts for the demise of this family, as in Ibsen.

In addition to strengthening the issue of class in *My Wild Duck*, the interpretive innovation of this performance points to another of the play's concerns: the asymmetrical power relation between men and women. Issues of class and power are clearly connected, in that it is the fate of the less well-off Gina to be coveted by richer men who have their own interests and desires at heart rather than hers. The men treat Gina as an object to be desired, even in a sense loved, but they see her as a means to an end rather than as a human being desirable in and of herself. In other words, by having Gina commit suicide rather than Hedvig, Borhany Marand strengthens the politics of gender in the performance. As the object of a struggle between rival males Gina is, as any woman in this society, extremely vulnerable, to the extent that she ultimately chooses to end her life.

Ideals and critique

The suicide of Gregers Werle is another significant innovation in this adaptation. This alteration to the source text probably has to do both with the wider politics of cultural exchange and the presence of censors. In his suicide letter, Gregers tells Hedvig the story of his life and explains to her why he will now take it. In Ibsen, Gregers says to Dr Relling that if 'you are right and I am wrong [...] then life is not worth living.' There the question of whether or not life is worth living is part of a philosophical debate about truth and ideals and their significance in human life and society. In the Moaser Theatre Group's version, however, this more abstract and theoretical discussion about truth, knowledge and consequence is excised from the text and from the character's personal motivations.

The Iranian Gregers' motivation to interfere in Hjalmar and Gina's marriage, revealing to Hjalmar the role that his father has played in

Gina's (and consequently in Hedvig's) life, has to do with private selfish desires rather than a rigorous concern for truth and ideals. This Gregers confesses in his last letter: he has been hopelessly in love with Gina ever since she came to nurse his mother at their house. Gina was also the reason behind Gregers' flight to Høydal after his mother's death: he had been his father's rival for Gina and lost. His jealousy and rivalry revive when, on his return, he learns that Gina is now married to his old friend Hjalmar. He cannot turn away, he has to interfere and try somehow to win Gina from Hjalmar. And so, because he desires her, Gregers tells Hjalmar the 'truth' about Gina.

Borhany Marand's *My Wild Duck* makes for impressive theatre. It calls for accomplished actors who, in both the framing story and the play, are able to embody the pain of lives wasted and destroyed by errors whose consequences are still alive and active, although they lie many years back. What interests me, however, are the political aspects of the changes to the role of Gregers Werle. Borhany Marand's Gregers is motivated by desire and personal feeling rather than by rigid, abstract ideas and demands for truth and ideals: the effect is to transform the 'Gregers Werle problem' into a private individual one. The question is whether this dramaturgical choice was a result of (self-)censorship. In other words, was it seen as necessary to rewrite the aspects of this character, which could lead the audience to draw an 'undesirable' parallel between the figure of Gregers and more general issues concerning fanaticism, ideal demands and the desire to interfere in other people's lives, such as a parallel to local political leaders and their ruthless insistence on knowing the absolute truth and on forcing everyone to live by it? Gregers in Ibsen demands that truth and ideal be put first regardless of any consequence. When the text shows that this can have catastrophic human consequences it could well be read politically, as a critique of a local regime more than willing to insist on its version of truth and 'Islamic ideals'.

Because Iran has a solid tradition of Ibsen performances, it is clear that audiences would notice something as radical as changing the discussion between Relling and Gregers into a private discussion between rivals. This re-interpretation 'speaks' doubly, as it were, through the evident modification of the performance text. As noted above, this doubleness is part of what makes censorship difficult to understand and delimit; when something is cut or changed in order to satisfy the demands of censorship, the censored material will still be 'present', even in its silence and invisibility. Sigmund Freud knew from experience about censorship. It was a central part of his theory of the psyche that our conscious psychological life rests on suppressed or 'censored' material, and regardless of how we view his theory as such, it can throw light on how censorship works when it comes to a classic play. As in the psychological symptom, the repressed speaks through absence, alteration, displacement and compression. It is a fact that Ibsen's plays are still censored in different ways but it is also clear that a 'classic' such as an Ibsen play is often adapted to circumvent the censor, to smuggle in the subversive precisely at the place changed by censorship. The classic becomes ventriloquist.

Visual signs: *The Master Builder* from Beijing

China has had a strong Ibsen tradition ever since central intellectuals within the May 4th Movement took him to heart in the 1920s and 1930s.[41] The dominant Chinese view of his plays has shifted several times since then, but Ibsen has mainly been seen as a naturalist, and *A Doll's House* is without a doubt his best-known play in China.[42] Since China's opening up, however, plays such as *Hedda Gabler*, *An Enemy of the People*, *The Lady From the Sea* and perhaps above all *Peer Gynt* have also attracted the attention of China's theatres. Knowing the scale and speed of the building boom in urban China, one might expect *The Master Builder* to attract the attention of the world's fastest growing economy. But Lin Zhaohua's 2006 staging of the play did not connect in any obvious sense with current social or political issues.

Lin is one of the masters of Chinese theatre. Born in 1936, he has made his mark on Chinese theatre during the last four decades. His work is contested and often seen as avant-gardist, not least because Lin has been a key figure in the little theatre movement in China, together with people such as Gao Xingjian, whose plays he has staged a number of times. Although there has never been an overt political aspect to his work within the theatre, some of his productions have been interpreted as indirectly relating to volatile political issues within Chinese society. Most famous among these is probably his 1989 version of *Hamlet*, performed only a few months after the army's crackdown on student demonstrations at Tiananmen Square.[43]

Lin's *Master Builder* was a major success, and has toured extensively within China and internationally.[44] The production followed Ibsen's text faithfully, with a strong emphasis on the relationship between the Master Builder and the young Hilde Wangel. This interpretation was reflected in the casting: the two main roles were played by star Chinese actors, well known in film and television. Pu Cunxin's Halvard Solness was a powerful presence, even though for much of the performance he was immobile, seated in a large leather armchair with his feet on a footrest. Tao Hong's Hilde Wangel, however, was vibrant and energetic. Positive, charming and seductive, she moved about the stage engaging with each of the actors.

While being faithful to Ibsen's text, the *mise en scène* was innovative in most respects. The performance opens with Solness sitting in his red armchair, feet up on the red footrest. Next to him is a pair of boots; a few steps further away is a small table or shelf with a wreath resting against it. Solness is on stage from the beginning and does not leave the stage until at the last moment he walks up a white staircase and out of sight. Hilde remains on stage from the time she enters. The continued presence of these characters on stage when Ibsen's stage directions would require them to be off, imparts a distinctly non-realistic dimension to the *mise en scène*. Thus Solness and Hilde listen as Dr Herdal discusses his mental state with Aline; while Hilde is present when Solness and Aline talk about her.

The bareness of the stage gives it the abstract character of an open space in which meaning can be invested. The bare stage strips away meaning yet invites semiosis, even allegoresis; its openness enhances the significance of any object or body introduced onto it. As the sole property on stage, the large, glaringly red leather armchair in which Solness rests as if enthroned necessarily acquires surplus meaning. And because this play is about a confrontation between a younger generation and its oppressive forebears, and therefore about social change and transpositions of power, it is not difficult to imagine that the older authoritarian man at rest in his red chair signifies a power other than himself. This is not to suggest that Lin's version of *The Master Builder* should be read as a straightforward, unequivocal allegory stating that the 'red' Party (CCP) is oppressive and should be overthrown. Rather it is that the invitation to semiosis opens up a field of meaning that points to larger social and political issues. In other words, a system-critical reading of this staging of the play would have been possible had Solness's chair been of another colour, but the fact that it is so evidently red invites this line of interpretation.

Contemporary China is undergoing constant change and in most instances the changes are towards liberalisation. Chinese media and art today are free and open when compared to the state of affairs during Mao's rule. But the Chinese state still has myriad forms of censorship at its disposal, and its laws insist that 'all public acts should uphold socialism and support Party leadership.'[45] Open protest against these principles would therefore not pass the censors, and if by some accident it did, there would be serious repercussions for the artist. But through the mastery of his art, Lin is able to open a field of signification that may point in directions that the censors would find 'undesirable'. And if there are different messages or meanings passing under the radar of the censorship agencies that have a stake in this performance, this is probably in part due to the fact that they are mediated by non-linguistic, visual signs.

Having said this, it is important to note that the semiotics of the performance is anything but simplistic. Part of the richness of Lin's *mise en scène* is the juxtaposition of Solness's red chair with Hilde's red dress. The colour red is associated in this way with the ageing master builder's repressive force, but also with the new generation's liberation. This ambivalence is of artistic importance to the performance, but it also has political significance. Furthermore, the knitted dress that Tao Hong wears is not only red, it also has a floral pattern, which makes a semiotic connection to one of the most startling visual effects of the *mise en scène* towards the end of the play, when Hilde begins to 'plant' flowers on stage. Once Hilde has reached her goal, and convinced Solness to attempt 'the impossible' and climb to the top of the tower, she moves about, throwing flowers onto the stage floor. The flowers have arrow tips, so that they stand where she throws them.

Hilde's silent action supplements the ongoing action and dialogue: it passes unremarked by the other figures on stage, who go about their business and deliver their lines as if nothing unusual is taking place. She fills the stage floor with blooming flowers; a silent action only tenuously connected with the main action of the play. It functions as a supplement, communication by sign and gesture, which implies a

Figure 3.4 *The Master Builder*, directed by Lin Zhaohua (2006), Lin Zhaohua Theatre Studio. Hilde (Tao Hong) to the left next to Solness (Pu Cunxin) (Photo: Zhou Wei).

symbolism specific to its Chinese context. The action of planting flowers in bloom, of letting flowers bloom 'here and now', connotes an important incident in modern Chinese history known as the Hundred Flowers Campaign after Mao Tse-Tung's slogan 'Let a hundred flowers blossom and a hundred schools of thought contend.' Circulated in 1956, and probably influenced by Nikita Krushchev's critique of the late Joseph Stalin, Mao's slogan invited Chinese intellectuals and other citizens to critique the development of Chinese society and CCP politics. The slogan was taken up by other CCP leaders and Mao elaborated on the issue in his speech at the Eleventh Session (Enlarged) of the Supreme State Conference in February 1957.[46] Mao argued that although the revolution and Party rule had removed the basic antagonistic contradiction between exploiters and exploited in China, so that the country was now 'united as one', this did 'not mean that contradictions no longer exists in our country' (Mao Tse-Tung, 2007: 130). Mao called for critique and open discussion in order to solve residual non-antagonistic contradictions within Chinese society. He prescribed argument, discussion, 'painstaking reasoning, and not crude coercion' as the way forward in the arts, culture and science, and to 'help us get rid of bureaucracy' (Mao Tse-Tung, 2007: 155, 161). The flowers of critique did blossom during the winter and spring of 1957:

> Although most intellectuals were wary when they first heard Mao's call to 'Let a hundred flowers bloom', they lost their inhibitions as praise was lavished on those who came forward with criticism. The outpouring of criticism that followed apparently took Mao by surprise; he abruptly reversed course and angrily accused the critics of harbouring rightist ideology and opposing the party.[47]

During the veritable purge of all dissenting views that followed the 'Hundred Flowers Campaign' period of criticism and debate, more than half of the country's educated elite were punished or severely critiqued and stigmatised.[48]

Before his speech on 'the correct handling of contradictions among the people' was printed in June 1957, Mao Tse-Tung 'went over the verbatim record and made certain additions'[49] that signal the shift about to take place. This printed version of his speech is interesting because it contains traces from both phases of this history, which saw the opening up of liberal critique and its reversal. In this deeply ambiguous text, Mao espouses liberty, free discussion, dissent, openness to critique, and demands that the party and its cadres refrain from 'crude methods of suppression', while boasting of the 'elimination' and 'cleaning out' of counter-revolutionaries: 'Not to have a correct political orientation is like not having a soul' (Mao Tse-Tung, 2007: 151). The speech concludes with six political criteria 'for distinguishing fragrant flowers from poisonous weeds' (Mao Tse-Tung, 2007: 157). The most important of these criteria – all potential matters of life or death – state that words and deeds 'should be beneficial, and not harmful, to socialist transformation and socialist construction [...] and should help to strengthen, and not shake off or weaken, the leadership of the Communist Party' (Mao Tse-Tung, 2007: 158).

The sinister repressive import of this text lies in its ambiguity; it can be re-interpreted to any purpose, such that any honest opinion construed as a weakening of Party leadership can lead to serious charges. The consequences of being branded a 'poisonous weed', a person without 'a soul', are less than promising. However, the major legacy of Mao's text was the promise of liberal-minded, rational discussion of political issues: the moment of openness and the toleration of different schools of thought that had preceded the persecutions and purges. This earlier positive connotation is the main import of the blooming flowers in Lin Zhaohua's production of *The Master Builder*. The old ruling force seated in the red chair relaxes his grip. Solness allows Hilde to make 'a hundred flowers' bloom; he abstains from 'crude methods' of repression, setting Ragnar Brovik and Kaja Fosli free; he states that he will no longer interfere in practical matters, building only 'castles in the air'; and he walks away, leaving the flowers to bloom in peace.

The supplement of this silent action, Hilde's strewing the stage floor with blooming flowers, gives the words spoken on stage a new resonance, an added layer of meaning for those 'connoisseur' audiences who can make the reflexive connection. Furthermore, the visual elements of the *mise en scène* that I have analysed here are interrelated, they pull in the same direction, pointing towards a much broader field of political and ideological struggle. However, it is important to stress that while this reading is possible, and in my view correct, it is in no way necessary.[50] The performance can certainly be enjoyed without the inference that I have drawn here. And even if one recognises the visual allusiveness of the *mise en scène*, one need not interpret it in a system critical way because the signs themselves are ambivalent. This is especially true of the flower scene; even if the allusion to Mao and the 'Hundred Flowers Campaign' is noticed, it need not be interpreted as critique, because it does have support in Mao's (even more ambivalent) text. It could be seen as an innocent pointing towards Chairman Mao's wisdom, with no topical dimension and certainly no necessary connection to recent Chinese history, such as the tragic events that took place at Tiananmen Square in 1989.

Concluding conjectures

This study of four productions from three different cultures cannot claim to be empirically representative, but these examples may still be grounds for some tentative theorising. One trait that these excellent and extremely different Ibsen productions share is a double inflection – of realism and plot. While all four adaptations maintain a strong realistic form of representation, they inflect this form through different techniques and devices. Mehrjui's *Sara* bends realism in response to a strict necessity generated by censorship itself; Borhany Marand introduces a meta-level in order to frame the core action of *The Wild Duck*; Lin invests a virtually empty stage with supplementary significance through a few added props and actions; while, in similar but very different ways, Le Hung's *Doll's House* introduces scenographic elements and actions that have symbolic significance. In their different ways, all four productions activate supplements that tend to inflect the otherwise dominant realism of the adaptation.

A similar inflection takes place when it comes to plot. Consistent with Peter Brooks' definition of plot as 'the design and intention of narrative, what shapes a story and gives it a certain direction or intent of meaning',[51] each of these adaptations reshapes the plot, bends it in new directions, towards discourses with a local resonance. It is important to note, however, that the plots are not destroyed or deconstructed, but changed through an inflection that gives them an additional dimension. Even the Iranian *My Wild Duck*, in which the story is most radically changed, retains major aspects of the source plot. Borhany Marand has on the one hand added a new layer of plot, a meta-story concerning the playwright Hedvig and her struggle with the plot we see performed on stage, and on the other hand changed and deleted some aspects of the inner story, Ibsen's plot. These adaptations of the plot serve to strengthen discursive aspects concerning gender and class. Some of these elements supplement the plot through replacements or additions, but the most contested and potentially dangerous aspects of the performance are communicated via the opposite strategy of cutting; that is, through what is *not* present, what is mute.

In a much stronger sense, Lin's *Master Builder* and Le Hung's *Doll's House* illustrate what I would call the strategy of the parallel supplement. While adhering quite closely to Ibsen's plot, each adds actions and visual elements that supplement and potentially redirect what Brooks calls the 'design and intention of the narrative' presented on stage. It is, however, important to stress the open potentiality of this parallel supplement; it relies on an invitation to interpretation that has to be seen and accepted in order to be realised. Not unlike Derrida's logic of the supplement, the additions to the main realist plot line introduce elements of indirection and inauthenticity.[52] They are ambivalent to the extent that they can be invisible – not necessarily seen – but when recognised they can disrupt the absorptive quality of the plot. They are thus reflexive, relying on interpretation: when activated they can usurp the main plot and become the main thing.

The danger of invoking Derrida is that certain kinds of prejudice would have it that we are then about to enter the abyss of interpretation;

where we will end up with infinite chains of signifiers without signifieds. My point, however, is that while the specific logic of the supplement establishes the crucial *possibility* of the abyss of interpretation, this emptiness or openness of the abyss functions specifically as an escape route, a safety valve. In other words, a specific critical utterance or meaning is communicated clearly to the knowing audience, those 'tuned in' to this frequency, but simultaneously there is recourse to the claim of emptiness, endless ambivalence, indecision in response to possible prosecution. The supplement can pass under the radar of censorship only by virtue of its double claims to full authentic specificity and elusive ambiguity.

Among the most interesting findings in the preceding analysis, although not the most surprising, is the nuanced use of allegory, the modest invitation to allegoresis that can be seen in all four productions. Even the marionettes that open Le Hung's Vietnamese version of *A Doll's House* do not demand an allegorical reading. Although the marionettes clearly invite allegoresis, the 'other' meaning spoken in public remains ambiguous.[53] Not only are multiple allegorical possibilities encoded, the codes themselves are ambiguous. And because this multiple coding seems so deliberate, we need recourse to the facts of censorship to fully comprehend it. The understanding of these artistic expressions relies on knowledge of the power struggles and conflicts that permeate their cultures and societies. In the words of Angus Fletcher:

> At the heart of any allegory will be found this conflict of authorities. One ideal will be pitted against another [...] Allegories are far less often the dull systems that they are reputed to be than they are symbolic power struggles.[54]

Even although the existence of state censorship in these three cultures informs the ways in which each *mise en scène* can be read, it is important to emphasise that none is a mechanical effect of censorship. Although elements of the *mise en scène* will be better understood if the fact of censorship is taken into account, they cannot be deduced from censorship rules and regulations. These four versions of Ibsen in practice embody conscious reflexive responses to a situation dominated by censorship: they are not mechanical responses to the censor's intervention. In this sense they are testimony to a relative autonomy of art within heavily censored contexts. As such they are important not only for their aesthetic value but as proofs of human courage and intelligence.

4

Three Chinese Dolls

During the first half of the twentieth century China experienced unprecedented and accelerating social and cultural change. While representing a period of change – in many ways for the better – it was also a period characterised by tremendous suffering and violence. Moving through feudal Qing dynasty rule, through the War-Lord period (1916–1928), Nationalist takeover and (mis-)rule, Japanese, Russian and Western invasions into its territory, the civil war and ensuing communist revolution, the Chinese people suffered and prevailed. And in addition to these political conflicts and upheavals, came several droughts and periods of famine, the worst of which took place in 1920/21.[1] This period of turbulent change is the historical and material context for the introduction of Henrik Ibsen to China. In a situation characterised by a social, political and economic structure in decay and fissure, Ibsen was taken up by leading intellectual figures within the 'new culture movement' and the later May 4th Movement during the first decades of the twentieth century.[2] These intellectuals sought radical change in Chinese society, and they used Ibsen as a kind of literary 'agent' in order to promote change and progress. Lu Xun, generally regarded as the most important Chinese author of the twentieth century, introduced Ibsen in essays as early as 1907, while still studying in Japan. And the philosopher Hu Shi, who had studied under John Dewey at Cornell, pushed forward his agenda of change through a new individualism and freedom of thought in the essay 'Ibsenism' in the journal *New Youth* in 1918.[3]

The many different intellectuals and artists who participated in the introduction and domestication of Ibsen into China, during what is often called the 'first Westernisation', saw Ibsen as a progressive dramatist whose plays the Chinese people should learn from in order to modernise and liberate themselves from the shackles of feudalism. According to He Chengzhou, what united the:

> Chinese intellectuals during the 'first westernization' in China [was] the unanimous expectation of change, economically, socially and politically. What was most crucial for the nation, according to the intellectuals then, was to awaken the people by showing them the truth. The construction of modern literature was done for this purpose. So was the introduction of foreign literature.[4]

Ibsen was, however, put to use in the early twentieth-century Chinese context as part of an effort to introduce new forms of theatre and drama, *huaju* or spoken drama, which certainly had a modernising and Westernising logic of its own. Many of his plays were translated and discussed, but none can rival *A Doll's House* in importance and centrality within the Chinese context. This first phase in the history of the Chinese Ibsen reception has been thoroughly researched and is well documented.[5]

The complex history of Ibsen within the People's Republic of China (PRC), however, has not been subject to the same detailed analysis and scrutiny. In the following I will discuss three very different versions of *A Doll's House* from three phases of modern Chinese history: the 1956 production commemorating the fifty-year anniversary of Ibsen's death; the 1998 intercultural performance featuring a Norwegian Nora in an otherwise Chinese cast; and the Chinese–Norwegian modern dance performance of the play from 2010.[6] They are chosen not only because they are important landmarks within the history of Chinese Ibsen performances, but also because they in different ways point to the politics of cultural exchange. These three stagings of *A Doll's House* share the fact that they all constitute cultural exchanges, not only in the artistic sense, but also by involving politics at a more official level within the Chinese–

Norwegian interchange. They represent different phases in the modern history of Chinese theatre, specifically showing the shifts in its relationship with Western drama. Hence a central aspect in the following will be to investigate how the complex relation between these productions and their local context is influenced also by a shifting Chinese *use* of 'foreign', Western Others, here in the shape of a Norwegian dramatist. In order to understand these three cases of Ibsen in practice, it is necessary to relate them to the complex negotiations of China's relationship with its Western Other, often giving rise to the discursive mechanisms termed 'Chinese Occidentalism' by Xiaomei Chen.[7] These discourses range from what Chen calls 'official Occidentalism' – the use of a demonised stereotype of the hostile West in order to suppress opposition at home – to what she calls 'anti-official Occidentalism', which has the opposite goal of protest and liberation (Chen, 2002b: 3–6). Spanning over fifty years of the turbulent history of the PRC, the three productions will also substantiate my introductory stress on the necessity of seeing Ibsen's plays in practice, not as objects but as relational processes. What we will see is how the changing relational conditions determine the shapes given to this one play in what is after all a relatively short time, and that they can hardly be understood without a strong emphasis on the context(s) from which they originate.

Beijing *Doll's House: Nora* (1956)

The relationship between Norway and the PRC was remarkably good from the outset, not least considering the vast distance between the countries both in terms of geography and ideology. In spite of the ideological antagonism so strongly marked during the early years of the cold war, Norway was one of the first countries to recognise the PRC – in February 1950 – and in direct opposition to US policies. The Chinese authorities could be seen as reciprocating through the remarkably high level of its diplomatic representation in Oslo from early on, noted also by other Western powers.[8] It has even been speculated that the performance in 1956 could be seen as signalling a similar kind of appreciation by the Chinese authorities, but there is no documentation to support this theory.[9] When *A Doll's House* was put on stage in 1956, it was in any case the first major performance of an Ibsen play in the PRC. This was an important year in the history of the young communist state. Experiencing the first signs of economic growth after having consolidated its power and implemented the first five-year plan, the communist leadership decided to try to win a greater proportion of the intellectuals over to its side through the 'Hundred Flowers Campaign'.[10] This short period of thaw was designed to create a climate of productive, 'non-antagonistic' opposition and critique to further strengthen the party and its support among the former elites who were after all still hanging on to the 'values of the old bourgeois world'.[11] This also created a much more open atmosphere in relation to art and literature originating in Western Europe.

On 17 October 1955, the Chinese press released the news that the World Peace Council had decided to celebrate ten 'giants of world culture' in 1956, and among them Henrik Ibsen. This did not, however, give rise to an unchecked enthusiasm at the Norwegian Embassy in Beijing. Judging from the correspondence between the Embassy and the Ministry in Oslo, the response is better described as anxious and uncertain. On behalf of the Embassy, the acting Chargé d'Affairs, Nicolai Geelmuyden, wrote to the Ministry of Foreign Affairs three days later asking for instructions on what to do should the Embassy be approached by Chinese authorities on the occasion.[12] What caused the anxiety, however, was not the Chinese authorities' decision to make a major event out of the fiftieth anniversary of Henrik Ibsen's death, but the involvement of the World Peace Council (WPC). This organisation was founded in Warsaw in 1948, and its official goals and purposes were to promote world peace and national sovereignty, and to fight imperialism and atomic weapons, among other things.

The problem with the WPC and its involvement in a cultural event was that it was perceived by the Western powers as a communist 'front organisation', purely used for propaganda purposes, and controlled by the Soviet Union.[13] In the same letter Geelmuyden reminded the ministry that similar events had taken place in 1955, when Schiller, Montesquieu and Hans Christian Andersen were celebrated on their respective anniversaries, under the auspices of the WPC. It was the East German Embassy that was invited to the Schiller event, and all Western representatives declined to go. During the Andersen event the Danish ambassador had participated: 'He felt compelled to go, while the rest of the Western representatives kept away after consultation with the British chargé d'affaires who had received direct orders not to attend any arrangement done under the auspices of the WPC'.[14] In light of the possible ideological and political difficulties, Geelmuyden stressed the need for guidelines and said that he would in any case await further instruction before responding to a possible advance from the Chinese authorities. While the Embassy kept asking for instructions through the following months, the Norwegian authorities in Oslo started the process of political clarification.

In a memorandum from Odd Jacobsen of the 'Third Political Office' of the Ministry of Foreign Affairs, dated 15 November 1955 (NA, B1622), official policy was outlined in three points. First, it stressed that Norway should continue to stay away from the WPC and all its activities, so as not to do anything that could contribute to an increase in the prestige of the WPC. Second, as far as Ibsen was concerned, the Ministry doubted that the WPC could give any valuable contribution to the spreading of knowledge about the dramatist: 'Instead there is every reason to fear that Ibsen's writings can be used for propaganda purposes (for example his critique of Prussian militarism)'.[15] They did not, however, see any reason for Norwegian representatives in China to stay away from 'events that are not seen as propaganda, for example performances of Ibsen's plays', should they not be emphasised as parts of WPC activities.[16] In light of the fact that several other members of NATO might have to 'face similar problems', the memo concluded with the suggestion that Norway should raise the issue within the Alliance to ensure a common understanding among the member states.[17]

In a secret note on 5 December 1955, the Ministry said that they wished to discuss the matter with other Western powers before deciding on which line to take, and instructed the Embassy to 'be reserved towards possible approaches from Chinese organizations'.[18] The Embassy kept expressing its concern while asking for specific orders throughout the winter,[19] and on 22 March the Embassy wrote to Oslo saying that they would be grateful if the Ministry 'had the opportunity to give its instructions to the Embassy as soon as possible',[20] because they had then been approached by the Chinese. The local authorities had decided to make a much larger event out of the celebration of Ibsen and George Bernard Shaw than of the other notabilities of cultural history. They planned a large exhibition, a seminar/public meeting, screening of a film about Ibsen and Norway (if the Embassy could find one), and they planned a staging of *A Doll's House*. They asked the Embassy to assist in finding pictures of Norwegian daily life in Ibsen's time, photos from Norwegian Ibsen productions and names of potential Norwegian experts who could be invited to speak at the public meeting.

In a secret letter from 9 April, the Embassy was instructed to keep to the policy outlined in the memo from 15 November; they could participate and contribute to arrangements put up in the honour of Henrik Ibsen, as long as it was not seen as 'propaganda' and the WPC was not fronted as the organiser. The political instruction, then, was to keep out of politics when it came to Ibsen, meaning that purely artistic events were acceptable. And in a letter on 9 May, the Embassy informed Oslo about successful meetings with the Chinese Vice-Minister for Culture, Xie Yen, himself an Ibsen expert and playwright, and Sheng Tse-Pei of the Ministry of Foreign Affairs in Beijing about the coming collaboration: the Chinese director Wu Xue was invited to Oslo for the Ibsen week to be held there in May two weeks later (from the 23rd to the 29th of May) and the Norwegian director Gerda Ring was invited to Beijing to act as artistic advisor for Wu's staging of *A Doll's House*. It is with clear relief that the Ambassador concludes his letter with the information that the official organisers of the Beijing event will be different Chinese arts organisations, above all the All China Federation of Stage Artists and the

Chinese Association of Dramatists, and not the WPC. He also reported that he had raised the issue directly in his meeting with the ministry, and that the Chinese understood the problem: 'Mr Sheng was aware that the World Peace Council was something of a stumbling block for us, and said laughingly that the Peace Council would be kept in the background'.[21] The sensitivity shown by the Chinese organisers in this regard was again mentioned with gratitude in the Embassy report to the Ministry after the event, where the Ambassador even claimed that, 'The World Peace Council did not enter the picture and was not mentioned in any of the official speeches'.[22]

After different, quite subtle negotiations on both sides, the end result was a major, successful celebration of Ibsen on the fiftieth anniversary of his death. The Chinese motivation was repeatedly stressed during the events as being a result of the prominent role Ibsen had played in Chinese history since the days of the May 4th Movement. Because there was a similar connection to George Bernard Shaw, and both of them being dramatists, the Ibsen events were launched through a large meeting in joint commemoration of the two on 27 July in The Main Hall at the Peking Hotel. This was at the time Beijing's largest assembly hall, and the audience counted close to 2,000 people. The meeting was opened by the Minister of Culture, Shen Yen-Ping – better known under the name Mao Tun, at the time considered to be China's leading author – followed by Tien Han, Chairman of the Union of Chinese Stage Artists. After them, Lennox Robinson and Rubeigh James Minney talked about George Bernard Shaw and their relationship to the Irish dramatist,[23] followed by the Norwegian Director Gerda Ring, who gave a lecture on Ibsen. Having listened to the lectures and speeches, the audience was presented with three scenes from Shaw's plays *The Apple Cart* and *Mrs Warren's Profession*. The evening was concluded with a ball, and during the meeting everyone present was given a new Chinese translation of three of Ibsen's plays. The Embassy, together with Norwegian and Chinese newspapers, reported enthusiastically about a highly successful meeting where no expenses were spared. The following day, *A Doll's House* had its premiere in the packed 3,000-seat China

Youth Art Theatre. The performance was originally planned only for a few nights, but due to its success it stayed on the repertoire for the whole season, and also toured the big cities of China. In addition, the theatre gathered a full house for a public meeting on the morning of Sunday 28 July, with Wu Xue, Gerda Ring and the Norwegian director and critic Gerhard Knoop among the speakers.

The 1956 event was entirely a Chinese initiative, and took place only because the Chinese wanted to commemorate the fiftieth anniversary of Henrik Ibsen's death. The fact that the events had a Norwegian component was also a result of Chinese invitation and initiative. And almost all the expenses were covered by the Chinese state; the only real expense on the Norwegian side was the invitation of Wu and his interpreter, where travel and living expenses during the Ibsen week in Oslo were covered. The Chinese on their part had already invited Mrs Gerda Ring to stay in Beijing for a month, and they also invited Gerhard Knoop for the festival itself. Both parties were very happy with the events afterwards, the Chinese praising the effort made by the Embassy in all kinds of practical matters. The Norwegians enthusiastically praised the celebration, and the production of *A Doll's House* in particular. The Embassy repeatedly underscored that the WPC had been kept out of it, and that 'the memory of the great figure of culture was celebrated without ulterior motives of a political nature'.[24] The irony of this last statement is of course that the correspondence shows that the celebration was full of 'ulterior' and 'political' motives, not least on the Norwegian side. The conclusion from the Embassy saying that the Ibsen festival had become 'good propaganda for Norway' tells the same story.[25] Both sides in this cultural exchange, it seems fair to say, were highly conscious of the political and ideological stakes involved.

Furthermore, in light of the speeches and lectures from the Shaw/Ibsen meeting on 27 July, it does seem a pretty long way down the path of euphemism to say that politics were kept in the background. In fact, and contrary to the Embassy report, the very first sentence of Mao Tun's opening speech stated that '[in] response to the call of the World Peace Council, the Chinese people have convened this meeting here today'.[26] He did not keep on stressing the WPC, but what he and the other Chinese speaker, Tien Han, continually emphasised was a clear-cut political, Marxist reading of Shaw and Ibsen. In accord with the rhetoric of the WPC, he praised the two dramatists for loving 'peace', 'freedom', 'democracy', and for opposing war, etc. His concluding remarks about Ibsen were that:

> We commemorate him because his works encourage mankind to strive for freedom and liberation, because they criticise the petty and the vulgar, because they reveal the misery that the patriarchal system brings.

Mao Tun's speech is interesting also because it illustrates how dependent on context the meaning of words and concepts are; his use of these 'positive' words from the Western, enlightenment tradition of political thinking – 'freedom', 'peace', 'liberation' – had very different meanings and implications than what they would have in a Western context. And of course the new Chinese regime would take the opportunity, not only to demonstrate the Chinese familiarity with Ibsen and Shaw, but also to state how they conceived of the two dramatists' relevance to the contemporary Chinese situation. The main speaker, Tien Han, gave a detailed and well-informed lecture on Shaw and Ibsen and their relationship to the new China, based on a Marxist view of art and aesthetics. Shaw was generally praised for his leftist leanings, but with the slight reservation implied in Tien's quoting Lenin's characterisation of him as a 'good man fallen among Fabians' (Tien, 1956: 13).[27] Ibsen, being far more difficult to rephrase as a socialist, was interpreted as a great artist, the father of modern, realist-progressive drama. His political potential was stressed through readings of *An Enemy of the People* – where Stockmann was seen as 'a staunch fighter against the ugliness of capitalism' and the play as a 'merciless exposure of the bourgeoisie' – but also *Brand, Ghosts, The Lady from the Sea* and of course *A Doll's House* were given due attention.[28]

The Chinese documents on the performance were almost without exception structured around three basic elements: first, a strong emphasis on the historical background of Ibsen's dramas in China; second, a consistent investment of specific left-wing political ideas in the plays; and third, a discussion of the possible relevance of Ibsen in post-revolutionary China. In the programme leaflet for the performance, the director Wu Xue underscores the relation to the May 4th Movement, and claimed that Ibsen was introduced to China by Lu Xun, a writer greatly appreciated and adopted by the Communist Party.[29] In addition, the programme links *A Doll's House* to the historic struggle of the CCP by telling the story of important productions of the play from 1921, 1923, 1934 and 1948, all of them purportedly with links to the Party: the first one made possible through the assistance of a 'secret faction of the communist party', the last one performed by the CCP troupe 'Budu Drama Society'. This 1948 performance was, according to the programme, censored, but the artists disobeyed the censorship rules and stuck to the original script upon which the:

> ... secretary of the drama society Chen Qianmou (member of the communist party) was seized (and went on to die a martyr's death). These harsh practices of the reactionaries enticed the fury of the entire drama society, and they pushed the performance forward for more than a month. They played for full houses every night, affirming the support of the society while dealing a severe blow to the reactionaries.[30]

The different official Chinese documents concerning the *Nora* performance in 1956 emphasise the genuinely *Chinese* Ibsen tradition, with the added political stress. Of course, Ibsen was never a clear-cut communist avant-garde writer in pre-revolutionary China, but that the Chinese Ibsen was from the outset linked to social energies in opposition to the old Confucian, feudal China seems evident. The CCP version of this story is interesting in its attempt to assimilate Ibsen as part of the communist struggle *and* as ideological ally and forerunner. The problem, however, is not only one of similarity, of how to overcome difference, how to make *A Doll's House* legitimate – but perhaps even more of how to maintain and negotiate the reality of difference. In other words, an additional difficulty for the post-revolutionary Chinese theatre seems to have been that this nineteenth-century European dramatist could not be seen as *too* topical within the new, communist reality. The crucial issue concerns historical difference, in Wu Xue's words, that Ibsen reminds us of historical progress – that '[t]he age of Nora is gone never to return', because the Chinese reality has changed decisively:

> As for our generation, the chief foundation for married life should be based on mutual respect, mutual love and mutual aid. This is the kind of family life that Ibsen yearned for half a century ago. Regarding the question of women's rights, they have already been firmly endorsed by the PRC, in a way that differs greatly from the prattle of the capitalist's newspapers. (Wu, 1956: 3)

In the course of one generation, then, Ibsen had fundamentally speaking gone from being a forerunner and political ally, to being decisively part of the *old* world, the previous stage of bourgeois capitalism. But it was only the progressive, communist states that had left this stage behind them; it did exist as a reality in the enemy camp of the 'reactionaries' in the West. Embracing Ibsen within the new reality of the PRC could therefore be seen as ideologically ambiguous, a path to be trod with caution. And it is a cautious Wu who ventures the idea that there may be – even within the new era of Chinese communism – remnants from the old order when it comes to gender:

> But if we look for remaining patterns of that time's mentality today, are there not still women like Nora, the way she was before she left, to be found? Women whose spiritual lives are completely restrained by the trivial matters surrounding them, with no greater ideals for their lives and their careers? And are there not also husbands like Helmer; self-loving, self-serving, and hypocritically immoral? (Wu, 1956: 3)

In spite of the success of liberation, then, there are remnants of the old age still alive, and Wu concludes by saying that 'Nora is a play that withstands the toll of time.'[31] These finer points of ideologico-political negotiation are at stake in the Chinese documents on the performance, as in the performance itself; the critical and radical Ibsen is highlighted, but simultaneously distanced, put down. What we see here are clearly the contours of the effects of what Xiaomei Chen calls 'official occidentalism' that is the use of the West as a stereotyped enemy to serve internal political ends – the dangers of being labelled a Western 'agent', in any sense of the word, were clear enough. The Hundred Flowers Campaign was the first major, if ever so brief, period of thaw, also in relation to the Western Other, but the 'West', it would seem, could not be embraced too univocally – a distance had to be negotiated.

In contrast to the Chinese negotiation of explicitly political aspects of the writer and his cultural background, the Norwegian side of this cultural exchange wanted to avoid politics, albeit in an ambivalent and politically charged way. Gerda Ring's speech at the public meeting on 27 July warned against tying Ibsen too strongly to topical issues or the form of realism itself – instead she propagated an Ibsen image in the timeless, tragic vein: Ibsen was 'representative of the monumental classical drama, poetic and symbolic [...] to be considered a poet, and not merely a polemical mouthpiece of a certain trend of ideas.' Gerda Ring, as the Norwegian Embassy, did not want politics but the existentialist poet, 'as an interpreter of human conditions'.[32] When juxtaposed, however, what appears is not a contrast between a political and a non-political point of view, but rather the difference between two ways of formulating the political. *Not* wanting to see oppression or conflict in terms of class or gender in a work of art is a political statement in itself. And of course Gerda Ring's interpretation of Ibsen has its own cultural background; she emphasises the need to do something new, to bring Ibsen in touch with her own time within the European theatre of the 1950s. And that seems to her to imply a distancing in relation to politics in the direct sense, which is symptomatic of the early post-war era. The 1950s could clearly be seen as a period of, if not backlash then at least a re-consolidation and strengthening of the traditional gender roles in Norway and Europe.

This ideological trend is easily registered in the Norwegian reception of *A Doll's House*, because the play in the 1950s was to be regarded as *not* a feminist text but as a timeless, 'marital' or existential tragedy.

In spite of the multi-layered and conflicting forms of misunderstanding at play here, the cultural exchange and co-operation was experienced as highly successful and rewarding by all involved parties. Li Chao, Secretary General of the Union of Chinese Artists, wrote a letter to the Norwegian Embassy in September 1956, where he stated that:

> although this was the first case of co-operation between Chinese and Norwegians, the co-operation was more than close. The performance of 'Nora' gave Chinese art circles and large audiences greater understanding of the Norwegian people, and with understanding real friendship was born. [. . .] We hope that the great and traditional cultures of Norway and China will prosper in mutual friendship in the future. (11 September 1956, NA: 485)

Due to the events of the following decades in China, it was to take almost 25 years until the next major Ibsen performance in the country. But somehow the Ibsen tradition never died, and after the Cultural Revolution it was to be resumed – both as performance and as intercultural co-operation.

The performance

Set in China's most prestigious theatre, the China Youth Theatre, with a prominent director and China's finest actors, the 1956 performance made a strong impression on Chinese and Norwegian reviewers alike.[33] There are no recordings of this performance, but it is well documented so that those of us not fortunate enough to have seen it, can get a relatively good impression of what it could have been like. In addition to the many written accounts, there are rich visual records of the performance in the form of stage photos, in colour as well as black and

white.[34] The photos are astonishingly well kept and of high quality.
When looking at them two things spring to mind: first, seen as visual
evidence of cultural exchange and co-operation, the performance
photos testify to a surprisingly mono-lateral process, almost a one-way
street; and second, the leftist or Marxist political stress we found in the
Chinese discourse surrounding the performance is not visible.

The first point concerns the most conspicuous – almost startling –
fact about the photos, namely that the actors at first glance could be
mistaken for being Europeans, and not Chinese. At least a superficial
look at the photo of Nora from the opening scene, where she has just
come home from shopping – still wearing her outdoor clothes, arms
full of boxes and gifts – will not reveal that this is a Chinese woman. Her
hair is golden blond, her skin light, cheeks red (presumably from the
cold outside), and she is wearing winter clothes, a thick jacket with fur
coating and a small fur hat. Down to the last detail the theatre has
worked hard to create the image of an 'authentic' Western woman of the
bourgeoisie, wearing an expensive looking purple dress, jewel earrings
and a wedding ring on her right hand, Norwegian style.[35]

And the same goes for the rest of the people on stage; they all
look distinctly 'Western' – and they all carry strong visible signs of their
class background. The women are wearing expensive-looking, heavy,
long (silk) dresses, and the men appear in long dinner jackets, with
starched white (silk) shirts, ties or neatly tied bow ties. Even the three
blonde, light-skinned children are dressed up – the two boys in suits,
with white shirts, neck-scarves and knickerbockers, the girl in a dress
with some elements from Norwegian folk costumes. And as can be seen
upon closer scrutiny, not only are the details of clothing and make-up
given attention, but the actors also perform with exquisite wigs and
false noses giving them a Western profile. The substantial effort to
'Westernise' the characters on stage is matched by the effort (and
money) the Chinese theatre have put into the designing of the stage as
authentically Western bourgeoisie living quarters; the high ceiling with
stucco and chandelier, and the walls covered with 'historically correct'
wallpaper, heavy drapery and paintings. There are two major paintings

on the living room walls, one of them depicting a ship sailing off from a coastline looking genuine enough to give off an aura of nineteenth-century Norwegian nation-building, the other of a 'classical' motif of Roman architecture; St Peter's Square with the dome in the background (Figure 4.1). This gives the stage an Italian ambience concordant with

Figure 4.1 Dancing the tarantella; *A Doll's House*, China Youth Theatre, directed by Wu Xue (1956). From left to right: Nora (Ji Shuping), Helmer (Yu Chun) and Rank (Du Peng) (Photo courtesy of The National Library of Norway).

the tarantella dance, but also a religious placement within Christianity. It is, however, also in correspondence with the iconography of the Norwegian theatre tradition that from the beginning had a habit of having a reproduction of Rafael's 'Madonna and Child' on the rear-wall of the set.[36] The furniture is heavy and expensive, even with gold painting on some of the heavy wooden frames, otherwise resembling mahogany. The huge double doors on the back wall have massive, carved and decorated frames, almost like columns along the sides. In addition, there is a piano, thick carpets on the floor and even a tiled stove on stage. Down to the smallest visual details, the theatre has meticulously sought to achieve full illusion of this being Ibsen's Norwegian world.

This was also an observation made by Gerhard Knoop and Gerda Ring in their reports in the Scandinavian press, where they enthusiastically claimed that the language was the only thing that really prevented the performance from passing as 'Norwegian'.[37] Apart from minor 'mistakes' in details, the *mise en scène* was in Knoop's words 'a Norwegian living room! [...] on the whole: honest, authentic and filled with the tobacco-brown, intimate, cosy atmosphere of the 1880s'.[38] The photos do, however, not only tell us that Wu and the Youth Theatre in Beijing want the actors and the set to appear as authentically Norwegian and bourgeois as possible, but that this aspect of the performance is to be found even in the bodies of the actors, such as in their very gestures, poses and movements. One moment within the play that almost always will be photographed is the tarantella. In Beijing, Nora is seen wearing a grey silk skirt and a waist-short burgundy jacket with white lacework scarf and sleeves. Placed in front, Nora is given a background that also tells a story – not only through the gaze of the two men behind her, but also through the painting of St Peter's Square. What is most interesting, however, is the pose itself: her body turned sideways with her face turned towards the audience and the camera, she is holding a tambourine high in the air with her right arm, and the left pointedly resting on her hip. It is worth noting that this pose is not to be found in the play itself, as the stage directions only tell us that Nora dances; this pose, then, is carried by the theatrical tradition itself, *not* by the text as such. In other words, what is so striking with this pose in the Beijing performance is above all its reference to the *Norwegian* tradition of staging the play. This pose is to be found in the very first staging of the play in Copenhagen in 1879, and repeated in Oslo during the following decades. In Norway, it has lived its life through performances of *A Doll's House* all the way up to 1990.[39] The same point could be made in relation to the rest of the photos; they all seem to depict bodily gestures and positions modelled on Scandinavian poses – whether it is the picture of Nora lighting Dr Rank's cigar, her playing with the children, or the ending of the play. The photos from the performance all indicate how specific gestures and poses were imported into Chinese theatre by Wu in 1956, through the help of a Norwegian instructor acting as artistic advisor.

In fact, what springs to mind when reading the reviews and looking at the photos from the performance is more the concept of imitation than one of exchange or co-operation. This is not to say that the performance was in any way weak; it seems to have been extremely strong and successful. And still there can be no doubt that imitation of the authentic, 'Norwegian' way of doing the play was the *raison d'etre* of the *mise en scène*. This is what Wu Xue wanted, and in order to secure this result he used his visit to Norway in May 1956 to collect stage photos, see Norwegian Ibsen performances and interview artists and other experts – in addition to inviting Gerda Ring to spend a month in Beijing, giving advice on how to perfect the performance as *authentically foreign*.[40] Hence it also goes without saying that there was no Norwegian pressure at play in shaping the performance; it was a Chinese initiative, and the Chinese knew what they wanted.

Apart from being a great success, artistically and in terms of audience turnout, the 1956 *Doll's House* in Beijing draws attention through its way of handling cultural difference. In spite of the many speakers and writers emphasising Ibsen's importance in Chinese history, the performance was constructed so as to make him not in any sense local but as foreign as possible – culturally, historically and politically. This choice, and its success on stage and in reviews, has to be understood in light of its cultural and political context. This was an official event – a result of decisions within the CCP and the state apparatus – and the performance was to fit within the policies outlined at the time. It therefore seems obvious that it should be understood within the context of the ongoing Hundred Flowers Campaign, which meant an opening up towards other opinions and expressions than the official party-line *and* at the same time towards the outside world and the West. But it seems equally important to remember that the Hundred Flowers Campaign never meant total freedom to express any kind of opinion. Mao made it very clear from the outset that one had to keep the distinction between 'flowers' and 'poisonous weeds' clear – and that the latter would not be tolerated.[41]

Not least because the articles and speeches on the occasion emphasised that the play had a history of being used subversively in China – as indirect or allegorical critique of feudalism and 'the reactionaries' – it seems reasonable to infer that Wu and the Youth Theatre would want to make sure that the same allegorical aspects of this version were not activated as potential critique of the CCP. This seems, then, to have been secured by making it a 'Western' performance about problems now relevant primarily to an 'other' culture, specifically Western capitalism. From this point of view, it also becomes clear that there is a political aspect to the shaping of the *mise en scène*; that the Marxist or Maoist perspective created or even *demanded* the Westernising traits in the performance, and hence that our two points above are in fact interrelated. The reason that the Marxist perspective was absent in the performance is to be found in the very same Marxist perspective, and the reason for the 'Norwegian-ness' of the performance is correspondingly to be found in the specifically *Chinese* situation. Hence the political meaning of the performance was in this sense diametrically opposite to the one lauded by Ring and Knoop. Where they perceived the performance as a victory for the unpolitical, ahistorical and transcultural work of art, the Chinese saw it as deeply political and culturally *specific*.

If read in the light of Xiaomei Chen's concept 'occidentalism', this first instance of a cultural co-operation between Norway and the PRC would seem in a strangely over-determined fashion to be influenced both by its official and unofficial form.[42] It is part of official occidentalism to claim that Ibsen is above all an honest critic of Western Capitalism, which is essentialised as a hostile and oppressive other, a discursive move that criticises this Other while simultaneously praising the state of affairs internally: that is, this historical stage is surpassed by the Chinese Revolution, and Nora's drama testifies to this historical reality. In Xiaomei Chen's words, this discourse has 'the consolidation of a particular group within domestic politics' and this group's 'domestic oppression of political opponents' (Chen, 2002b: 5) as its main purpose. However, the sheer success of the production does indicate that it was able to address problems that the audience felt to be pressing. The many statements claiming that the problems within the play were not surpassed once and for all, and that liberation was an ongoing process, indicate that the performance could be seen to give vent to social energies more critical of the state of affairs within the PRC. Hence it seems just as clear that the performance was invested with the opposite 'anti-official' form of occidentalism, 'using the Western Other as a metaphor for a political liberation against ideological oppression' (Chen, 2002b: 5). This is hinted at many places in the discussions of the play, but only one of these draws explicitly on an audience response. Wu Xue recorded a conversation he overheard after one of the performances, which could well summarise this double discourse:

One night after the performance, I overheard the conversation between a couple:

Wife: You have to reflect upon yourself!

Husband: What do I have to reflect?

Wife: What to reflect? Nothing is more clear. I feel that you are like Helmer!

Husband: Nonsense. In our society, there is no Helmer.

Wife: It's not nonsense. I have the reason to say that. What I am referring to is that your mind is full of the ideas and attitudes Helmer has towards women.[43]

Through the retelling of this small dialogue between two members of the audience, Wu was able to give a poignant expression of the core ideological conflict at stake in the performance. Some commentators have claimed, as the husband in the dialogue, that the main point was that real progress had taken place, that a woman could now criticise her husband and tell him to reflect and improve, hence she was better off than her sisters in the West, and divorce was basically unnecessary. However, the wife's point would probably be that history, in her own experience, does not work in this way; old thoughts, beliefs and habits die hard, ideology will live on, and Nora's problem cannot be – is not – solved that easily. Even though the play was performed as foreign, it clearly, and through this foreignising, opened up an identity space for the Chinese audience – above all for the women.

Another aspect of this mini-dialogue is that it gives expression to the relationship between cultures; the husband expressing cultural superiority, while the wife is at least implying that something can still be learnt from others. And it is not difficult to find a similar kind of ambiguity in relation to the other culture in the Norwegian material. If the Chinese material contains clear signs of occidentalism, the Norwegians are by no means free of orientalist prejudice. In his first note to the Ministry in Oslo, Nicolai Geelmuyden informed that the WPC would celebrate ten giants of world culture, and lists eight of them – Rembrandt, Heine, Dostoyevsky, etc. – by name, with the additional 'an Indian and a Japanese whose name I have not found out yet'. The sense of superiority implicit in the fact that he did not deem it necessary to find the names of the Japanese painter Toyo Oda and the Indian poet Kalidasa does speak volumes. And in the newspaper reports by Knoop and Ring, there are passages where the Chinese are described as small, almost like children, that are somewhat distressing to a reader of today. I also find it slightly disquieting to see the degree of certainty with which the Norwegians express their 'knowledge' of the true and genuine Ibsen; there is a surprising degree of authority verging on chauvinism in their sense of ownership of him. But at the same time, both Gerda Ring and Gerhard Knoop tell stories about genuine cultural encounters where they have learned with humility; while on the one hand describing her mission as one of 'correcting mistakes and misconceptions', Gerda Ring also admitted, on the other hand, that her stay in China often made her feel that she came from a 'culturally underdeveloped' country, when compared to the Chinese. The Chinese and Norwegian artists alike seem to have learned from each other. They saw the experience as mutually enriching, as a source of optimism, that, in Gerda Ring's words, 'art can build bridges across borders, much stronger bridges than all the political speeches of the world'.[44]

Both parties in this first cultural co-operation between the PRC and Norway saw it as immensely successful. As we have seen, it was a success riddled with misunderstandings and conflicting ways of interpreting the other. The story of this production shows how misunderstandings are part of cultural encounters. Misunderstanding should not be seen as a deviation in relation to an absolute truth or certainty, but as a productive step in negotiating with each other on the basis of good will. This, of course, also goes for the different encounters that constitute this book; my encounters with materials from cultures where I am a stranger, and in turn your, the reader's, encounter with my account. I am certain that I misunderstand in myriad ways, as I am sure my reader(s) in turn might do. An interesting aspect of Wu Xue's 'Nora', then, is that it is a story about cultural exchange as foreignising; the production sought difference and strangeness, not similarity and appropriation. In order to make the play work in the local Chinese context, the Beijing Youth Theatre tried to make it as Norwegian as possible. And the reasons for this were purely local. Gerda Ring and Wu Xue both loved the performance they had succeeded in creating, and they praised each other's contributions to the end result, but they interpreted it differently, almost in opposite ways. Hence the story of this production shows us the relational nature of cultural exchange, that content *is* context. Without an understanding of the material and artistic context, cultural exchange cannot be analysed – which gives reason for humility, also on my part.

Culture and/or gender: *A Doll's House* in the 'New Era' (Beijing 1998)

The celebration of the Ibsen anniversary in 1956 was by far the grandest and most expensive official Ibsen event in China to date. As we have seen, 1956 was a special year in the history of the PRC, but the increased tolerance towards multiple, and even opposing, views on the world propagated during the 'Hundred Flowers Campaign' was soon to be followed by renewed anti-rightist campaigns that made it increasingly dangerous to be seen as promoting bourgeois, Western culture. During the ten years of the 'The Great Proletarian Cultural Revolution', from 1966 up until Mao's death in 1976, only the (eight) 'model plays' designed to promote proletarian values and help remove all bourgeois values and feelings were allowed on stage in the PRC.[45] After Deng Xiaoping's return to power and with the introduction of the 'New Era' policies of opening up and reform, the cultural milieu also changed rapidly.

Among the major productions of Ibsen in the following years, are certainly the 1982 *Peer Gynt* at the China Central Theatre Academy and the China Central Experimental Theatre productions of *An Enemy of the People* in 1996 and *A Doll's House* in 1998, all of them in Beijing. They differ strongly from Wu Xue's staging in their different localising efforts, seeking a more direct relevance and actuality. The production of *Peer Gynt* in the early 1980s could be seen as having a transitional character in this respect. Some elements originating in Norwegian folklore were adapted to a Chinese reality, but the general thrust of the performance was to design it as an 'authentically Norwegian' version of the play, and similar to the 1956 performance of *A Doll's House* in that respect. It became a major success, in Xiaomei Chen's words, 'not because [the audience] understood the play in its original Norwegian terms, but rather because it evoked for them their own immediate Cultural-Revolutionary reality' (Chen, 2002b: 52). While being staged with an emphasis on its Norwegian-ness, the play successfully addressed the difficulties every member of the audience had faced during the years of the Cultural Revolution: problems concerning selfhood and survival, the necessity of 'going roundabout' in situations where 'being oneself' could lead to persecutions and labour camps. Previously Ibsen had been seen mainly as a realist, critical of bourgeois capitalism. Hence the choice of *Peer Gynt*, and the staging of it with romantic and symbolic elements intact, point to new directions within the Ibsen tradition in the PRC.[46]

In the rather insignificant role of Monseigneur Ballon in this *Peer Gynt* production, we find Wu Xiaojiang. Wu was to become important in the story of Ibsen in China during the 1990s, because he later embarked on a successful career as a director, and directed first *An Enemy of the People* in 1996 and then *A Doll's House* in 1998 at the China Central Experimental Theatre.[47] Wu's stagings of Ibsen represent new trends both in financial and artistic terms. While the 1956 version of *A Doll's House* represented a Chinese initiative, financed one hundred per cent by the Chinese, Wu's productions were partly financed by Norwegian state agencies. This signals an important change in Chinese politics; in 1956 it would have been utterly impossible to do a theatre performance in Beijing with outside funding, from a Western, capitalist country.[48] It could easily be seen as interference or even infiltration in a country set on self-sufficiency and socialism. With the 'New Era' policies of the Deng regime, culture was to become increasingly commercialised, and the theatres lost more and more of their previous secure funding from the state.[49] The 1996 production of *An Enemy of the People* was sponsored by the Norwegian Agency for Development Cooperation (NORAD). The funding was later expanded through Norwegian business sponsorship, which paid for the production to go to Oslo and participate at the Ibsen Festival. While in Oslo, the director Wu met with the Norwegian actress Agnethe Haaland. She was then about to move to Beijing together with her husband, Erling Borgen, who was to start his three-year assignment as the China correspondent for Norway's National Broadcasting (NRK). This meeting resulted in the plans for a new Chinese production of *A Doll's House* – and another funding application. In her application, Agnethe Haaland stressed Ibsen's importance in China and several innovative traits in the planned production. With the enthusiastic support from the Norwegian Embassy in Beijing, and after some negotiations with NORAD and the Ministry, the application was granted.

Wu Xiaojiang's productions represent the final departure from the previous tradition of 'faithful', authentically European and manifestly 'foreignising' rendering of classics from the Western canon.[50] Wu's general view was, in his own words, that 'what the play could say to today's Chinese should be more important than conveying the precise meaning of the play.'[51] In *An Enemy of the People*, this desire to address local problems more directly was communicated through the introduction of 'indirect' symbolic devices, an unspecified, abstract space and set design, alienation effects and specifically 'Chinese' elements. The most obviously topical aspect of Wu's staging of *An Enemy of the People* was the critique of the severe ecological problems China faced in the wake of its industrial success. The concept of pollution and the critique of environmental issues, however, were given a wider, more encompassing meaning. In his directorial statement Wu made this explicit:

> We may be able to catch up with those more advanced countries in another decade, but we may also sacrifice our fresh air, clean water, and our traditional values in terms of honesty and modesty. I am convinced that we will have to pay a very high price to get those valuable things back in the future if we cannot prevent pollution now. (Wu, 2001: 80)

The effects of ten to fifteen years of reform and opening up, for Wu, were not only an economic growth that could make Mao Tse-Tung's old utopian goal of catching up 'with those more advanced countries' seem possible, but also an alarming pollution of natural *and* cultural environment alike. The performance was not about 'a small town in Norway over one hundred years ago' but the Chinese 'living and cultural environment today', and the goal was to 'make a statement about resisting pollution in order to protect our humanity and natural environment' (Wu, 2001: 80).

The allegorical potential in *An Enemy of the People* is obvious enough. What does the pollution stand for? Who are the real polluters? The unsettling feeling of there being a spiritual and moral pollution sifting into the fabric of Chinese culture, morality and humanity from the outside, was paradoxically expressed enough and addressed by Wu and the theatre through the staging of a foreign, Western classic. While explaining that he had chosen *An Enemy of the People* because of its ability to address these larger issues, Wu stated that *A Doll's House*, even though better known in China, was less suitable 'because it mainly focuses on the problems of an individual.'[52] However, he changed his mind in this respect as he discovered how to utilise this 'individual story' to address larger cultural and political issues through an intercultural version of *A Doll's House*. The cultural problems facing China after almost two decades of reform were represented through a cross-cultural cast, with the action placed in the pre-revolutionary China of the 1930s. Wu's preoccupation with cultural tensions between the local and the foreign, between the Western and the Chinese, within China, however, has its immediate social and historical background.

The changes of the 'New Era'

According to a Chinese saying, 'Policy may change three times in a single day,'[53] and when studying the history of modern China it is tempting, almost at every point, to characterise the period under scrutiny with phrases like 'unprecedented change' or 'radical shifts'. Indeed it is difficult to think of a society in world history that has undergone as many radical changes as the Chinese have within the last generation. And these are not just the obvious changes in terms of economy, standard of living, building of infrastructure and modern mega-cities, but also cultural, linguistic, religious and everyday political changes in what could be termed 'the ordinary' parts of life. These many-faceted changes constitute the backdrop for Wu's work with

Ibsen in the 1990s, with an increasing focus on the changing relationship between the domestic and the foreign, Self and Other, Chinese and Non-Chinese. Alongside the many domestic changes, the relationship between 'Chinese' and 'Foreign' underwent substantial change. The previous suspicion and latent animosity towards the foreign, capitalist Other were to a large extent replaced by admiration during the 1980s as China became increasingly oriented towards the West, and especially the United States, as a model to learn from. Many leading intellectuals during the 1980s held up the Western intellectual and academic tradition as being superior to the Chinese. Hence the relationship between self and other underwent a quite substantial shift also within the cultural field, visible not only through the increased influx of foreign culture, but also through new and more critical views on Chinese tradition and history itself. The most famous example of the latter is probably the extremely popular and controversial TV series, *He Shang* (*River Elegy*) from 1988, which gave a highly critical exposition of Chinese history – contrasted with a positively painted Western tradition.[54]

The New Era's honeymoon days of almost unequivocally positive sentiments towards the West seem to have ended quite abruptly in 1989. Being in themselves examples of cultural misapprehension, the events of 4 June 1989 at Tiananmen Square changed the feelings of many Westerners towards the Chinese state in a much more negative manner than what was the case internally. Contrary to Western expectation, what followed Tiananmen was not that the regime lost support, but in many ways the opposite:

> Indeed, one of the real ironies of recent Chinese society is that in the 1980s, a time in which the leadership pushed hard to make reforms [...] intellectuals were increasingly alienated by the government and disbelieving of its propaganda. Contrarily, in the 1990s, a time when most outsiders would agree that the government had little interest in [...] reform, students and the intellectual community were more believing of government propaganda [...] and more supportive of their government generally.[55]

One reason that this development seemed almost incomprehensible to many Western commentators was probably that the demonstrations in Tiananmen Square themselves were misapprehended as pro-Western in the ideological sense. But the demonstrations during the spring of 1989 in Beijing and other Chinese cities were never *for* the introduction of Western democracy in China. The more than one million people on the streets of Beijing 'were first and foremost demonstrating against *corruption* among political leaders and for more job opportunities.'[56] They were, in other words, not demonstrating against the state *per se*, but against some of the deeply felt problems caused by the reform process.[57] According to the important critical intellectual and professor at Tsinghua University, Wang Hui, himself a participant in the demonstrations, the mass gatherings at Tienanmen Square during the spring of 1989 were the culmination of a broad 'social movement' responding to a deep 'crisis of legitimacy' created by the negative aspects of the reform process.[58] Wang Hui has analysed the complex reasons that led to the defeat and dissolution of the 1989 social movement, ranging from state violence and repression, to China's relation to the outside world.[59] After a few years of readjustment, Deng Xiaoping made his Southern tour in 1992, signalling renewed and strengthened economic reform and opening up, after which the 'fundamental questions raised by the 1989 movement were set aside' (Wang, 2003: 82). The movement of 1989 was increasingly seen as an instance of excessive radicalism that potentially and/or in reality lead to chaos, and intellectuals and students shifted their attention towards the market, China's ancient traditions, neo-conservatism, the new left or nationalism.[60]

The gradual but speedy normalising of Chinese society and economy in the continued tracks of 'New Era' neoliberal economic policy was during the 1990s accompanied by a strong growth in nationalist sentiment. This new nationalism not only meant a growth in feelings of national pride, it was also directed outwards towards the Western (and in particular American) Other. And what is more, the strong nationalist feeling was shared by large sections of the elites, and ordinary Chinese alike.[61] The decade following 1989 saw large, popular and nationalist protests, both in the streets and on the Internet, and in other mass media. Following China's defeat in its bid to host the 2000 Olympics in 1993, during the Taiwan Strait Crisis in 1995/96 and most violently after the bombing of the Chinese Embassy in Belgrade in 1999, ordinary Chinese took to the streets in their thousands to protest against the West, and to protest against the United States in particular.[62] This more aggressive and parochial nationalism could also be seen in popular media such as television, as it also found strong expressions in the official cultures of political speeches, editorials and mainstream media reporting.[63] And not least, the stronger nationalist, and anti-Western, sentiment was also given aggressive expressions within the elite culture, through books such as *China Can Say No!* (1993) and *The Plot to Demonize China* (1997).[64]

The growth and intensification of nationalism and anti-Western sentiments in China after 1989 have been interpreted and explained in different ways. In my view it seems obvious that Chinese nationalism, like most nationalisms, is a highly over-determined phenomenon with both external and internal causes. When a country is severely critiqued and subjected to suspicion and even sanctions abroad, as China was in the aftermath of 4 June 1989, it could easily be seen as threatening in ways that might give rise to a stronger nationalism internally. The new forms of social (and cultural) insecurity created by the emergence of a brutal capitalism, albeit with 'Chinese characteristics', could easily give grounds for nationalist sentiments – especially if nurtured by a strong state apparatus – as could the enormous increase in the physical presence of foreigners, and Westerners in particular, within China.[65] A similar feeling of vulnerability could well follow from the mere fact that the Chinese economy went from being largely home-based and controlled by the state, to becoming almost completely export-driven, and dependent on the outside world, in not much more than a decade.[66] Most important, however, in our context here, is to see the strengthening of Chinese nationalism during the 1990s as a *real* phenomenon influencing Chinese culture and thinking. It should, in other words, not be written off as a mere result of state and party manipulation and propaganda.[67] The expressions of a new form of nationalism across the board in Chinese society during the 1990s were not just a safety valve opened up by the CCP to diverge discontent. The nationalist and anti-foreign sentiment in Chinese culture was a real issue addressed by Wu in his performance of *A Doll's House*.

The adaptation

The fact that Agnethe Haaland was 'the first foreign actress on the Capital city's spoken drama stage' emphasised that the relationship between self and other was of central importance to the production.[68] The specific adaptations of the story of the play should be seen within the same context. In terms of time and place, the action was placed in an unspecified city in the north of China during the 1930s. Agnethe Haaland's Nora is a Norwegian woman married to a Chinese man, Han Ermao, played by Li Jian Yi. Han Ermao met Nora while studying in Europe, and he brought his Norwegian wife to China, where they settled and had three children. He became seriously ill with tuberculosis a few years after their arrival, and she borrowed money from Ke Luotai ('Krogstad') to pay for the expensive medicines necessary to save his life. She repays him by putting aside money meant to cover her own personal needs, in addition to what she can earn as a translator. In other words, structurally speaking Ibsen's plot, but with the important change in terms of time and space and, above all, the intercultural aspect of the story. This aspect is highlighted in the performance not only by Agnethe Haaland's presence on stage, but also linguistically. Nora speaks some Chinese but for the most part she speaks English, while the rest of the cast speak Chinese with some English words and phrases thrown in. The fiction, then, is that she can speak some Chinese and understand a lot more – the Chinese on stage also understand her English, within the fiction that is – in reality they do not speak English at all. They all wear traditional Chinese clothes of the period being depicted, and they live in a traditional *siheyuan*, Chinese courtyard house. The performance space is small and intimate, but divided into the courtyard, a sitting room, a corridor and a back gate.

The most conspicuous cultural encounter in the *mise en scène* was, however, constituted by the mixing of Western style realistic drama, *huaju*, and traditional Chinese opera, *xiju*. The performance opened in complete darkness with the mild tones of an *erhu*, a traditional Chinese stringed instrument, flowing onto the stage. Shortly after a dim, blue light fell over the musician, Rong Jun, in the right-hand corner of the stage. She was seated behind a thin, transparent veil, and after one minute, Zhang Juping, a well-known Peking Opera actor, entered the stage and delivered a song from the opera *Farewell my Concubine*.[69] This opening set the tone for a performance focusing on cultural meetings and conflicts. The Peking Opera elements reappeared in a few small instances during the performance. Through the inclusion of Peking Opera techniques within the otherwise realistic staging, the *mise en scène* also represented an inter-weaving of theatre cultures. This constitutes a fairly accurate, neutral description of the intercultural aspects of the performance – and one in line with what was said by most reviewers both in China and in Norway. It does, however, not address the far more interesting and important question of the *meaning* of the formal interculturalism of the performance. While most reviewers claimed that the Peking Opera elements functioned as parallel and commentary, it seems more accurate to say that they functioned as *contrast* and *opposition*. This should already be clear from the content of the specific Peking Opera – *Farewell my Concubine* – inserted into this version of *A Doll's House*. The opera tells the story of Xiang Yu, the General and 'Hegemon-King of Western Chu', who fought a losing battle over the rule of China against Liu Bang, who was later to found the Han Dynasty. In the opera, Xiang Yu is surrounded by enemy forces and facing certain destruction, when his favourite concubine Consort Yu begs permission to die alongside him. He denies her request, upon which she sings a song that distracts him with its beauty to the degree that she can get hold of his sword and commit suicide with it. Her song goes: 'The Han army has conquered our land/ We are surrounded by Chu songs/ My lord's spirits are low/ Why then should I live?'

Farewell my Concubine is certainly parallel to *A Doll's House* in the sense that it tells a story about a strong woman in a man's world, a woman with her own mind – but more than anything it is a story about a woman willing and wanting to live for a man, a woman whose life is devoid of meaning without the man she lives for. She commits suicide when his defeat is imminent; she has nothing more to live for. In this sense she represents a contrast and an opposition to the Western woman who refuses to live for the man, who demands sacrifice from him, and who will leave him and seek her own autonomy when she realises that he will not sacrifice anything for her. Through the insertion of the story of the concubine, Consort Yu, Wu's version of Ibsen's play establishes a cultural opposition between a traditional and 'Chinese' female hero on the one hand and a modern and 'Western' one on the other.

The realistic action itself, however, opens with Helmer and Rank making calligraphy banners serving as decorations for the upcoming celebration of the Chinese New Year, which replaces Ibsen's Christmas holiday. As the men compare their 'New Year Couplets', Nora arrives carrying presents for the children. From the moment she enters the stage cultural difference and potential conflict is emphasised. She walks over to Helmer, embraces him and starts kissing him. While they are kissing, Dr Rank turns away from them with embarrassment, and mutters 'Are you done?' Helmer makes the comment that: 'Chinese are not used to this. You haven't changed this habit in these years.' In the following, the three of them keep a light, slightly flirting tone, and as they fool around, Rank says to Helmer that 'Foreign goods are better than the Chinese goods after all. It makes me jealous.' Nora is present while he refers to her as a foreign 'product' or 'goods', which does not seem to bother her. She does, however, object by saying (in English) that 'I have been living here for four years, and you still treat me as a foreigner. We eat Chinese food every day, and the children speak Chinese. I love Peking Opera. Everything inside is Chinese, except my skin and hair.'

This is certainly an exaggeration, which is made clear by the many different ways in which her foreignness is stressed. She talks about the virtues of a Chinese wife (as being frugal, for instance), and Helmer keeps on instructing her about the responsibilities following their status as a family 'with face'. He also addresses her from the beginning as his 'foreign doll', which she seems to find pleasure in, until we reach the last act. One effect of this emphasis on cultural difference, and on Nora's project of cultural assimilation, is that she is constantly instructed and corrected. The cross-cultural aspect of the performance, then, gives it a 'Pygmalionesque' character – this Nora is Helmer's Alathea. He shapes and educates her, constantly trying to make her adapt, become 'Chinese', which changes the balance between them; she is foreign, and he knows best what is required of a Chinese wife. Han Ermao is also more direct and suspicious than Ibsen's Helmer, for example in the sense that he suspects her of lying to him several times during the beginning of the play. When she suggests that they could borrow some money on the prospects of his new, improved salary, he asks her directly if she has made the mistake of taking up a loan without him knowing it. Her denial, then, clearly makes her more dubious in the moral sense than what is usually the case.

However, Nora is not depicted as completely inferior, even in the cultural sense, because these scenes make Han Ermao seem quite rigid and old-fashioned. There is also an interesting use of comic elements in some of the cultural and linguistic exchanges in the performance. In the scenes with Ke Luotai, where Nora is at her weakest, being threatened by the man who controls her destiny, this version of the play involves a lot of comedy. The main element contributing to the comic effect and strong laughter from the audience is this Krogstad's lacking control of the English language. Whenever he tries to bring some English words and phrases into his speech, the audience laughs aloud. Hence there is actually a strong cultural ambiguity at play here, where the audience and the performance itself vacillates between seeing Nora as an unwelcome and inferior foreigner, and of her being the superior and more 'modern', sophisticated and urban person.

Helmer's explicit goal is to transform his Nora into 'a perfect Chinese wife', and the cultural difference is a constant source of worry (and pride) for him. When they discuss whether he should fire Krogstad or not, the decisive point for Helmer is that he cannot change his mind and let Ke Luontai stay, because he would then 'become a laughing stock' for listening to his 'foreign wife whatever she says'. A 'good wife' in China, he says, is called 'a good inside helper' (*xian nei zhu*), that is one who stays home and does not interfere. Upon her protests he gives a seeming concession to her cultural background by saying that he knows that people in her country would talk of 'gender equality', and concludes with the suggestion that they should 'share this burden together'. Sharing, however, still means that his decision is beyond dispute; they will share the decision he makes. At this point in the action we see for the first time how the gender issues are layered upon the cultural issues, as Helmer stresses that gender equality is a Western notion. Cultural differences and underlying cultural conflicts are emphasised from the outset, but from here onwards they are intertwined with and in some ways exacerbated by the gender difference and conflict.

Hence as Nora sees the world closing in on her, and has to recognise that Krogstad will reveal her secret, her main worry is that this will make Han Ermao 'completely lose face'. The same double layering of conflicts is highlighted in the 'tarantella scene'. Nora here wears a traditional Chinese opera costume, and rehearses a double act, first a Norwegian folk song-and-dance number together with Helmer, and then a solo song from the Peking Opera, *Farewell my Concubine*. It is during the Norwegian folk dance that she shows a little of the agony she usually expresses in the tarantella as she becomes more uncontrolled. In this version, however, it is above all a comic act, at least judging from the laughter in the audience. It would seem that much of the comedy stems from Han Ermao's pretty helpless attempts at doing the 'foreign' folk dance. While Nora sings the Peking Opera song, however, she performs without interruption or instruction from her husband – and gets spontaneous applause from the audience.

When they return from the party, Helmer is very happy with his 'foreign doll'; she has done both Norwegian and Chinese traditional culture with success, and everyone had been silent, he says, in spite of her 'foreign accent', while she sang the song from *Farewell my Concubine*. Almost every aspect of the *mise en scène* – stage design, time and place, and details of action and plot – places this Norwegian Nora in very Chinese circumstances. The cultural conflict between her and the surroundings are strengthened and accentuated. And it seems important that Nora from the outset tries her best to assimilate. She has learned the language, and tries to adapt to the customs and unspoken rules of the culture; she knows how to prepare for the spring festival, how to cook, how to toast, and she even takes lessons in Peking Opera. But there is no avail; when catastrophe closes in on them, cultural conflicts and tensions come to the fore and simultaneously strengthen and redirect the other conflicts of the play. As Han Ermao leaves the stage to go into his study to go through his correspondence, the final reckoning between the spouses is introduced or framed through a short sequence where Zhang Juping returns and performs a Peking Opera dance, while Nora is seen kneeling down with hands folded as in Christian prayer (Figure 4.2). After this tableau of cultural difference, Han Ermao enters. Infuriated to the brink of physical violence he yells out his anger and frustration:

> **Helmer**: Since I brought you home to China, I have been worried that you were going to give me trouble. I taught you the Chinese ways of the world in every detail, but you still messed up and gave me such a headache. In the beginning, people reminded me that I would never understand a foreign woman's mind. If women are the source of trouble, then a foreign woman is a scourge! Now you reward me like this in the end!
>
> **Nora**: I rewarded you! I saved your life!

He claims that she has destroyed him, left him at the mercy of a scoundrel, Ke Luotai, who can now decide whether or not he will lose face for good. And what annoys him even more, seems to be that

Figure 4.2 *A Doll's House*, Beijing, directed by Wu Xiaojiang (1998). From left to right: Nora (Agnethe Haaland), musician (Rong Jun) and 'Chinese Opera Nora' (Zhang Juping) (Photo: China National Contemporary Theatre).

'disaster and ruin' are brought upon him by 'a foreign doll'. The cultural framing is further emphasised when Nora hints at her thoughts of suicide as a way out of her misery:

> **Helmer**: Ha, bring up your foreign theories again? – Women are independent; men and women should be equal. It does not work in China! So you think you are a foreigner and have some advantages? In their eyes, you are still a woman. You are my wife, living in my house! All you did would be counted on me. Yes, Ke Luotai will use this and publish the story all the same. People will think I'm hiding behind you – a foreign woman! I will never get clean again. You have completely destroyed me, now you see!

At this point in the play Nora experiences the full strength of the impasse she is caught in; there is no way out – not even death will give any real escape. The barriers that have closed in on her have to do with legal matters, as in Ibsen, but far more with gender *and* culture. In Ibsen's text, Helmer's accusations centre on three aspects: (i) what Nora did was illegal, she is a criminal; (ii) she is a woman, and does not understand society; and (iii) she has inherited deep moral flaws from her father – and whether this last aspect is strictly hereditary or a result of her upbringing is an open question. The third issue is not present in Wu's version, but is replaced by culture, that is by her status as foreigner. One obvious result is that the problems surrounding the inequality in the upbringing and education of boys and girls are left out of the discussion, which also gives Nora's stated aim of re-educating herself at the ending of the play a different meaning. From Han Ermao's perspective, it is her status as a woman *and* a foreigner that makes it impossible for him to conceive of a way out of the trap he feels caught in. His choice of hygienic vocabulary gives his accusations an ominous trait; she has contaminated him, made him dirty in ways that make it impossible ever to 'get *clean* again'.

After receiving Krogstad's second letter, he feels cleansed all the same, and instructs Nora that she is forgiven. But because she does not understand the 'complexity of the Chinese society', she will in the future have to 'listen to' him, and refrain from 'making decisions on your own', he tells her. Upon her first protests he claims that he both understands and loves her and refers to their children. Having children together, however, does not carry the same weight for her:

Nora: So many Chinese women are busy having children. They imagine that is the tie of love! But that is a fraud. A fraud perpetrated by you men. A Chinese fraud!

Helmer: I warn you, now you are hurting our national virtue and my self-esteem! Of course I can forgive you for that, but you should know that you have many of the foreigner's faults. You like pointing fingers at Chinese affairs.

In the following she does far more than point her finger. She dismisses what he calls love, and claims that he is only in love with his 'foreign doll', and the sense of pride it gives him. For her it means never to be seen and respected; she has been like 'a Peking Opera actress', singing and dancing in his house, and performing at parties:

> **Nora:** [...] People applaud me. They think I am happy. Actually, I am not! Actresses can take off their make-up. But I cannot. I am forever a foreigner!
>
> **Helmer:** Finished? Don't bring up the theories of women's liberation and feminism here. Nobody hears you, and neither do they care about it. You are a foreigner and your role is to perform as a cute foreigner.
>
> **Nora:** I am not a performer.

What the crisis after Ke Luotai's first letter gives her is a radical experience of being Other, of being, as woman and foreigner, outside of society. And when she laments the fact that she is not seen as a genuine person or individual, that she is othered and given a role she cannot escape from, she is cut off, and told not to bring in her 'Western' ideas. She should accept her role as 'cute foreigner'. With some meta-dramatic irony she claims not to be an actress. The ending of this intercultural version of *A Doll's House*, then, has to do with notions of individuality and authenticity; she wants to be allowed to be *herself*, as a woman and as an individual from another culture. This, however, is out of the question:

> **Helmer:** Com'on! Why is it that you want people to dislike you? To see a true you? You are a foreigner, and that is an objective truth. We are used to you as a foreigner! It is just like the French trams on the streets, people think they are comfortable to sit in, and Chinese drivers can drive them. You don't have to let everyone know, that the French guys who made the trams ate half-cooked steak and raw vegetables just like barbarians.

The alternative to acting the 'foreign doll' is to be disliked. In Nora's case, there is no room for a 'true you', she has to adapt by repressing her difference as much as possible. And the metaphor chosen to illustrate this point tells its own stories: 'just like' a French tram – comfortable to sit in and can be driven by a Chinese (man) – she should try to conceal the fact that she is a barbarian, or at least that there are barbarous aspects in her cultural background. In instances like this one, we can see clearly how close Han Ermao's nationalism is to tipping over into a xenophobia bordering on racism. He claims that foreigners and foreign things carry traces of their origin in 'barbaric' cultures, as a few minutes later he also claims that 'Chineseness' is a matter of blood, or race: 'Between the Chinese people, we don't have to discover or discuss "new" values. The moral values and culture is in our blood.'

In light of China's millennia-old history of being the 'Middle Kingdom', it can come as no surprise that it also has an ancient history of seeing itself as the centre of the world, and of viewing outsiders as 'barbarians'. That this history also has its possible racist traits is clear enough.[70] In connection with Han Ermao's dismissal of new, modern and Western ideas in the name of a tradition that runs in the blood, it is important, however, to remember the historical setting. The action of the play is placed in feudal China of the 1930s, and it should be noted that Han Ermao proves to be a representative of that society. Judging from reviews of the performance as well as the live recording of it, it seems safe to say that the audience did not share his views wholeheartedly. In the concluding scenes of the play, the audience laughs at him as he becomes desperate when Nora prepares her departure. And this, it should be said, in spite of her very harsh words about China and Chinese culture. She says that she cannot bear the 'Chinese way of thinking any longer', and asks:

> Does the philosophy of Confucius teach you Chinese to be such mediocre human beings? If that's true, I want to curse such a morality and culture.

When she has her say, she not only criticises her husband and a patriarchal society, but repeatedly points to it as being a *Chinese* patriarchy. She blames Chinese *culture* as such, and curses it, or, more precisely, she curses Han Ermao's version of this culture. She makes it very clear that she wants a divorce and that she does not care that it means that he will 'lose face completely', as he laments. Her status as an outsider and a foreigner gives her the strength to say no to a whole culture:

> **Nora:** I don't care! [...] I am a foreigner! I am not your ugly, uneducated, Chinese wife!

The cultural aspects of the performance, then, seems to give it a harsher and more final ending, as they both deliver strong insults towards the 'other' culture. On Nora's side, however, there is a certain conciliatory potential as she states that she wants to go out into Chinese society and learn more about it. What she rejects is in this sense the feudal, patriarchal version of China, and not Chinese culture as such. She is completely estranged from Han Ermao's China, to the extent that it even encompasses her own children, as she makes clear in what are her last words in the performance: 'I am not qualified to be a good Chinese mother. They are not like me. None of them.' The last scene, then, leads to her being alienated from her husband and her children, which seems harsh, not least because they are toddlers. The performance ends with Han Ermao's repeated screaming her name, but it seems only to be the screams of a man realising that he will lose face.

This intercultural performance of *A Doll's House* ends with a culture clash – Nora curses Chinese culture, and Helmer certainly has his say about Western influence. And what is more, the disaster seems inevitable. Hence it can come as no surprise that several critics have interpreted Wu's *A Doll's House* as a production that 'condemns international marriage as a destructive social practice'.[71] But as Conceison also notes, Wu's goal with his Ibsen productions were more far-reaching, and this *Doll's House* performance set in the 1930s should be seen as a 'direct allegory for the 1990s' (Conceison, 2001: 290). Wu himself has explicated what he perceived as the background and context to read the allegorical thrust of the performance against:

> During this time of overall opening, divorce rates and crime rates have risen; gambling, pornography, and theft are overflowing; every

traditional moral and moderate life attitude of Chinese people is being bashed into the corner [...] modernization has brought a modern social illness. The ideals and values we held so firmly in the past have been abandoned [...] it is only natural to turn back to Chinese traditional morality and ethnic pride in search of solutions.[72]

Audience members, and censors, who came to the show with the view that China was threatened by the influx of foreign culture, by a cultural pollution, could certainly find confirmation through the performance they were watching. At the same time, however, they would just as certainly be challenged, not least because allegory can be difficult to control, and it is by no means given that the production should be seen as a simplistic critique of modernisation, reform and opening up, and a defence of traditional values in the name of 'ethnic pride'. A major obstacle for such a reading lies in the way that the adaptation plays culture out against gender. In other words, if seen as a bid for a return to 'traditional values', these values are at the same time exposed as being sexist, repressive and feudal, because their main representative on stage is Han Ermao. Reading the production as a critique of opening up and influx of foreign influence would mean siding with Han Ermao and his old-fashioned, pre-revolutionary views and attitudes, saying for example that authentic 'Chineseness' equals anti-feminism. It would also mean to condemn Nora, who is after all a hero of the Chinese tradition dating back to the May 4th Movement. It would also be tantamount to taking a cultural stand against universalism, and ultimately to be against the performance itself, because it is inter- or cross-cultural through and through.[73] In other words, a chauvinistic reading of the adaptation, both in terms of culture and gender, could be seen as self-defeating, contradictory.

Given the fact that Wu's adaptation invites allegorical readings along broader nationalist lines, it is equally clear that the same invitation could open for readings of the production along opposite lines, such as a critique of growing nationalist chauvinism. According to Bettina S. Entell, this is not at all an uncommon trait in the Chinese use of plays from the Western canon:

> [T]he foreign play acquires allegorical and metaphorical meanings
> and may become a convenient and safe vehicle for social and
> political criticism. Under the guise of the foreign play, distanced
> from the immediate cultural context, otherwise taboo subjects may
> be examined.[74]

The Chinese government was at the time supportive of criticism of the
West and of nationalist defence of traditional Chinese values, and this
could in fact have been Wu's strategy to sell and package the production.
What makes it a strong and sophisticated production, however, is
above all that it successfully investigated an unresolved ideological
conflict, or conflicts. It let the conflict and its opposites stand, unresolved,
within the production. Its importance, then, lies in the fact that it
succeeded in opening these ideological conflicts in a situation where
they were pressing and deeply felt within Chinese culture and society.
This situation meant that it negotiated unresolved ideological tensions,
and that it *could* make a difference, by not giving unequivocal answers.

Dancing dolls (Beijing 2010)

Cultural tensions or conflicts are not openly stated or visualised as such
in my third example, the modern dance version of *A Doll's House* at
Beijing Capital Theatre in October 2010, starring China's most famous
modern dancer, Jin Xing. Like the two productions discussed above,
this was the result of a cross-cultural co-operation, but of a very
different kind on almost every level. The idea, initiative and funding for
this production was Norwegian, but it included both Norwegian and
Chinese artists. In 1956 it would have been inconceivable to have a
production on a Chinese stage funded by a Western state, with foreign
artists – in 1998 it was still not without difficulties to have one foreign
actress on stage in a Chinese production with partial funding from
outside. Neither of these elements posed difficulties for the Chinese
authorities 12 years later, in 2010. Hence it is symptomatic of significant
changes in Chinese culture, and in the relation between China and its

Western, Norwegian, 'Other'. The ideological complexities surrounding this production are many, and some of them are located at the macro-political level. The fact that the Chinese could welcome and collaborate on a dance production, but with spoken word – in Norwegian – on a major stage in the capital, could be seen as a sign of strength and assertiveness. The presence of foreign culture, and mixed with the local, was not seen as a threat. That the Norwegian authorities, like those of so many other Western countries, would encourage and support a production like this one, is also a clear sign of their wish (or need) to be present and visible as friendly powers in the culture of the emerging economic giant.

Soft power is a central goal for both parties in this relationship. While the West has wanted to increase its presence on a cultural level in China, the Chinese have been just as eager to increase its own soft power within the area of culture.[75] Abroad, China uses large amounts of money to become a more positive cultural presence, through cultural export, artistic tours, exhibitions, Confucius Institutes, and so on. Domestically the policy seems still to be to 'let the foreign serve China', but not under the same kind of detailed supervision and control that one saw earlier. Within certain limits Deng Xiaoping and the succeeding regimes have wished to support 'the rise of a new "individual creative spirit", assuring that there would no longer be any bureaucratic interference in artistic creation.'[76] Ultimately this probably had an economic rationale behind it, but it has loosened the control of the cultural sphere, and as long as no-one tries to import art and culture that goes directly against the regime, there is a consistent acceptance of the fact that, in Deng's laconic words, 'when you open the door some flies will get in' (Ferrari, 2012: 25). Market mechanisms have, however, taken over much of the control of the arts scene, as the cultural sphere has been massively commercialised during the last few decades. The government permitted private theatre companies to set up in 2005,[77] and new theatre and dance groups now make a living outside of the state-supported system, or in interchange with the government funded theatres, with artists working in both private and state systems. Jin

Xing's theatre is a typical free group in this regard, doing avant-garde *and* broader commercial work simultaneously.

Funding and re-funding

The production in 2010 had a quite extensive pre-history in Norway. It started in 2006 as part of a full-day tour of Telemark, the region where Ibsen was born, where each part of the tour was accompanied by extracts from Ibsen's texts. It was called 'Henrik Ibsen – An Educational Tour', and took the participants through the Skien region on what the organisers called a 'Bildungsreise' by bus and boat, across lakes and on canals where they were served excerpts of *Catiline, Peer Gynt, Brand, Pillars of Society, The Wild Duck, A Doll's House, The Lady from the Sea, Hedda Gabler, The Feast at Solhoug, Lady Inger of Østraat, The Vikings at Helgeland, The Pretenders, An Enemy of the People* and finally back in Skien, *When We Dead Awaken*. The part from *A Doll's House* consisted of a 30-minute-long dance and theatre version of some scenes from the play. A mix of pure tourism and art, in other words, where one targeted audience were business executives who 'believe that leading other people is something more than administration.'[78] The sponsors were local municipalities, tourist agencies and local businesses – in addition to 'Ibsen 2006'.[79] It was quite successful in terms of audience turnout, with 3,552 participants in the 19 events, even in light of it being fully financed and the tickets free, according to the records of the theatre.[80] It was in any case a major achievement by a small regional theatre such as the Teater Ibsen in Skien.

They did, however, have even bigger ambitions for the dance part of the 'Bildungs-tour', which had already been developed into a full-night production, combining dance and spoken word theatre, with the aim of taking it to China. Funded by the Ministry of Foreign Affairs, Inger Buresund, then artistic director of Teater Ibsen, together with administrative director Gry Wie, choreographer Un-Magritt Nordseth, and stage designer Katrine Tolo, had all been to Beijing in

December 2005 to make agreements with sponsors and co-operating Chinese artists and theatre institutions.[81] In December 2006, the expanded production, called 'Hunting for Nora', was staged in Beijing, with a Norwegian cast for all main roles, and with Norwegian as the language spoken on stage. The Chinese part of the production consisted mainly of four female dancers, wearing the same red dresses as the Norwegian Nora, and hence appearing to be a kind of multiplication of the character, with Chinese characteristics, so to speak. The added dancers were, according to Nordseth, supposed to function 'almost like a choir, to expand the play to be about "all of us".'[82] What the 'us' in this statement referred to – universally, all human beings, all women, or Chinese (and Norwegian) women – was not made explicit. This goal was in any case obfuscated through the choice of performance language, because this choice inevitably made the Norwegians able to speak, but the Chinese performers mute. In addition, there was a visibly 'Chinese' element to the production through the stage design consisting of deep red panes and light walls made with Chinese paper-cutting techniques, by the artist Qiao Xiaogang. The ambition was not only to take the production to Beijing once, but to tour China and Norway, and use it as a starting point for a project running over several years. This project was to include a 'new production' in 2008, but they had 'not yet decided which play by Ibsen' to choose for the next production.[83] 'Hunting for Nora' was performed twice in Beijing, with an estimated audience of two thousand people.[84] It did not tour, and there were only the two performances in Beijing on 14 and 15 December. Because 'Hunting for Nora' was so well funded, however, it did not seem to be reliant on tours or even ticket sales.[85] For the two performances in Beijing, the theatre received almost 1.2 million Norwegian Kroner (approximately 200,000 USD) in public funding, in addition to the 500,000 NOK put up by the theatre in Skien (which is also, strictly speaking, taxpayers' money).

In 2007, Inger Buresund left as artistic director of the Teater Ibsen in Skien to become manager of the 'Ibsen Awards', also based in Skien.[86] She only kept this job for two years, and in 2010 established a commercial firm called 'Ibsen International Ltd'. This company's proclaimed 'mission' is to initiate 'international collaborations in the fields of art and culture through a genuinely intercultural dialogue based on transparency, tolerance and mutual respect' (http://ibseninternational.com/about/). According to the same website, the firm 'believes in the creative potential embedded in the encounter with the Other'. These are obviously quite benign and potentially important ideals, but their formulation simultaneously gives rise to a number of questions; what does a 'genuinely intercultural dialogue' look like, and how is it facilitated? Who is the 'Other' in this genuine dialogic encounter? Who defines it, from whose point of view, and according to which criteria, and what constitutes the radical otherness signalled by the capital letter? It might seem unfair to require a reflection on issues as complex as these from a commercial company, but then they are bound by the company's own ideals and not least by the fact that it aims to work within a specifically contested, conflicting field. Furthermore, in its commercial goals of promoting, facilitating and supporting artistic projects, Ibsen International specifically aims to 'implement [...] projects taking Henrik Ibsen's works and core themes as a departure point'. These core themes are said to be 'human rights, gender equality, preservation of the environment, individual liberty, fight against corruption, positive process of globalisation', and in the 2010 application for funding from the Ministry of Foreign Affairs, Buresund added 'free speech, idealism' and what she called 'positive political power'. These themes are as positive as they are empty. Lofty and unsubstantiated ideals supposedly connected to Ibsen, and formulated in a way that makes it hard to imagine anyone disagreeing with their importance; who are against fighting corruption, against free speech, individual liberty or positive political power? Even a theme like gender equality would probably not find opponents – even though a Christian fundamentalist right-winger and a Muslim women's activist would not give the same content to it. And the link to Ibsen and his plays is equally empty; where does Ibsen have human rights and the positive process of globalisation as his theme, and what does this mean more specifically? All important issues, and equally contested ones – issues and problems central to conflicts and violent clashes between different values and interests – if part of artistic projects, ought to be spelled out with these conflicts in mind, not effaced as empty words that everyone should, and in fact do, agree to (on the level of rhetoric). Alarmingly, formulations like these seem to presuppose common ground, sameness, and hence to testify to a certain disavowal of possible difference and conflicting interests.

A similar pattern becomes visible through the financial background of the production. It was part of the larger project called 'Ibsen in China', which included two other productions, a student festival and a seminar. The total budget for the China project was in excess of 3.5 million NOK, where they applied for 1,749,000 NOK from the Ministry of Foreign affairs, and of this the dance version of *A Doll's House* received 600,000 NOK directly from the Ministry, plus approximately 150,000 for the Norwegian producer and another 100,000 for travel expenses, accounting and other expenses. In addition, they obtained 107,000 from Teater Ibsen and 17,677 from the Norwegian Opera and Ballet. In total, this production received at least 974,677 Norwegian Kroner (around 162,000 USD) in support from the MFA and other Norwegian agencies.[87] To sum up, then, if one counts in the funding for 'Hunting for Nora' and the shorter version done in Telemark as part of the 'Bildungsreise' in 2006, there was at least 3 million NOK (more than 500,000 USD) in public funding behind the two performances of 'A Doll's House' with Jin Xing in Beijing, 23 and 24 October 2010. This estimate certainly testifies to Ibsen International's strong ability to get funding applications through the Ministry of Foreign Affairs, as it also shows how eager to be visible in China the official Norway had become. In financial terms this was neither a Chinese nor an inter-cultural production; it was a Norwegian production redone with stronger Chinese presence on stage. The question, then, is whether or not the financial background is indicative of the artistic meaning of the production, or, in other words, whether it was able to transcend the initial one-sidedness and become genuinely intercultural, a meaningful 'encounter with the Other'?

Sino-Norwegian dance

At first glance, the 2010 production 'A Doll's House' is more or less identical to 'Hunting for Nora'; they reuse the stage design, both productions take around ninety minutes, and the choreography is the same. The only significant difference lies in the fact that the Chinese presence was stronger in the 2010 production, on two levels: (i) not only minor roles, but three of the main characters were performed by Chinese dancers: Nora (Jin Xing), Helmer (Han Bin) and Krogstad (Wang Tao); and (ii) the introduction of Chinese actors in lead roles meant that the production had to be bilingual. In other words, the Norwegian dancer-actors spoke Norwegian and the Chinese spoke Mandarin. The potential communication problems occurring with two very different languages spoken on stage were solved by the use of subtitles, with translations in English. There is no doubt in my mind that the bilingual nature of the production was necessary, because it made the Chinese performers speaking beings, equal to the Norwegians in this sense. It also made the production more complex, pointing to cultural difference and possibilities of misunderstanding. In a more indirect sense, the use of English subtitles could be seen as pointing to the strength of this language as the lingua franca of our day. This last point is not without ambiguities, because it could also be seen as inadvertently suggesting that there is a third meta-standpoint, a neutral terrain in the English language, from which to mediate or efface the differences of the other tongues, or it could even mean that the 'overall hermeneutics of the production was regulated through English', as Rustom Bharucha has claimed in relation to another intercultural production.[88] Not necessarily 'wrong', this simply points to the fact that the targeted audience was a specific class of cosmopolitan, English-speaking people without any strong local connection – maybe part of what was called 'positive globalisation' in the application for funding? There are in any case still difficulties with regard to the intercultural tensions in the production, in spite of the improvement that the bilingualism represents.

Based on the plans, reports, reviews and press material for the production, it seems obvious that the casting of Jin Xing as Nora was not just the crux of the performance, but really the only reason for restaging it. Jin Xing is an extraordinary dancer with an extraordinary life-story. When born in 1967 she was a boy, who at the age of nine entered the famous military dance ensemble in Shenyang. At the age of 17, Jin Xing was awarded 'Best dancer of China', and two years later became the first Chinese dancer to be sent to the United States to develop further. As in China she received several awards and great reviews in the West. In 1993 she returned to China and had a sex-change operation there at the age of twenty-seven. She now leads her own company, the Jin Xing Dance Theatre in Shanghai, she has her own show on Chinese TV, has adopted three children and lives with her German husband in Shanghai.[89]

Being a national celebrity and a world-class dancer, Jin Xing clearly improved the possibilities of the production, in terms of publicity and artistic quality. Being who she is, one would have thought that this might also be grasped as an opportunity to interrogate gender roles and sexual identity in more profound ways. This possibility was, however, nowhere on the horizon of the production. It focused above all on surface, beauty and spectacle, and if there was any kind of deeper focus in the performance it was solely on an individual struggle for liberation, which is in line with what Jin Xing stands for as a person. She is very much aware of the fact that what she has accomplished both as an artist and as an individual is extraordinary, but she has never placed her own personal struggle within a larger political or structural setting. In her biography, she insists on being an un-political artist, she is grateful towards the Party for having helped her, and she boasts her success through consumerist ideals; she flies first-class, drives a Porsche, and plans to buy a Maserati too – and her 'heroine' and ideal is strangely – or should I say grotesquely – enough Jiang Qing, Chairman Mao's wife, who furious at Mao's philandering 'threw all her energy into the arts and produced the ten major masterpieces of the Cultural Revolution' (sic.) (Jin, 2007: 195). In the autobiography there is little sign of awareness on her part that she might also have an ideological position, or function for the Chinese authorities; her story is one about personal liberation against all odds, but a strictly individual story used to project a positive image of a new, more liberal China.

Initially the production was planned with the Norwegian dancer Kristian Alm in the role of Helmer, but that was changed in the process. The choice of a Chinese dancer for the part of Helmer was probably made so as not to get into the contested ideological and political issues that were explored by Wu in the 1998 production. Had the Chinese Nora been married to a Norwegian Helmer, one would have taken a greater risk, and entered into a terrain that has its topical aspects within the Chinese situation. The cross-cultural aspects were instead introduced through the two Norwegian dancers in the roles of Dr Rank (Lars Jacob Holm) and Kristine Linde (Henriette Blakstad). The production consists of dancers from very different traditions – the Chinese characterised by their strong classical training in combination with modern dance techniques from the United States and the Norwegian in a different European modern dance tradition – but there is no visible trace of any attempt at making these different traditions work together; they co-exist on stage, but without being marked as different. The difficulties that this casting creates, however, lies more in the interpersonal and intercultural constellations on stage. In *A Doll's House*, Nora is in conflict with, and has to liberate herself from ideological and political structures that she finds oppressive, for example patriarchy, and these structures are represented on stage by her husband Helmer and by Krogstad, her initial adversary, the person who sets the conflicts in motion through his demands and threats. Her friends and allies on stage, the people who show her understanding and compassion, who offer help and advice, are Dr Rank and Kristine Linde. Jin Xing's Nora (and the other Chinese Noras on stage), then, is in conflict with two Chinese adversaries, Helmer and Krogstad, while supported by the two Norwegian 'helpers', Ms Linde and Rank. Because the understanding that Nora receives in the course of the action is given to her by these two Western 'helpers', it is hard not to think of Spivak's phrase of brown women being saved from brown men by whites[90] while seeing the performance. Staging this conflict between the characters in the play in cultural terms, as in this production, gives rise to several difficulties. And these difficulties are further exacerbated by the uneven power relations in the production as a whole, because all positions with artistic power are held by Norwegians: director/choreographer (Nordseth), producer (Buresund), dramaturge (Tom Remlov), set and costume designer (Kathrine Tolo), composer (Jørgen Munkeby) and lighting designer (Erik Spets Sandvik) . . .

The major weakness of the production, however, lies in the choreography. It starts with the so-called chorus of five Noras appearing one by one dancing in slow elegant movements. After a few minutes they leave and Nora enters together with the maid carrying a Christmas tree. She eats a macaroon, and Helmer arrives. He instantly takes control and starts examining her, looking for traces of sweets in her mouth (which he opens as if examining the teeth of a horse at an auction). The choreography, then, gives Helmer power and prominence from the outset. He is in complete control not only of the space on stage, where he will dance around and excel in showing off through summersaults and pirouettes, but he is also in control of Nora's body, which he constantly corrects, fixes in specific poses and choreographs in the most minute detail. This is done, I presume, in order to pass the message to the audience that this man is the 'star' in his own and his wife's life, that he is in charge and that this woman is his doll. Because a lot of dialogue is cut, this visual display of the power relations between them could be seen as necessary. While having the advantage of being simple and unequivocal, it does lose some of the tension and complexity inherent in the choreography of the play. If one takes time to examine Ibsen's text in some detail, one has to notice how Helmer's verbal attempts to control his wife are contradicted by the bodily movements within the stage space. In the simplest instance: he says, 'do not eat macaroons', she says, 'no, of course not', and eats a macaroon. And more subtle, she says, 'Come out here . . .', he answers, 'don't disturb!', and then 'opens the door', comes in – and 'goes over to her', she 'goes over to the stove [. . .] he follows', she 'goes over to the table to the right' [he walks] 'over to her', she 'takes his arm', etc. In other words, Nora is in control of the space on stage – Helmer follows her, she directs him as she controls the movements of the others later on, the only exception being the scenes with Krogstad. This point is sometimes changed in stagings of the play, as it is here – but in this case where so much of Nora's verbal assertiveness is left out, it does change the interpretation by making her much more submissive, almost purely decorative, a beauty in and through submission. In Nordseth's version Nora (and her five replicas) follow Helmer's smallest signs; he waves his hand, she comes, he adjusts her arms or legs and she stands accordingly – often on one leg – and she is lifted, or she kneels down and he drops coins around her, which she picks up once he has left the room.[91]

This pattern is repeated in the scenes between Nora and Linde, and later with Krogstad. Linde picks Nora up and carries her around the room, while the opposite is never the case. One person lifting and carrying the other in this way does necessarily imply lack of power and strength in the object being lifted – a pattern which is nowhere as strong as in the scenes with Krogstad. The same meaning is conveyed through Nora sitting on the floor, or kneeling down, while the others stand above her. The point that Nora is a doll, a plaything and a subaltern being, is made extremely explicit in this production. Power is choreographed as asymmetrical to the degree that the Nora figures are reduced to purely dominated, beautiful objects of desire. In a sequence before the intermission, this point is strengthened as Nora dances with five men – Helmer, Rank, Krogstad and two 'ghosts of Krogstad' as they are called in the list of characters. They pull and drag her, she tries to escape or to seek refuge in Helmer but is rejected, pulled away, lifted up and passed from one man to the other in an endless exchange. The meaning seems to be that this woman is exchange value, that she is caught in a system of male dominance where there is no escape. The problem, however, is that this system seems to be reproduced in and through the performance itself – the Nora character is never portrayed as autonomous person, but as object of desire, a beautiful being – where the spectacle of her (Asian) beauty is the main thing. This trait is even stronger in the scene where Nora tries to persuade Helmer into not firing Krogstad. Here he dances with all five Noras, and they swarm around him eager to please him as he lifts one or two at a time. They get down on all fours and crawl around while he sits on their backs, before lying down with four of them as in a harem, while they smilingly stroke and caress him. This clearly also carries a message, but it is done without negativity or resistance – the audience is invited to share male pleasure, not female suffering (if there is any in this scene). And in the tarantella, where there is supposed to be both suffering and protest, there is only beauty, control and elegance in this version – spectacle for the audience on and off stage.[92]

The lack of cultural sensitivity can also be found on other levels of choreography in the production, for example in the relationship between Kristine Linde and Nils Krogstad. This couple is often understood and staged as parallel and as a contrast to Nora and Thorvald. However, in this version the element of contrast is taken one step further, because the Western Ms Linde is portrayed as the only strong woman on stage. Henriette Blakstad's Kristine Linde is tall and strong; physically dominating she has strength and initiative. When related to Helmer's physical dominance of the five Noras, this constitutes a strangely culturalised contrast between the females on stage. Not only does she lift and carry Nora around, she can stand her ground physically in relation to all the men. And in the final scene with Krogstad, Kristine has the initiative, not only verbally but also physically. She even bends him back and lies him down on the floor with herself on top of him. This is in itself fine, but it is highly problematic when it is the privilege of the Western woman only to have physical initiative in this dance of cultures (and genders). Not surprisingly, the ending is equally ill-conceived. Nora and Helmer seem to dance their conflict, but without any physical shift in the power relations presented; he is the strong one, lifting her and directing her movements in detail. And when the five Noras reappear, there is no realignment or turning of the tables; he is still the controlling centre with the Noras circling around him. When they leave in the end, he is left alone on the enormous stage, with a single spotlight on him. Hence the dance ends with Helmer alone and left out; an arrogant man, but not a bad guy as the choreography gives him the entire sympathy of the production as it ends with his feeble 'Nora!'

In spite of its stated goals of being both political and intercultural, this production comes across as having been neither. The result of the emphasis on beauty and spectacle is that what one could call the decorative aspects of the dance and the (female) dancers is foregrounded. The women, the Noras, are there for the men of the performance in the same sense that they are there for the audience, as beautiful bodies in movement. The women are in other words depicted as being there for the man, Helmer, to serve and to please, without this fact of the performance ever being negated, transgressed or challenged from within the performance itself. It is there as the most basic fact of the surface of the production, and the spectacle of the surface is all there is. Hence the audience is very fundamentally invited to place themselves in Helmer's position. And like the gender politics of the production, the intercultural aspects are flawed, and for the same reasons. The Chinese aspects of stage design, casting and language are mere décor, there being no resistance or difficulty in any of them. Because this production was redone in the vain hope of moving effortlessly between cultures, of touring internationally, it was designed to transcend the culturally specific by making culture into a decorative element. In this sense it completely disregarded the basic element pointed to by Rustom Bharucha's reminder '[t]he intercultural, one can never afford to forget, is also intercontextual.'[93] In an intercultural production, the cultures and contexts brought together will have to be addressed and negotiated as different. This was done in both of the previously discussed productions from 1956 and 1998, with interesting and challenging results. And this is perhaps most basically what is missing in Nordseth's version of *A Doll's House* – there is really no context except that of the commercial spectacle itself, which is the same as no context at all. The commitment to the other context, the context of the Other, that was strongly felt in Wu Xue's use of the Norwegian text and his locally anchored investigations into the otherness of the Norwegian context in 1956, or in Wu Xiaojiang and Agnethe Haaland's intercultural approach to doing Ibsen in 1998, strangely evaporated in 2010. Strangely, since the twenty-first century, with its accelerating globalisation, could (and should) have brought stronger, not weaker awareness of the contextual and cultural tensions at stake.

This conundrum should, however, be understood on the basis of the broader changes in context that I hinted at in the beginning of this chapter. We have here come full circle in more than one sense from the Chinese celebration of the Ibsen anniversary in 1956. Wu's production then was the result of a Chinese initiative, it was one hundred per cent funded by the Chinese, and the artists involved could not for a second forget the different cultures and contexts involved in the production. In 2010 the situation was reversed, the production a Norwegian initiative, funded by the Norwegians, and flown in with a preconceived layout in artistic, ideological and political terms. Hence it was also much easier to let go of both contexts. Instead of the relation to a local specificity we get non-relational, global sameness, the cultural expression of neoliberal globalisation. And in this sense there is a strong symmetry between the development in China and the West, as culture becomes increasingly commodified, reduced to a commercial product. And the sheer possibility of a company like Ibsen International speaks volumes: a commercial firm, with an annual turnover in excess of two million Norwegian Kroner – most of which is public funds, a public–private partnership within the cultural sphere. The complexity of the link to commercialism can be illustrated through Ibsen International's strong emphasis on the possibility of building business connections through its Ibsen events during the World Expo in Shanghai in 2010. They proposed showing excerpts from the show in the Norwegian pavilion, to take the show in full to Shanghai and offer tickets to the EXPO2010, and also informed that several of the 'artists involved are good communicators also of other messages' and could be utilised as such 'if desirable'.[94] From the highly politicised context of 1956, we are here in the neoliberal world of brokers and consultants, commercial go-betweens in art as 'useful'. The 'projects' are argued not through artistic strength and relevance, but based on a supposed ability to be of use to further business enterprises in China. As the funding possibilities grow and diversify through public and private sources set to increase soft power in China (and elsewhere), the danger of 'Ibsen' becoming 'Ibsen-industry' is what we see in this production. Ibsen, in practice, becoming 'Ibsen ltd.inc.'

Peer Gynt in Africa: Some Notes on the Dangers and Ambiguities of Interculturalism

Can one be a non-Orientalist?[1]

The first Ibsen performance in Africa took place in Cairo in 1892, according to the performance database, IbsenStage. It was the touring version of *A Doll's House*, with Janet Achurch in the lead role, directed by her husband Charles Charrington. They took the play to Australia, New Zealand, San Francisco, Colombo and Calcutta, before stopping in Cairo and Alexandria on their way home to Britain. Ibsen himself had, as we shall see shortly, visited Egypt long before, when he participated in the celebrations of the opening of the Suez Canal in 1869. Both these non-related pieces of information point to the fact that the history of Ibsen in Africa is in multiple ways connected to empire and imperialism. The fact that there exists strong African traditions of performing Ibsen is not easy to explain without any reference to empire, or more directly put, Western colonialism and its after-effects. The soft and hard power of the West contributes to the dissemination of Western culture into its satellites. As we will see in this chapter, this is by no means a simple process or a one-way street. There are no cultural 'pushers' out there forcing Western culture on other people, and there are certainly no passive and docile recipients in the 'other' end. This being the case, it would still be disingenuous to claim that influence is not exerted or that economic inequality does not make an impact. The richer countries of the world use a small, but increasing, part of their wealth on so-called soft diplomacy or soft power, often by supporting culture in poorer countries.[2] In the Norwegian case this means that a theatre can get much needed economic support to stage an Ibsen play. This is not in any way a practice that I am against or critical of in principle; I find it only fair and reasonable that Western countries should try to support cultural sectors in countries where they have contributed to produce the general poverty in question. But it has to be done in ways that do not add insult to injury, by being able to negotiate the specificities of place and local context.[3] Hence the three cases discussed in this chapter are not chosen to illustrate the practice of Ibsen in Africa in a sweeping manner, but because they all have their own focus on an African setting – which gives rise to different but related sets of ideological and political difficulties. The focus in the following will be on *how* they take place (or take the place) in Africa.

Before getting into the details, however, let us maintain the bird's eye perspective a little longer and bring time, or timing, into the equation. When we examine the historical data on Ibsen in performance gathered in IbsenStage, we find a recurring pattern with peaks around special years, such as anniversaries. We have already touched on this phenomenon here and there in the preceding chapters – Beijing 1956, Santiago 2006, Hanoi 2006. Régis Debray has made the point that institutions play a pivotal role in the transmission of culture,[4] and in the case of authors' anniversaries we meet two institutions working in tandem: theatres and state agencies. When planning a season's repertoire, a theatre will often glance at upcoming anniversaries, and nation states can at the same time offer extra funding to promote 'their' authors. In Ibsen's case, there are distinct peaks in numbers of productions in 1928 (one hundred years after birth), 1956 (fifty years after death), 1978 and, above all, in 2006. I checked the number of productions for each of these 'Ibsen years' against the number of productions three years before and three years after each of them, and it turns out that in every case the number of Ibsen productions double or triple in these 'special' years.[5] In the case of 2006, one cannot know exactly how many of the 325 Ibsen productions were a direct result of Norwegian state sponsorship, because we do not have the data. And some of the productions that *were* sponsored could of course have taken place in any case. It is a fact, however, that the Norwegian state set aside a substantial amount of money to promote Ibsen-related activities that year. It was also done in a well-planned way, with a 'National committee' appointed several years ahead with the responsibility to co-ordinate and plan activities. The total budget for the years 2002 to 2006 was 68.3 million NOK (approximately 11.3 million USD), with 47.5 million for 2006 alone.[6] The objects sponsored spanned from the Ibsen Museum in Oslo, to very different activities: productions of plays, tours, seminars, exhibitions, workshops, lectures, books, articles, etc. These are all examples of factors that need to be taken into account when analysing Ibsen in practice. Ibsen's works clearly extended their way through the British (and German and Japanese) Empire in the nineteenth century, and it is obvious that his works, and those of other canonical Western dramatists, spread out across the globe in part as a result of the money and power that these Western powers will muster for the cause of transmitting what they see as their values and their culture. The research into this field is in its early phases, because we need more data and not least we need comparative data in order to understand the role of states in the transmission of culture and theatre.

The two productions analysed in this chapter are both adaptations of *Peer Gynt* that took place in Africa in 2006, with Norwegian funding, although on a very different scale. The first was done in Zimbabwe, by the New Horizon Theatre Company, and directed by the African theatre activist Robert McLaren. The other took place at the Giza Plateau outside Cairo, directed by the Norwegian manager of the Centennial celebration of the Ibsen year, Bentein Baardson. The latter was as official and highbrow as can be; the former was grass roots and had a strong educational aspect to it. These productions are extremes, in many ways opposites in the way they use Ibsen's text. And Ibsen's *text* will be the starting point for the discussion. *Peer Gynt* holds a special place within Ibsen's oeuvre, being the only play outside his cycle of realistic plays regularly performed on stage across the world. It is a wild, almost anarchical text, and the action frequently moves in time and space. The only places within these many movements that are given geographical specificity are the African scenes in Act 4 – the coast of Morocco, and unequivocally: 'Near the village of Gizeh. The great Sphinx carved out of the rock. In the far distance the spires and minarets of Cairo.'[7] In the introduction I argued that there is no original, no pure and uncontaminated source outside of culture. Ibsen's texts represent versions, historically and culturally changing entities or processes of meaning, themselves sites for contestation and negotiation of meaning and power. In the case of *Peer Gynt*, these ideological complexities are embedded in the text *as well as* in performances of it. The central question in the text is what it means to be oneself, what the self is and how it is to be realised in full life. This is more often than not understood on an individual and existentialist level. But the question of the self is throughout the play also posed along political and social lines, and one can make the argument that what Peer truly lacks is sociality, that is community and acknowledgement of others – on individual *and* cultural levels. In other words, the text is deeply entrenched in ideologico-political questions concerning culture, imperialism, and even orientalism, questions which a performance of the play has to address and relate to. If not, they may well return with a vengeance.

The orient in the text[8]

Some literal facts: the fourth act of *Peer Gynt* takes place in Africa; the people who live there are Africans; the world depicted is dominated by a capitalist economy where colonialism plays an important role. When reading the text that much is clear, but when reading the literature on the play these facts seem to disappear. Elisabeth Oxfeldt's book *Nordic Orientalism* is the major exception to this rule.[9] Where more traditional scholars have read important passages in the fourth act symbolically or allegorically, or simply neglected them completely, Oxfeldt has shown that they contribute significantly to the play, among other things by placing Peer in a capitalist world system in which everything can be commodified. Among the commodities that Peer himself mentions as the basis for his fortune at the beginning of the fourth act, we find both human beings (i.e. slaves) and sacred objects (idols and Bibles). Most important, however, is that Oxfeldt situates the text in a colonialist context, taking the African setting at face value. In the first three acts, Peer's carefree vacillation and egoism are characteristics of him as a person and of Norway as a nation, while in the fourth act they are extended to becoming characteristic *Western* features in the encounter with Africa, an instance of what we today refer to as orientalism. For example, Oxfeldt shows how Peer personifies the Western traveller's 'improving eye', the eye that only sees its surroundings as an arena for – profitable – improvements and 'modernisations'. What little he notices of local culture is phrased in terms of lack and deficiency, which is also one of orientalism's characteristics.[10] Peer takes little interest, for example, in his African surroundings as such, but is all the more obsessed with ideas of colonising, such as digging canals, irrigating, removing the 'foul stench', building towns, setting up 'factories' and, not least, establishing 'fresh, healthy culture' (Ibsen, 1993: 93 and Ibsen 1972: 344). So, the local forces need help to get things moving, Africa has to become 'Gyntiana'!

Granted that the geographical setting in the fourth act must be given specific meaning, the critique of Peer could, by extension, be seen as a criticism of a particular Western attitude to the orient. According to Oxfeldt – and this is where I part with her – what in the end saves *Peer Gynt* from being simply another manifestation of the orientalism of the day is that the multi-layered irony in the text undermines Peer's outlook. Peer's prejudices and stereotypical attitudes to the orient and oriental people are exposed to laughter in such a way that the text serves as a critique of the hegemonic orientalism of its time. Because 'Ibsen writes at a critical distance [. . .] and renders this depiction with irony' (Oxfeldt, 2005: 150), the text transcends the standard orientalism of the period. This is, in my view, to underestimate the dangers and ambiguities latent in the clash of cultures in the text. The oriental stereotypes are simply too many and all-pervasive to be suspended through a reference to dramatic irony. This can be illustrated by looking briefly at how the Anitra character is introduced in the text:

> (*The tent of an Arab Sheik, standing alone in an oasis.* Peer Gynt, *in his eastern robes reclines on cushions. He is drinking coffee and smoking a long pipe.* Anitra *and a group of girls are dancing and singing for him.*)
> CHORUS OF GIRLS. The Prophet is come!
> The Prophet, the lord, the all-knowing,
> To us, to us he has come
> Riding over the sand!
> (*Oxford Ibsen*, 1972: 346)

The orientalist clichés follow on each other's heels here, and they may be overdone, driven into hyperbole to the extent that it is hard to take them at face value today. Even so, the parodic exaggerations or ironic qualities can never safeguard the text from being caught up in the same orientalist clichés. Ibsen's text cannot be saved from the fact that these scenes ridicule Islam and Muslims in a way that will be perceived by many as offensive. For what Ibsen does at the beginning of the scene with Anitra is to have Peer fool the Arabs by making himself out to be the *Prophet*. Not *a* prophet, that is, but *the* Prophet – not a neutral expression to any Muslim. Even to many secular Muslims, having Peer trick the faithful by pretending to be the prophet Mohammed will be at the limits of blasphemy. The next lines, Anitra's first speech on stage, run as follows:

> ANITRA. His stallion is milk-white
> Like the rivers of Paradise.
> Bow every knee and head! [...]
> He, the unexampled,
> Came across the desert,
> Arrayed like a son of the earth.
> Kaba, Kaba stands empty;-
> He himself proclaims it!
> (*Oxford Ibsen*, 1972: 346)

The idea that a river of milk flows through Paradise is in accord with the Koran, and the Prophet comes through the desert in the person of a 'son of earth', but the reference to the 'empty' Kaba is more remarkable. Kaba, the holy building in Mecca, the goal of Muslim pilgrimages, *is* empty – as it is supposed to be, because Mohammed himself threw out the idols that were there in pre-Islamic times. Anitra's speech seems to imply that she believes Mohammed to have appeared, in spite of the display of faulty knowledge of Islam.[11] Not least in light of the attitude in Islamic societies towards the display of the female body in dance – openly, what is more, to satisfy the gaze of a lustful Western man, as in Peer's case – it becomes clear that these scenes can at least not be read as unambiguous criticism of Western orientalism, simply because the possible critique is represented through stereotype, and they remain stereotypes of a perturbing kind. Oxfeldt's work is important above all due to her insistence of the significance of the African setting, and the ideological tensions that thereby become apparent are recalcitrant. They cannot be effaced or subdued, be it in textual analysis or stage performance. Oxfeldt's reading reminds us of the many ways that the discourse and ideology of orientalism is still in function. She could also be said to open the text for a discussion of what one could call the privileges of having a voice, which is a difficult question, but one worth bringing up. For the notion that this Western author in the 1860s had seen through orientalism, and critiqued it thoroughly, and in a sense done the job for the Egyptians and Moroccans themselves, does carry some alarming aspects.[12]

During the Ibsen year 2006, the point was repeatedly made, for reasons that I will return to, that Egypt was the only culture outside Europe that Ibsen had taken a special interest in. Egypt also plays a role in Ibsen's biography, because he was invited to the opening of the Suez Canal, as one of two Norwegian representatives chosen by the Swedish King, Carl XV, in 1869. The visit to Egypt did not have obvious results in Ibsen's writings, but he said many years later, in 1890, that his visit 'to Egypt . . . was the most interesting and instructive period in my life.' No wonder that he saw it as a memorable experience, because he had taken part in what must have been one of the most lavish celebrations in world history. The Egyptian viceroy, the Khedive Ismail, invited 1,600 foreign guests for a two-month-long stay, with all expenses covered, travel, meals and pocket money included. It started on the boat from Malta, where they were treated with four meals per day, and a dinner consisting of eleven courses and all the wine they could wish for, with a similar meal served at midnight. They visited Alexandria and Cairo, and went on a boat trip on the Nile all the way up to the cataracts. The Khedive's wildly generous expenditure on this occasion has its sinister side in and through the stark poverty that characterised the country outside its privileged few. Ibsen's Norwegian travel companion was the Egyptologist Jens Daniel Carolus Lieblein. He was at the time a research fellow at the University in Kristiania (Oslo), a few years later (1876) to be appointed professor of Egyptology. Lieblein wrote several articles for the Norwegian newspaper *Morgenbladet*, where he reported from the whole journey and the opening ceremony itself. His general outlook is that of an external, colonising subject, facing an inferior people, but he does show an important sensibility for his surroundings by reflecting on the fact that the whole two-month party would have to be paid for by the 'poor Fellah', and *he* is already 'poor enough, without us in addition coming here to eat his last remaining lamb.'[13]

Ibsen himself had planned to write a lengthy travel description, and he kept a diary on his trip. This is lost and all we have from his hand is a short sketch called 'Abydos'. It covers eleven pages in the Centenary Edition of Ibsen's works, and describes the journey to the ancient city of Abydos. What strikes a reader used to Ibsen's terse prose, are the many poetic descriptions of nature and scenery. The writer was obviously quite infatuated with Egypt in many ways. But there is no sign of compassion with the local population, and certainly no feeling of guilt for taking part in the lavish expenditure of the celebrations. Ibsen enjoyed the 'Khedive's Havannah cigars' as much as having people 'waving away the flies' around him. After a while Ibsen discovers that 'underneath the seemingly meaningless chaos of screams, gestures and actions there lies a certain order; all of this is after all expressions of a social life, that also has its law and rule' and the nations of the world, he concludes, 'in their basic core are not as different as one is inclined to believe.'[14] But he also states that one 'sees no sign of family life; no social connection between men. The Oriental only knows superiors or subordinates, never his equals [...] A lethargic dreamlike half-life seems to have put its veil over the Oriental.' In order to 'force through a whole new civilisation', he continues, one cannot build on the existing state of affairs, but has to 'recreate the whole spiritual habitus of every individual' and 'to a certain extent do violence to the nationality itself.' This is something that only the 'most intrepid and autocratic government can force through' (Ibsen, 1930: 344), he says, and warns against any kind of naïve belief in human rights or democracy if one is to solve the task at hand.

Now, I do not mean to say that Ibsen was a kind of colonialist monster in disguise, but rather to claim that he was of his world; like his literature he was personally in most ways a product of his own society and the discourse and ideology that dominated his class. His texts are secular – part of culture *and* empire – and he was himself not a 'beautiful soul' elated above the turmoil of his time. So the same ambiguities that we found in *Peer Gynt* are also to be found in the person Henrik Ibsen. The importance of this ambiguity is that it shows that there is no access to a position outside of ideology – and this is perhaps the lesson to be learned: that the most culturally biased and orientalist would be to assume that we and Ibsen can talk from a vantage point outside of orientalism.

Peer Gynt in Africa – Zimbabwe

The two productions discussed in the following were to my knowledge the only performances of *Peer Gynt* in Africa in 2006 – as mentioned, one in Zimbabwe and one in Egypt. These two versions of *Peer Gynt* were both sponsored by Norwegian authorities, albeit on a very different scale. Both were adaptations of the play, and both were done, in Robert McLaren's words, with the explicit goal to 'contribute towards mutual understanding through cultural exchange'.[15] In the Zimbabwean case, there was certainly some cultural exchange taking place in and through the production itself, that is in its negotiation between a Norwegian text from the nineteenth century and an African reality of the twenty-first century. McLaren's plan was also to take the production to Norway, but this part of the project had to be cancelled due to lack of funding. In addition to the projected goal of realising an exchange between cultures, they both aimed to give the performance a local anchoring in and relevant to African culture. They were also both recorded for television.[16] Apart from these commonalities, the two versions of *Peer Gynt* were as different as can be. The 'New Horizon Theatre Company' is a young professional theatre company, and the actors have all graduated from either CHIPAWO, a Zimbabwean arts education organisation working with children and young people, mainly from disadvantaged backgrounds, or the Zimbabwean Academy of Arts Education for Development.[17] It is a professional company, established with the purpose of giving new graduates an opportunity to work and build their careers further.

The production certainly had elements from a strong tradition of theatre for development, and the achievement of the actors testified to the quality of the education they had been given. Not least in light of their age, the youngest actors being 16 and the 'oldest' 24, it was an impressive performance on their part. There was no tradition of performing Ibsen in Zimbabwe before this, and one could not count on the play or its author being known to the public, hence it was deemed necessary to adapt the play to a contemporary Zimbabwean reality. The adaptation by Robert McLaren and Stephen Chifunyise does, however, come across as surprisingly faithful to the text. As the title, 'A Journey to Yourself', indicates, the main focus was on Peer's journey and search for identity. It connected to local forms of storytelling, while at the same time focusing on the modern challenge of how to negotiate an identity for an individual stretched between the demands of a living rural tradition and modern city life. Hence the story of this Peer – called Peter Gwindi and performed by the 23-year-old Nqobile Khoza – is never an isolated existentialist endeavour but is played out through a constant tension and conflict between the needs and rights of the individual on the one hand and a village community permeated by tradition and family ties on the other. Much of the storyline is kept, and no major cuts done, except from the quite common omission of large parts of the fourth act.

The elements most culturally specific for Norwegian folklore are seamlessly changed into Zimbabwean traditions. Hence the trolls are changed into Mashavi, 'lost spirits' of people who had died in 'strange lands' without the required 'rituals to bring you home', and the Boyg becomes Ndiripohandipo – literally translated as 'I am here and I am not here', giving Peer the order to 'Go round'. In this way the adaptation is able to spell out conflicts between living folklore and modern life that are still very much alive within the local situation. Even more politically acute is the version given to the only scene kept from the fourth act, namely Peer's fateful meeting with the other wealthy travellers who steal his yacht in Morocco. In this version the meeting takes place in a suite in a luxury hotel in Johannesburg, and his companions are from South Africa, Nigeria, Cote d'Ivoire and Kenya. Peter Gwindi has made his fortune in the United States, profiting from the desperation and despair of the African diaspora, a 'lucrative business', he says, dealing in 'visas, work permits, study opportunities, foreign exchange, fuel, pornography, sex slaves, babies – such things'.

This brilliant scene opens the play to the darker sides of the global movements of people seeking to improve their lives, ranging from students and workers seeking work permits and visas, to victims of trafficking, children and body parts for sale. Always a buck to be made for the right person, which Peer is, now under the Anglicised name Peter Gingi. At the same time this scene is used to point towards more ambiguous politics within Zimbabwe, when Peter says that he plans to become 'King of the world' through the ultimate business deal with the Americans. Through his connections in high places he has learned that the United States and United Kingdom plan to invade Zimbabwe, and he most certainly does *not* plan to use his money to help his countrymen.

He plans to join forces with the invading Westerners to get his hands on all the golden contracts that follow in the wake of this new type of war. The introduction, almost in passing, of the idea of a coming American–British invasion of Zimbabwe is ambiguous to say the least. It does express an occidentalism of its own, a stereotype of a hostile West, ready to crush a poor African country at will. In addition, it has bearing on domestic politics, because Robert Mugabe has often enough played this occidentalist card in his struggle to hold onto power. And it is after all not without justification, on the background of wars in Iraq, Afghanistan, Libya, and increasing numbers of drone attacks in different parts of the world, including Africa. Within the logic of the adaptation, this set-up seems to be there to express both a critique of Mugabe and his rhetoric of anti-Western occidentalism, while at the same time to launch the idea that the Western powers are not benign, or to be trusted, like their servant Peter Gwindi. In respect to the intercultural aspects of the adaptation, it must be said to express an interesting twist, or radicalisation of this part of Ibsen's story. There Peer plans to help the Turks in crushing the Greek uprising, and he is in that sense a traitor to 'his' Christian-European culture – Peter, however, is willing to sell out not only religion and culture, but even his own nation and his countrymen (Figure 5.1).

In terms of props, stage design, costumes and equipment, it is a modest production, marked by the fact that the company had very limited resources at its disposal.[18] This limitation is fully compensated through the imaginative use of few props (most centrally a ladder, which can be a rooftop to place Amai Peter (Mother Aase – played by Chipo Basopo), a mountaintop, the entrance to a hut, etc.), local performance traditions (dance, song, music, storytelling), and the sheer energy of the actors. One further example to illustrate this point: because Zimbabwe does not have a coastline Peer's return home by ship is difficult. This problem is solved by Peter returning home on one of the notoriously dangerous minibus taxis that do the route from South Africa to Zimbabwe. Peter and his fellow passengers sit on small benches and are thrown around as the driver speeds up on the unlit

Figure 5.1 'A Journey to Yourself', Stephen Chifunyise and Robert McLaren's adaption of *Peer Gynt*, directed by Robert McLaren (2006). From left to right: Peter Gwindi (Nqobile Khoza) and Amai Peter/Mother Aase (Chipo Basopo) (Photo: Courtesy of Robert McLaren and New Horizon Theatre Company).

road; the Strange Passenger (Blessed Rukweza) appears with his morbid queries, and they crash. The essence of the text is there – but localised to a context that could not be more different from Ibsen's setting in his dramatic poem from 1867.

'A Journey to Yourself' was a great success; it premiered at the Harare International Festival of the Arts, and was since part of the main celebration of the Ibsen Centenary in Harare. It went on a national tour of Zimbabwe and finally ran for two weeks at the Reps Theatre in Harare in September/October 2006. Through small humoristic details it also reflected on the cultural difference itself, for example when one of the girls at the wedding in the beginning of the play declines to dance with Peter, using the excuse that she dances like 'a Westerner' who 'can't keep the rhythm'. Hence it is part of the performance that Africans have their own stereotypes about foreigners. In form and content, the production represents an interesting negotiation between different cultural meanings. What made it so successful was, in other words, the ability to negotiate with humour, and give form to cultural tension between Ibsen's text, European culture, global tensions and local African reality. This kind of cultural sensitivity was not the most dominant trait of the other performance of *Peer Gynt* done in Africa in 2006.

Peer Gynt on the Giza Plateau

The context for the staging of *Peer Gynt* on the Giza plateau could not have been more different than the staging in Harare. This performance was the official conclusion and celebration of the Ibsen year 2006, and it caused a heated debate in Norway, mainly because of the expenditure, which was more than 13 million NOK.[19] The audience on the premiere night – when I saw it – had a remarkably high level of notability; Mrs Mubarak of Egypt, the Norwegian Queen Sonja, former prime minister of Norway, Kjell Magne Bondevik and other leading politicians, in addition to a great number of business executives who were there representing the different sponsors of the Ibsen year 2006. The central argument for the design of the production at this site was that it was to be seen as a meeting of cultures, an international theatre event bridging gaps between cultures. The point of departure was as follows: the performance ran two nights, first as a 'dress rehearsal' on 26 October and then as a 'premiere' on 27 October. Norwegian spectators were in the majority on both nights. The play was radically shortened, and performed in Norwegian, by Norwegian actors. Hence an important section of the audience was excluded through a decisive linguistic choice made from the outset, a fact that inevitably had an effect on the 'experience' of the performance, notwithstanding the small boards with subtitles (only visible from the front rows).[20] This aspect was further exacerbated in this case by the fact that the excluded part of the audience was the Egyptians, the 'host' culture. The action was accompanied by Cairo's symphony orchestra playing Grieg's national romantic music composed for the play (in Håkon Berge's arrangement). And the tone was set, so to speak, from the very beginning, opening with Norwegian folk music – a single Hardanger fiddle spreading its characteristic sound in the desert night. To the Norwegian part of the audience, this may have meant something (both positive and negative, I imagine), but what about the Egyptian spectators? In any case, the Norwegian element in the production was considerable.

In terms of timing, there were also alarming aspects to the production, because it took place at the conclusion of the Eid al Fitr celebrations after Ramadan. Because this is *the* major holiday and festivity in all Muslim countries, it might not be seen as the perfect time for a big event of foreign culture – the comment was made that Norwegians might not be too interested in having an Egyptian theatre production, with thousands of Egyptian audience members flown in, taking place in the centre of Oslo during Christmas. Not to mention what the stage crew, drivers, carpenters, mechanics, musicians and their trade unions would have to say . . . The heated debates and demonstrations following the publication of the Mohammed caricatures in Danish and Norwegian newspapers were only a few months before. In spite of these, and other difficult questions looming in the background, the question as to what kind of cultural encounter we had witnessed never occurred in any genuine sense to the Norwegian reviewers and journalists who were in Egypt to see *Peer Gynt*. The journalists present seemed fascinated by what they found exotic and unfamiliar in Egypt, virtually as tourists, but showed no awareness of, or commitment to, anything like a meeting of cultures. The absence of any discussion of the nature of this intercultural transfer is all the more striking, seeing that the actual meeting of cultures was explicitly stated to be the primary motivation for the production. There is no doubt in my mind that *Peer Gynt* could have formed an excellent basis for bringing the international Ibsen year to a modern conclusion. Given the increasing tension in recent years between east and west, occident and orient, the choice of Egypt as the arena might appear all the bolder. The choice of text *and* location were, however, primarily legitimated through the text and Ibsen's biography, as Bentein Baardson expressed it in the programme for the Giza performance: 'Egypt is the only country outside Europe towards which Ibsen bore a particular relation.'

Baardson himself constantly emphasised the cross-cultural aspect of the production, which was to convey 'cultural exchange' and not just be a Norwegian 'guest performance'.[21] Norway's major newspaper, *Aftenposten*, reported that the performance would consist of a 'globalised Peer [...] with the cultural encounter at its centre' (Skre, 2006). At the same time, it seemed as if the organisers preferred to rise above the whole problem, maintaining that the production was not intercultural, but rather acultural: 'No national costumes. No Anitra. We will remove all ethnic elements both on the Norwegian and on the Arab side, and place "Peer Gynt" in our own time', in the words of stage designer Ingeborg Kvamme (Skre, 2006). Basically, they believed that it was possible to ignore or transcend one's cultural self: 'Instead of digging out national costumes from a traditional store, the stage designer went to Armani in Milan, where she was able to buy a large portion of the 110 costumes at "friendly" prices' (Skre, 2006). Beyond the culturally specific and ethnic, then, we have the general and neutral, the Armani. No notion, surely, can be more culturally specific than this one.

The organisers of '*Peer Gynt* in Giza' insisted on the one hand that regard for the culturally specific was important, while on the other hand denying the existence of the cultural all together. The subsequent criticism, however, was primarily concerned with expenses and competence, and only to a minor extent with aesthetics and politics. Generally speaking, the performance was lauded and not reviewed in any critical sense of the word, and in the ensuing discussion the question of artistic value was largely evaded. The exceptions to this rule were Therese Bjørneboe in *Klassekampen* and Nehad Selaiha in *Al-Ahram*. In Therese Bjørneboe's opinion, the performance was more event and show than theatre. Her point was that 'the experience on offer was the driving force – with the Sphinx and the pyramids carrying the show' (*Klassekampen*, 28 October 2006). She saw the main objective and rationale of the production as a wish to give the visiting Norwegian spectators, and in particular the relatively large delegations from the senior management (with spouses) of the major commercial sponsors of the Ibsen year, an experience for life. And judging by the mood among the spectators after the show, it was a success in that regard. Bjørneboe's suggestion, then, was that the performance had to be reviewed as pure entertainment, a show designed for tourist experience, and not as theatre (and can the Sphinx and the pyramids ever get less than sixes in the reviewers' throw of the dice?).

At the very heart of this production, however, making it unique and quite different from any other production of *Peer Gynt*, was its relation to *place*, to the site for the performance. Baardson emphasised time and again that this setting, facing the Sphinx on the Giza plateau, is the only specific indication of place in Ibsen's text, and the aim was to make this the core or axis about which the whole production was to rotate (Figure 5.2). Hence the structure of the play was altered, from Ibsen's largely chronological presentation to a structure organised around Peer's encounter with the Sphinx, with the preceding events then shown retrospectively up to the meeting with the Sphinx, after which the play continued to the end, in a radically shortened form. If we look for it in Ibsen's text, however, 'Peer's meeting with the Sphinx' does not amount to much: '[Peer] observes the Sphinx attentively, now through his pince-nez, now through his cupped hand' (Ibsen, 1993: 112), and then makes a short monologue reflecting on what he sees. This little episode is in itself typical enough both of Peer and of a particular Western attitude to the orient: viewing it through his cupped hand he distances himself and isolates the viewed object, aiming for a purely aesthetic pleasure. And when he sets out to interpret what he sees, he incorporates it in his own, indeed private experience:

Peer Gynt. Now where in the world have I met before
a half-forgotten something that's like this chimera? [...]
   Ha, I remember the fellow!
It must be the Boyg – one clout, he was yellow, –
that's so to say, I dreamt it, – my fever was high. –
(Ibsen, 1993: 112–13)

In the preceding scene he believes he recognises the Mountain King in the statue of Memnon, and here he appears to believe that the Sphinx 'is' the Boyg. This little scene exemplifies an ingrained mechanism in Peer, his inability to relate to the external and unfamiliar. He lives through many and different adventures, but lacks the ability to genuinely experience them. He remains the same, without the ability to change through experience. Instead Peer takes possession of everything 'other' or alien, whether figures or persons he meets or texts he has read or heard about: they are all appropriated as parts of his own. In this sense, the scene shows how Peer is already enclosed in the 'self's cask' (Ibsen, 1993: 117), with little ability to see what is different or foreign – a mechanism in many ways characteristic of orientalism.

Another important aspect of the Sphinx in Ibsen is that Peer does *not* manage to engage it in conversation; it is, as we learn from the list of 'the characters' in the text, a 'mute person'. And this brings us to the really striking feature of Bentein Baardson's version of *Peer Gynt*. For here the Sphinx is *not* silent. Baardson's Sphinx speaks, and what is more it speaks *Arabic*. It is inaccurate, therefore, to say that the text is performed in Norwegian. One Arab takes part, the Sphinx. Because this is a 'mute person' in Ibsen, it had to be made to speak – which Baardson did by having the Sphinx speak the Boyg's lines! Hence the Sphinx became not only a pivotal point in the play's action, but also a speaking character, the Arab of the performance. Introducing an Arabic element into the production, also in the linguistic sense, was in itself a good idea. But to do so by 'confirming' Peer's mistaken confusion of the Sphinx with the Boyg was *not* wise. For one thing, to do so misses the point that Peer is investing his own self and culture in the Sphinx. To choose the Boyg, of all the characters in the play, to give voice to the Sphinx's silence, gave rise to further problems. Although the Boyg can certainly be interpreted in various ways, one can hardly get away from the figure's fundamentally negative nature. In many ways the Boyg embodies (or vocalises: we do not *see* the Boyg, it is a *voice*) the leading character's main problem: his evasiveness, his inability to choose, his going roundabout. In Nehad Selaiha's opinion, both text and production contained orientalist elements, but to turn the Sphinx into the Boyg, she felt, was unforgivable:

> What can neither be defended nor justified, however, was the identification, right out at the beginning, then at two other points in the production [...] of the Sphinx with the slimy, amorphous, evil Boyg, the propagator of compromises, circumlocution and prevarication – the advocator of 'roundaboutness'. (*Al Ahram Weekly*, 1–7 November 2006)

To make the Sphinx in the production into a negative entity, certainly testifies to insufficient understanding of the local context; to Egyptians the Sphinx is a positive symbol, and something they take pride in. Selaiha therefore appeared to regard it as a virtual insult when Baardson made the Sphinx into the Boyg, not only by giving Ibsen's mute person the Boyg's lines, but also by giving it the same position in the structure of action. In Ibsen's version, Peer is driven from refuge to refuge at the end of the second act: first when the trolls in the Hall of the Mountain King nearly take his life, and next when the Boyg almost has him down for good. In the text, these heathen and pre-modern primeval forces are overcome as follows:

> **Peer Gynt**. Too dear to buy an hour's more life
>   for such a wearing game of strife.
>   (*collapses*)
> **Birds**. Boyg, he's fallen! Now bind him! Bind him!
>   (*Church bells and hymn singing far in the distance.*)
> **The Boyg** (*crumbles to nothing and gasps*).
>   He was too strong. There were women behind him.
> (Ibsen, 1993: 52)

In Bentein Baardson's version, Peer's lines were Norwegian, while the Cairo opera choir gave Arabic voice to the 'Birds', and Mohammed Wafik Aly Helmy performed the Sphinx/Boyg's lines in Arabic. In other words, when this Norwegian Peer is on the verge of being crushed by the archaic Arabic force, church bells toll – upon which the Arab gives way and 'crumbles to nothing' with a gasp. It does not take much interpretative imagination or analytical effort to see what at this point is as plain as day, the Arab in this performance is a negative force, perhaps even the play's fundamental problem, and this figure or force is overcome with the help of unambiguously Christian symbols.

What was to be the core or very hub of this production – Peer's meeting with the Sphinx – was simply its main problem. 'Peer Gynt in Giza' was meant, for the first time in the play's history, to use the play's 'Egyptian dimension' as its 'main axis', as former minister of culture in Norway, Lars Roar Langslet put it in the programme. It was precisely as a meeting of cultures that the production was to achieve its importance and be of global significance: 'The Egyptian–Norwegian *Peer Gynt* in Giza also has its deepest meaning as a road map to brotherhood and peace between peoples,' Langslet continued, in all modesty. But it is precisely in a serious intercultural perspective that the production failed most drastically. The production's basic idea, the director's contribution – to make the meeting with the Sphinx its pivotal point by giving it the Boyg's lines and, what is more, in Arabic – consists of having the action in *Peer Gynt* revolve around a meeting between a western Peer and a foreign, oriental Other. The oriental is the spokesman for the Boyg's 'go roundabout' doctrine, and is on the point of taking Peer's life when it is overcome by the sound of church bells. Where the text is ambiguous – on the one hand, marked by oriental clichés that were typical of their day, but on the other, full of ironic exaggerations that may ridicule and partly undermine the same clichés, the production was far more unequivocally orientalistic.

Nor was that quality limited to the vital Sphinx scene. Ellen Rees has for example focused on visual aspects of the characters on stage and shown how the production also 'presents essentialized ethnic stereotypes based on physical characteristics', because all the characters that the audience 'are meant to sympathise with are blond'.[22] These are Peer's mother Aase (Lise Fjeldstad), Solvejg (Silje Reinåmo), and more than anything Peer himself whose hair was 'bleached the palest possible shade of blond, making the character into a rather frightening Billy

Figure 5.2 *Peer Gynt at Giza*, directed by Bentein Baardson (2006). Peer: Bjarte Hjelmeland (Photo: Heiko Junge/NTB Scanpix).

Idol-like icon of modern and aggressive manhood' (Rees, 2014: 123–4). That only these three are blonde, while the others have had their hair coloured black, dark, red, or green, might not have been conspicuous in another production, but it certainly was in this one. It was probably not a result of ill will – nevertheless it was hard not to see it as making a point on the semiotic level of visual imagery, not least due to its constructed, thought out and artificial nature. Furthermore, after Peer's meeting with the Arabic Boyg, the production continued with two scenes from the third act, 'Mother Aase's death' and a very brief 'leave-taking from Solvejg', before Peer was shown arriving in Egypt with a full caravan of Bedouins.

The caravan came down the road from the pyramids above, and in the darkness it became strangely uncertain whether this was really part of the production or not. Nehad Selaiha saw it as yet another example of how the production at times deteriorated to blatantly orientalistic exoticism. When Peer then rode up to the stage on a white Arab horse, the predominant impression was not one of irony or critical distance.[23] And his meeting with his Armani-dressed fellow travellers consisted of lines from the beginning of the act interwoven with the monologue in which he dreams of colonising the country and founding Gyntiana with its capital Peeropolis. There was an opportunity here to realise the play's critical potential in a post-colonial context, but instead the focus was narrowed down to Peer's personal megalomania. And as the performance proceeded, it became more and more focused on a traditional idealistic interpretation, with its emphasis on existential individualism and (quasi) religious reconciliation. Ibsen – in my view – leaves his ending open and ambiguous, whereas Baardson single-mindedly went for a tableau of reconciliation in which an ever-young, blonde and innocent Solvejg guarantees reconciliation both at the personal and at the religious level. Reinåmo as Solvejg, certainly did the best she could, but was almost exclusively cast as 'blonde, very young, virgin character'.

Leaving the gender politics of the performance to the reader's imagination, I wish in conclusion to look closer at the ending of the performance. As I said, a strong argument could be made for Ibsen's ending being open and ambiguous, not least because of the different ironies mobilised through Solvejg's blindness and age. And in this respect the image itself is important: what Ibsen's stage directions say is that Peer 'clings to her tightly, burying his face in her lap. A long silence. The sun rises' (Ibsen, 1993: 170). This leaves many aspects of the scene open, but it does state unequivocally that Peer is to 'bury' or hide his face in her lap, which may be seen as part of what has been the problem earlier in the play; he hides, escapes or evades problems, even here where the situation is at its most extreme. The image shown on stage in Baardson's version, however, was different; here Peer rests in her lap, being consoled in a fashion that conjures up another image, namely the *pieta* – the dead Christ resting, so to speak, in the Virgin Mary's lap. This image is often seen or felt in productions of *Peer Gynt* and it is a possible interpretation, but in this version, with its intercultural setting and focus, it gains an extra meaning that seems more than a little distressing. This is due to the way that the performance spells out the problem of the modern self: the struggle for selfhood had, in and through Peer's meeting with the Sphinx/Boyg, been cast in cultural terms, and to give the ending this form therefore also carried a cultural meaning that could be seen to say that there is salvation for the individual, in and through the image of God's son that has given his life for us – and this 'us' seemed inevitably to carry a certain exclusivity that in this setting was problematic, to say the least.

The Official Ibsen Year 2006, then, ended with a prolonged visual display, a tableau, with its own inescapable iconography. While Solvejg's song was performed, in Grieg's romantic version, the stage was occupied solely by the Solvejg/Peer image. The music, or lyrics, brought out a clearly religious message, while the visual meaning or iconography pointed in the same direction. In other words, this production strengthened and emphasised aspects of the text that point towards a strictly Christian reconciliation, while suppressing other aspects that point in different directions. This is of course in itself not a problem. A staging of this play may end by saying that the specifically modern problem of the self can only be solved and reconciled through Christ – but *this* performance could *not*. Because the question of the self in this performance had already been culturalised as a conflict between Arab, or Muslim, otherness, and Christian or Western hope and life, this specific ending was the worst possible. The question of the self was posed in cultural terms of conflict and hierarchy, and the production could thus be seen as making an almost aggressive orientalist point both at an individual and cultural or religious level. It is difficult, then, to see this production as a road map to brotherhood and peace. Indeed, it is rather fortunate that it did not bring about the opposite. Regarded as intercultural theatre, the result was a disaster. And the production can never rid itself of the fact that it was presented as an intercultural project, and therefore *must* be assessed as such. No doubt it was the expenditure that necessitated the overblown pretensions, which was rather a shame, for regarded as a tourist project, that was as pure commercial spectacle – in the tradition of the Khedives 'Aida' – as entertainment and 'an experience for life', it would still have been deeply ambiguous, but in those terms more defensible.

Between cultures

In relation to the theatre performance, the text is nothing more (nor less) than a template. Nevertheless, I wanted to point to the text in this chapter, because Ibsen's *Peer Gynt* is such a conflicting, contradictory template. I have tried to show very briefly that the text contains elements that are not only ambiguous; they are murky, in an ideological and political sense. Ibsen's text can obviously be read in many different ways, but I do wish that one would be more willing to take Elisabeth Oxfeldt's lead in addressing its 'darker' aspects. The orientalist elements in the play represent a challenge for readings and stagings alike; they bear witness to the historical situation of the text within a world system anno 1867, which are still with us, in the shape of the orientalism of the twenty-first century. There is a relational force at play here; the text cannot escape its relation to the asymmetrical distribution of power and resources in its context of origin, and neither could a realisation of it on stage in 2006. This does not mean that any given staging of the play necessarily has to include a critique of orientalism, but it has to be reflected on, if not explicitly addressed. Rustom Bharucha was probably the first to bring up the question of orientalism in *Peer Gynt*, in an essay he wrote on his own experiences from directing the play in Mysore, Karnataka, in 1995.[24] He rounded up his politically astute text by reflecting on the orientalism of the play, and on how his own 'critique of orientalism [...] was missing' in the production, that 'the subterranean orientalism within Ibsen's imaginary was allowed to function as a source of entertainment rather than critique' (Bharucha, 2000a: 83–4). He registers this trait in his own staging with mild humour and some surprise, defending it with the:

> claim that stereotypes can be played in different registers of fun in relation to different critical traditions of the Other [...] I realised, not without a sense of irony, that in criticising orientalism, one does not necessarily have to suppress one's own fantasy of the Arabian Nights. (Bharucha, 2000a: 84)

Bharucha's observation points to three important relations: to the text, and its subterranean orientalism, to the context of the production, itself highly over-determined, and to the fact that we are all within ideological space, we all have our fantasies, desires, images of the other. And as we have seen, 'A Journey to Yourself' deals with these fantasies, its own reverse orientalism, with humour and sharp wit. So the point is not that these fantasies have to be suppressed, but they do need to be dealt with critically, with humour, satirically, entertaining, allegorically ... This might be part of what *Peer Gynt* challenges us to do, a challenge completely neglected in the concluding celebration of the Ibsen year 2006.

The fundamental weakness of the *Peer Gynt* at Giza lay in the inability to see the matter from others' point of view. That was bad, because the play itself is concerned with the cultural and individual mechanisms of being engrossed in a self-centred perspective on the world, and because it contrasted so sharply with the organisers' own assessments and objectives. The performance displayed few signs of any reflection on the difference an Other point of view and position in the world makes. The official Ibsen Year accordingly concluded with a performance which more than anything else exhibited a typically Norwegian form of naïveté, the belief that because our intentions are good everything is in order. Put in other words, the situation was not taken seriously, and the situation or context for a performance will, not least, always be relationally (over)determined and impossible to control by 'intentions' on the part of the sender. This point was taken seriously by the New Horizon Theatre Company, and neglected completely by Baardson and the Norwegian professionals in charge of the celebration of the Ibsen year 2006. Baardson's *Peer Gynt* fell through because it adopted an arrogant and ignorant approach to the cultures *and* power relations it was situated within, and did not take in the dangers and ambiguities of interculturalism. But there are many indications that bringing the Ibsen year to a conclusion with an event that blocked communication was contrary to the organisers' intentions. That, too, makes it an interesting production, and a warning to all of us (me included). It is not *that* easy to be a non-orientalist.

Coda:
From Dhaka to Mabou Mines

Instead of trying to distil a forced essence or give a synoptic repetition of the previous chapters, I will end this book through a short reflection on two important factors in the practice of Ibsen not sufficiently covered by the preceding chapters, namely festivals on the one hand and individual 'auteurs' on the other, original artists or companies with the strength in terms of cultural capital that follows from an 'avant-garde' standing. Festivals of all kinds seem to be of increasing importance within the cultural economy. A Google search for any classic dramatist combined with the word festival will generate hits in the seven- or eight-digit range. In the last decade, there have been important annual, biannual or one-year theatre festivals focusing on Ibsen in Oslo, Dhaka, Lanesboro (MN), Beirut, Delhi, Hyderabad, Havana, Harare, Nanjing and Kolkata, just to mention some. The International Ibsen Festival in Oslo is clearly the most highbrow, prestigious and oldest of these festivals. It was inaugurated in 1990 and ran as an annual festival in the first years, but has been bi-annual since 1994. The impact of the Ibsen Festival at the National Theatre in Oslo could best be seen along three different dimensions. On the most local level, it committed the National Theatre to Ibsen in a much stronger sense than before; it had to make substantial productions for its own festival, the result being that it to some extent has become an 'Ibsen theatre'. On a broader national level, the festival's focus, at least during the first fifteen to twenty years, on bringing in Ibsen productions from other parts of the world, has strongly influenced and changed the

Norwegian tradition of doing Ibsen.[1] Last but not least, there is reason
to believe that the existence of the Ibsen Festival in Oslo may have
influenced theatres and directors outside of Norway to make Ibsen
productions with the hope of being invited to the festival. Hence it can
be seen as influencing both the quality and the quantity of Ibsen
productions both inside and outside of Norway.[2]

A very different kind of festival – and one with a very different kind
of importance and impact – took place in the capital of Bangladesh,
Dhaka, in 2009. Certainly among the largest Ibsen festivals to date, it
counted twenty-two different productions, from India, Pakistan, Iran,
Nepal and Egypt, in addition to the Bangladeshi productions. The
festival lasted ten days (from 12 to 22 November), during which they
had two to three shows per day, all of them with an almost full house, the
audience mainly consisting of young people. In addition to the theatre
performances, the festival featured a large art exhibition, film screenings,
discussions with directors and actors, theatre workshops, and a three-
day conference on Ibsen. I left the festival with an enthusiastic feeling of
having seen glimpses of what must be one of the most vital and vibrant
theatre communities in the world. The festival title was 'Ibsen through
new eyes', and we did get to see many new takes on the plays; from local
forms of village theatre to postmodern multimedia shows. The festival
was well funded, with local support from several ministries and
businesses, in addition to Indian and Norwegian state agencies. This had
made it possible to invite several important guest performances,[3] in
addition to commissioning thirteen Bangladeshi productions.

These productions were as different as can be, but they all shared a
common effort to localise Ibsen's plays, expressed through a diverse
range of adaptations. What seemed to be the common denominator for
most of the productions, on a very general level, was that they were all
part of an ongoing struggle over the meaning and function of secularism
in Bangladesh. Historically, Bangladesh has not had a strong tradition
for radical, fundamentalist interpretations of Islam. In Bangladesh and
the Bengali culture, Islam has been of a more syncretistic nature,
adapted to local culture. But this tradition has been under pressure

during the last few decades, and one has seen increasing tendencies towards a more political and fundamentalist Islam; this has become one of the main dividing lines in the highly politicised culture of the country. The festival in 2009, under the rule of the Awami league, which has mainly been a centre-left political party with a secularist line of political thinking, could be seen as a fragmented and pluralistic voicing of secularism. Hence the festival saw productions of plays such as *Brand* and *Ghosts*, which clearly voiced a critique of an increasing influence of political Islam in everyday life and politics. There were two versions of *Ghosts*, one done in proscenium style, but boldly adapted to local reality by Mohammed Bari and directed by Rokeya Rafique Baby. Even stronger, and far more striking, however, was the version called *Adrisha Paap* (literally meaning 'Invisible sin'), performed by a travelling group of village performers from the remote area of Rangpur in Northern Bangladesh, specialising in the folk theatre form called Kushan Gan.[4] In Kushan Gan, episodes from the *Ramayana* are traditionally dramatised, and are typically performed during religious festivals in temple precincts, outer courtyards or village squares. It is a theatrical form consisting not of dramatised spoken word, but of a narrator and a sub-narrator telling a story in constant interchange with dance and music. During narrative sequences, the performers will be seated in a square formation, which then delineates the borders around which they dance and sing during the musical parts of the performance. All dancers are male, but dressed as women.

The artists were poor and illiterate specialists within a traditional religious theatre form, and they developed the production in co-operation with the director Golam Sarwar and the National Theatre in Bangladesh. The formal elements of Kushan Gan were kept, with an adapted version of the story in *Ghosts* as narrative content. Had I not known in advance, I would probably not have guessed that the performance had anything to do with Ibsen or *Ghosts*. What made it such an enjoyable performance, even for an outsider like me, was the vigour and vitality with which they performed, full of beauty and a burlesque kind of physical humour. It was also astonishing to see how they had managed to make Ibsen's content into their own; the narrative of lies, power and deceptions in a European bourgeois environment had seamlessly become a sinister story of rural village life in Bangladesh. Central to the production was, according to Nilu, Mrs Alving's words about all the 'old dead doctrines and opinions and beliefs' that influence people's lives. One can easily imagine that this constitutes a contentious and important political and cultural theme within the group's home environment. This was a central aspect of the festival in Dhaka as a whole; that the productions were designed not just to be performed at the festival itself, but to have a longer life in performance. The festival gave the main narrator Kripa Sindhu Rao Sarkar, and the group, an opportunity for the first time to use their expertise within a traditional theatre form to develop a new production with a very different and secular content. The production is still performed in rural Bangladesh.

One noteworthy function of a festival dedicated to a single dramatist, like the one in Dhaka, is that it will encourage and even commission new versions of the plays, and thus contribute to what Bourdieu calls the 'consecration' of the artist.[5] The festivals in Oslo and Dhaka share this trait, as they also have in common that they contribute to cultural exchange, in bringing 'foreign' productions of the same playwright into a local situation. These two festivals are dedicated to a single dramatist, and more importance is normally attributed to the general international festival circuit – be it in Avignon, Berlin or Adelaide. And it would be disingenuous to deny that the access to the international festival system is easier for artists coming from global centres of economic and cultural capital. Hence one would not be surprised to see productions from major European theatres like the Schaubühne at major theatre festivals. The same is the case with an avant-garde company with tons of cultural capital and equally small (or varying) amounts of economic capital, like the off-Broadway theatre company Mabou Mines from New York. Established in 1970 – by JoAnne Akalaitis, Philip Glass, Ruth Maleczech, Lee Breuer and David Warrilow – Mabou Mines has become something of a contradiction in terms, a long-running (more than forty years practically qualifies to be called permanent) avant-garde theatre institution, known for its innovative work with the most diverse materials, from cartoons to epic poetry, from Shakespeare to Beckett.[6] In November 2003, their *DollHouse* premiered at St Ann's Warehouse in Brooklyn, directed by Lee Breuer who adapted the play together with Maude Mitchell (who also played Nora). It was immensely successful, had great reviews, has had a very long run in New York, and has visited thirty-three different places, in the United States, Europe, Australia and Asia. The Mabou Mines' *DollHouse* is in fact second only to Ostermeier's version of the same play in terms of tours and guest performances of an Ibsen production. It has not been performed on stage since 2011, but a full-length film version of the production was made in France (Arte TV France) in 2008, which has been broadcast throughout most of Europe and is available on DVD.

The Mabou Mines' own description of the opening of the production points to its decisive and defining traits: 'Nora comes home with a Christmas present. It is a dollhouse so large that the children can play inside. [...] Enter Torvald, Rank and Krogstad – we find that the men are the same size as the children.'[7] First, what becomes the set, walls, door, windows, is unpacked and folded out on stage by Nora and the maid, Helene (Margaret Lancaster), and is, like everything else on stage, double: simultaneously a meta-dramatic device, stating that 'this is art' and not 'reality', and at the same time a presentation of realistic everyday life. From the outset the production vacillates between the two modes; meta-dramatic estrangement and a realistic mirror effect. Second, this set and furniture fits perfectly for people who are around four feet, which is the actual height of the male actors on stage. The female characters, however, are close to six feet, and made to look even taller. The casting, in combination with the stage design, constantly makes the point that the social world of the stage reality is made to fit the men only; they move effortlessly around and sit comfortably in chairs and sofas, while the women crawl around to get through doors or sit on their knees to be of the same height as the men during conversation. In the words of the Mabou Mines' homepage again: 'Ibsen's feminism is metaphorically rendered as a parable of scale.' Had it not been for the extraordinary quality of the acting (and the intelligence of the adaptation), this would probably have been nothing but the driest of parables, an abstract point without life. But life, and the playfulness of fun, is one of the basic characteristics of this production. The extreme difference in body size, for instance, is obviously used to express many serious political and existential points, but it is also an occasion for a lot of comedy. This is also the case when it comes to the very acting style(s) of the production, which may be described as a constant shifting between realism, melodrama and Brechtian *Verfremdung*, often accompanied by a piano played on stage by Ning Yu.[8] All the actors speak with a strangely exaggerated kind of Scandinavian accent, the women in a high-pitched overly 'feminine' voice, the men in a dark 'manly' voice. The comic elements are funny, but always more than just fun. One small incident that could exemplify this strangely successful mixture is the scene towards the end of the play where Kristine Linde (Janet Girardeau) has her last conversation with the Helmers, and Thorvald (Mark Povinelli) lectures her on the aesthetic relation between knitting and embroidery. The latter is an elegant and graceful activity, while the former 'can never be anything but ugly', he says, and concludes with emphasis that knitting has 'something very *Chinese* about it'. Upon hearing this the pianist, Ning Yu slams down the fallboard and jumps to her feet about to run out in protest, but Helmer holds her back while Nora explains to her that 'it's in the text', and in the film version we actually get to see this very page in a Norwegian version of the text. She accepts this explanation and returns to her place at the piano.

According to Maude Mitchell, this moment in the production 'consistently gets the biggest laugh in the show'.[9] The occasion for Helmer's words about knitting in this version is that he hurts his behind by inadvertently sitting down on the sofa where Kristine has left her knitting, and the scene combines bodily and intellectual humour. But it also makes a number of serious points: behind the surface of this civilised middle-class man there lurks not only a strangely repressive aesthetics, but also sexism and racism. The very oddness of the 'excuse', and the social pressure established as the whole cast freezes, looking at

Ning Yu, also stages how victims of racism are often forced to 'take it' and not make a fuss. Equally characteristic of the production is that this is also a distinctly meta-dramatic moment, where the illusion breaks down as the actor points to the text outside the performance. Through its very irrelevance as an excuse for a racist remark, it also points to the authority of the text, which this production both respects and disrespects. Hence it also points to the ideology (or blind spots) of the text itself, which is not necessarily liberating in every respect, and the fact that it is Nora who excuses Helmer's remark may point to some limitations in her own perspective and liberation. In other words, it is both funny on a very basic level, while simultaneously having the Brechtian quality of making the spectator reflect on the relation to his or her own political context of everyday life.

Size clearly matters in this production, and the highly unusual difference in size between the men and women on stage is utilised to make a number of important points. The most fundamental is that the play between these bodies clearly displays that power relations are not based on any kind of natural order or fact (such as bodily size or strength), and that our social world is adapted to men and men's needs. That they succeed in making this point so effectively does in my view have more to do with acting style than actor size. Maude Mitchell as Nora makes the point that she is playing the role of woman through an acting style that constantly shifts between naturalism, melodrama and a very Brechtian distancing, a *gestus* that shows distance to the acting. She plays 'small', 'weak', 'beautiful', 'helpless', 'seductive', etc. in an ostentatious way which points to the performing itself. The effect, however, is not that the spectator can withdraw and enjoy the position of superior reflection from the outside, because the acting, 'unreal' and 'exaggerated', is also realistic in the sense that it closes the distance between Ibsen's nineteenth-century reality and the spectator's twenty-first century reality. Simultaneous estrangement and recognition might be a way of describing the effect. And this effect is maybe even stronger in regard to the male actors. They are able to perform their roles as 'men' with complete absorption all the way into gestures of exaggeration in a manner that makes them appear as vain posers, pure acts, while at the same time completely honest and authentic in their groundless, self-absorbed pompousness. Mark Povinelli, Ricardo Gil (Dr Rank) and Kristopher Medina (Krogstad) are extraordinary actors with the ability to bring out an extreme range of possibilities in the male characters; psychologically realistic and completely absorbed, while at the same time theatrically distanced they performed the melodrama, the humour, the vulnerability, the violence and the sordid sexuality in Ibsen's male characters almost effortlessly. And in the end they display to the full how egoistic and masturbatory (in more than one sense) this patriarchal masculinity is, while the performance is taken far out of any straightforward realism and into operatic meta- and melodrama. Nora and Thorvald's last dialogue is performed as an opera duet, with Nora throwing off her wig and clothes facing a new future outside of the dollhouse, but still completely within art – there is no naïve attempt to point towards a future or a social reality outside of the work of art here.

Adrisha Paap and Mabou Mines' *DollHouse*, then. What could be the point of bringing these two together in this last chapter? Apart from them being artistically and, I would say, politically successful, what do they have in common? Neither of them is realistic in the traditional sense. Both productions bring one of Ibsen's naturalistic plays into theatrical forms that do not have the realism effect as their main purpose. One puts Ibsen's narrative into Kushan Gan, the other mixes Stanislavskyan acting with Brechtian modes of epic drama. What these two productions share is, in other words, the fact that they are equally local to their cultural origin and background. One reason for my bringing them together is to be able to make the point that they are equally provincial. The Mabou Mines' *DollHouse* is certainly more central in a strictly geopolitical sense of power and economy, but not in artistic or cultural terms. The preceding two or three pages are also written as a self-reflexive pointing back to my introductory emphasis on my own cultural situation, because one of these productions is so infinitely much more strange to me. Hence I could go on and on about the Mabou Mines production, whereas I would soon run out of words about *Adrisha Paap*. This has to do with me, not the production, just as the fact that *Adrisha Paap* will never be invited to the Ibsen Festival has to do with the festival and its audience. And conversely, the Mabou Mines will never succeed should they wish to perform in a village in Rangpur. Cultural specificity or difference, in other words, matters in so many respects, or relations. These relational differences have been my main concern in much of this book, and in this diversity itself lies a conclusion of sorts.

Notes

Introduction

1 Pierre Bourdieu, *The Rules of Art. Genesis and Structure of the Literary Field*, Susan Emanuel (trans.), Cambridge: Polity Press, 1996, p. 171.
2 Knut Brynhildsvoll and Atle Kittang, 'Preface', *Ibsen Studies*, Vol. IV, No. 2 (2004), pp. 121–2.
3 On the denial of equal value, see Johannes Fabian, *Time and the Other. How Anthropology Makes its Object*, New York: Columbia University Press, 1983.
4 Edward Said, *Culture and Imperialism*, p. 65.

Chapter 1

1 Thomas Ostermeier, 'Ob es so oder so oder anders geht! Ein Gespräch mit den (zukünftigen) Theaterleitern Stefan Bachmann, Mathias Hartmann und Thomas Ostermeier', *Theaterheute. Jahrbuch 1999* (Hannover: Friedrich Verlag, 1999), p. 76.
2 Thomas Ostermeier, Sasha Waltz, Jochen Sandig and Jens Hilje, 'Der Auftrag', http://www.schaubuehne.de/uploads/Der-Auftrag.pdf [accessed May 2014].
3 The others, in addition to *A Doll's House*, are: *The Master Builder* (Burgtheater, Vienna, 2004); *Hedda Gabler* (Schaubühne, Berlin, 2005); *John Gabriel Borkmann* (Schaubühne, Berlin, 2008); two versions of *Ghosts* (at Stadsschouwburg, Amsterdam in 2011, and in 2013 at Théâtre Vidy, Lausanne) and *An Enemy of the People* (Schaubühne, Berlin, 2012).
4 The Schaubühne stopped performing *Nora* when the lead actress, Anne Tismer, left the company in 2008; *Borkmann* was on the repertoire from January 2009 to June 2011. *Hedda Gabler* and *An Enemy of the People* are still on the repertoire and tour regularly.
5 Estimate based on figures given to me by the Schaubühne, covering performances to 31 December 2013.
6 See https://ibsenstage.hf.uio.no

7 Prominent Norwegian directors such as Eirik Stubø and Alexander
   Mørk-Eidem have for example made versions of *Hedda Gabler* where the
   influence from Ostermeier and the Schaubühne is clear enough.

8 Having said that it is important to point out that German theatre has
   had its own dose of budget cuts, and there has been much talk of an
   ongoing 'crisis' in the country's theatre. Compared to other countries,
   however, German theatre must be considered extremely well funded.
   For a short introduction to this discussion see David Ashley Hughes,
   'Notes on the German Theatre Crisis', *The Drama Review*, Vol. 51,
   No. 4 (Winter 2007).

9 Anja Dürrschmidt (ed.), *Dem Einzelnen ein Ganzes/A Whole for the Parts.*
   Jan Pappelbaum Bühnen/Stages (Berlin: Theater der Zeit, 2006), p. 162

10 See Michel Foucault, *Discipline and Punish*, Alan Sheridan (trans.)
   (London: Penguin Books, 1987), p. 195ff.

11 Schüttler won Germany's Der Faust Award for best theatre actor and
   the Theater Heute prize for 'Actress of the Year' for the role of Hedda
   in 2006.

12 Løvborg, however, comes from real wealth and is above this kind of
   necessity; he can afford to let Tesman get the job, only to humiliate him all
   the more in the public eye.

13 As Slavoj Zizek puts it in *Living in the End Times* (London: Verso, 2010),
   p. 3: 'if there is an ideological experience at its purest, at its zero-level, then
   it occurs the moment we adopt an attitude of ironic distance, laughing at
   the follies in which we are ready to believe – it is at this moment of
   liberating laughter, when we look down on the absurdity of our faith, that
   we become pure subjects of ideology, that ideology exerts its strongest
   hold over us.'

14 For Hedda, this quality extends even to nature itself. When she pretends
   to show Løvborg photos from her honeymoon, she asks Tesman the
   name of the 'komischen Gipfel' (comical mountain peak). The mountains
   are no longer sublime or beautiful; they are comical, ridiculous, kitsch.

15 Oxfam, 'A Cautionary Tale. The true cost of austerity and inequality
   in Europe', http://www.oxfam.org/sites/www.oxfam.org/files/bp174-
   cautionary-tale-austerity-inequality-europe-120913-en_1.pdf
   [accessed September 2013].

16 See Richard G. Wilkinson and Kate Pickett, *The Spirit Level: Why more
   Equal Societies almost always do Better* (London: Allen Lane, 2009).

17 See Charles Spencer, 'Hedda Gabler: Shocking then, shocking now', *Telegraph*, 29 February 2008, http://www.telegraph.co.uk/culture/theatre/ drama/3671492/Hedda-Gabler-Shocking-then-shocking-now.html [accessed 24 January 2014]. It is hard not to think that gender comes into play in the many harsh critiques of the Hedda figure in this performance, as when Spencer, in common with some other male reviewers, continues 'that Hedda gets exactly what she deserves'.

18 Ibsen's Norwegian word 'makt' does not carry these explicitly violent connotations, but means 'power' or 'force'. Since 'makt' also exists in German as 'Macht', the choice of 'Gewalt' in the performance is significant.

19 *The Oxford Ibsen: The Lady From the Sea, Hedda Gabler, The Master Builder*, Vol. VII, James Walter McFarlane (ed. and trans.) (London: Oxford University Press, 1966), p. 268.

20 The most recent example is probably Franco Moretti, who in *The Bourgeois* characterises *An Enemy of the People* as 'Ibsen's only mediocre play' (London: Verso, 2013), p. 175.

21 Arthur Miller, *An Enemy of the People. An adaptation of the play by Henrik Ibsen* (New York: Penguin Books, 1979 [1950]), p. 10. For an impressive study of Ibsen's reception in Nazi Germany, see Uwe Englert, *Magus und Rechenmeister. Henrik Ibsens Werk auf den Bühnen des Dritten Reiches* (Tübingen: Francke Verlag, 2001).

22 The Invisible Committee, *The Coming Insurrection* (Cambridge MA: Semiotext(e), MIT Press, 2009), based on the expanded edition from 2009. The quote above is from pp. 32–3 in the English version.

23 The programme is a small book of seventy-seven pages. In addition to the extract from *The Coming Insurrection*, it contains a few pages from Colin Crouch's *Post-Democracy* (Cambridge: Polity Press, 2004); some letters from Ibsen in which he writes about the play; an extract from Michael Raab's essay 'In Jedem steckt ein Volksfeind' in *Amüsement und Schrecken*, Mennemeier and Reitz (eds) (Tübingen: Francke Verlag, 2006); Steven F. Sage's *Ibsen and Hitler* (New York: Avalon, 2006); David Brooks' *Bobos in Paradise. The New Upper Class and How They Got There* (New York: Simon and Schuster, 2000); and Ingo Schulze's 'Sich selbst wieder Ernst nehmen' *Süddeutsche Zeitung*, 12 January 2012, http://ingoschulze.com/text_ Sichselbstwieder.html [accessed September 2013].

24 Stockmann's speech starts and ends with Ibsen's text, but within this frame we find a fluent text consisting of bits and pieces from *The Coming*

Insurrection carefully sutured together; one paragraph from p. 92, followed
by others from pp. 29, 30, 32, 33, 34, 40, 41, 63, 68, 78 and 94.

25 Daniel Freitag, 'ein volksfeind' (thomas ostermeier) [sic],
    http://danielfreitag.com/track/ein-volksfeind-thomas-ostermeier
    [accessed October 2013].

26 I have seen the production twice in Berlin (Winter 2013) and once in
    Istanbul (May 2014).

27 *The Oxford Ibsen: An Enemy of the People, The Wild Duck, Rosmersholm*,
    Vol. VI, James Walter McFarlane (ed. and trans.) (London: Oxford
    University Press, 1960), p. 95.

28 The literal meaning of the German 'Nazi-Keule' is 'Nazi-club', meaning that
    the accusation of Nazi affinity is used to neutralise or knock an opponent
    down in a discussion; it is mostly used by the political right in German
    public life.

29 Ostermeier in personal interview, Oslo, 25 March 2014.

30 There are, however, reports to the opposite effect: in Buenos Aires, the
    attacks on the authorities, on stage and in the auditorium, became violent
    and some members of the audience physically tried to prevent Billing and
    Hovstad from throwing the water balloons at Stockmann.

31 See Thomas Ostermeier, 'Reading and Staging Ibsen' in *Ibsen Studies*,
    Vol. X, No. 2 (2010), p. 68ff, or in a very different perspective, Moretti,
    The Bourgeois, p. 169ff.

32 Schaubühne does document the public meetings on video, but I have not
    had access to these materials.

33 Charles Isherwood, 'An Ibsen who Rages over Ritalin and Economic
    Austerity Plans', *New York Times*, 7 November 2013. Jason Farago in the
    New Republic (18 November 2013), however, was excited and concluded
    that the production was 'depressingly relevant'.

34 Thomas Ostermeier told me this story during our conversations on 24 and
    25 March 2014.

35 Thomas Ostermeier, 'Die Zukunft des Theaters' in *TEXT + KRITIK.
    Zeitschrift für Literatur. Sonderband* (Richard Boorberg Verlag, Munich,
    2013).

36 Thomas Ostermeier, 'Reading and Staging . . .', p. 71.

37 Wolfgang Streeck, 'The Crises of Democratic Capitalism', *New Left Review*,
    No. 71 (September–October 2001), p. 6. See also *Post-Democracy* by Colin

Crouch (mentioned above, n. 23) or Peter Mair's different approach in *Ruling the Void. The Hollowing of Western Democracy* (London: Verso, 2013).

38 John Nichols and Robert W. McChesney, *Dollarocracy: How the Money and Media Election Complex is Destroying America* (New York: Nation Books, 2013).

Chapter 2

1 For a cold assessment of American involvement in the coup, see United States Senate Report, *Covert Action in Chile 1963–1973* (Washington DC: US Government Printing Office, 18 December 1975); Peter Kornbluh, *The Pinochet File: A Declassified Dossier on Atrocity and Accountability* (New York: The New Press, 2003); and Oscar Guardiola-Rivera, *Story of a Death Foretold: The Coup against Salvador Allende, 11 September 1973* (London: Bloomsbury, 2013).

2 The same CIA report estimates that 'more than 13,500 Chilean citizens had been quickly rounded up through raids and mass arrests aimed at officials of the deposed Popular Unity government, political activists, labour unions, factory workers and shantytown dwellers' (Kornbluh, *The Pinochet File*, p. 153). They were held at detention centres, sports stadiums and camps throughout the country where many were tortured and, not least important, all were witnesses to torture and the effects of torture.

3 Marco Antonio de la Parra, quoted in Naomi Klein, *The Shock Doctrine: The Rise of Disaster Capitalism* (London: Penguin, 2007), p. 111.

4 André Gunder Frank, *Economic Genocide in Chile: Monetarist Theory versus Humanity* (Nottingham: Spokesman Books, 1976).

5 See Eladio Cortés and Mirta Barrea-Marlys, *Encyclopedia of Latin American Theater* (Westport CN: Greenwood Press, 2003), p. 93.

6 Grinor Rojo, 'Chilean Theatre from 1957 to 1987', *Theatre Journal*, Vol. 41 (1989), p. 529.

7 The University of Chile was operating but strongly weakened as a result of having been targeted during the coup itself and afterwards: 'on 11 September 1973, the University of Chile's Drama School was shelled by army tanks, and a pyre was lit in its main hall with the store of props,

scenery, and costumes' (Enzo Cozzi, 'Political Theatre in Present-day Chile: a Duality of Approaches', *New Theatre Quarterly*, Vol. VI (1990), p. 119). Later on 'the military dismissed the entire faculty and expelled half of the student body' (Rojo, 'Chilean Theatre', p. 529).

8 Cozzi, 'Political Theatre', p. 123.

9 Juan Andrés Piña, personal interview, Santiago, 6 May 2013. See also Catherine M. Boyle, *Chilean Theater, 1973–1985: Marginality, Power, Selfhood* (London and Toronto: Fairleigh Dickinson University Press, 1992), p. 50ff.

10 The following discussion is built on the script, contemporary reviews, programme, photos of the performance, sketches and drawings for stage design and costumes, in addition to interviews with the following participants in the performance itself: Alejandro Castillo (director), Elsa Poblete (Nora), Hector Noguera (Helmer), Sergio Zapata (costume designer), the critic Piña, and Professor Maria de la Luz Hurtado who also acted as dramaturge for the performance.

11 In preparing for the performance the company did, however, discuss more topical aspects of the play. The director, Alejandro Castillo, told me that they had 'invented' a new kind of backstory for the Krogstad role, in which his past transgression was not to have forged a signature but to have been involved in an anarcho-syndicalist organisation.

12 Matteo Iribarren, personal interview, Santiago, 8 May 2013.

13 *La Nación*, Santiago, 27 September 1980.

14 Elsa Poblete, personal interview, Santiago, 7 May 2013.

15 Cf. Julieta Kirkwood, 'Women and Politics in Chile', *International Social Science Journal*, Vol. 35 (1983), p. 629ff; and Ana Corina Toledo, *Partizipation von Frauen während der Militärdiktatur in Chile (1973–1990)* (Spektrum Politikwissenschaft, Würtzburg: Ergon Verlag, 2001), p. 126ff.

16 Quoted in Patricia M. Chuchryk, 'From Dictatorship to Democracy: The Women's Movement in Chile', *The Women's Movement in Latin America. Participation and Democracy*, Jane S. Jaquette (ed.) (Boulder CO: Westview Press, 1994), p. 75.

17 This point was emphasised by Elsa Poblete and Maria de la Luz Hurtado during my interviews with them.

18 Cf. Toledo: *Partizipation von Frauen . . .*, p. 135ff.

19 Ian Watson and Susana Epstein, 'Theatre after the Dictatorships: Developments in Chile and Argentina', *New Theatre Quarterly*, Vol. XI (1995).

20 Watson and Epstein: 'Theatre after the Dictatorships', p. 43.

21 Watson and Epstein: 'Theatre after the Dictatorships', p. 45.

22 See David Harvey *The New Imperialism* (Oxford and New York: Oxford University Press, 2003); Duncan Green, *Silent Revolution: The Rise and Crisis of Market Economics in Latin America* (New York: Monthly Review Press, 2003), pp. 104ff., 112ff., 158; and Donald L. Huddle, 'Effects of Neoliberalism on Latin American Development and Poverty: Two Conflicting Views', *Economic Development and Cultural Change*, Vol. 45, No. 4 (1997).

23 Green, *Silent Revolution*, p. 158.

24 The continued presence of the painful memories of dictatorship, and the newer pressures of life under a brutal capitalism where 'only money counts', were recurring themes in almost all of my interviews with theatre artists in Chile.

25 Nelly Richard: *Cultural Residues: Chile in Transition* (Minneapolis MN: University of Minnesota Press, 2004), p. 112.

26 For a short discussion of Castro's testimonial theatre, see Nelly Richard, *The Insubordination of Signs. Political Change, Cultural Transformation, and Poetics of the Crisis*, Alice A. Nelson and Silvia R. Tandeciarz (trans.) (Durham, London: Duke University Press, 2004), pp. 19–21; and Catherine Boyle: 'Violence in Memory: Translation, Dramatisation and Performance of the Past in Chile' in Anny Brooksbank Jones and Ronaldo Munck (eds): *Cultural Politics in Latin America* (London: Palgrave Macmillan, 2000), p. 108ff.

27 The following discussion is based on reviews and articles, stage photos, a high-quality DVD recording of the performance, the script and interviews with Alfredo Castro, Amparo Noguera (Nora), Marcelo Alonso (Krogstad), Matteo Iribarren (Rank), Mireya Moreno (Elena), and several theatre artists and scholars who saw the performance.

28 Trying to chart Amparo Noguera's movements on stage becomes an almost impossible task. Counting only major bodily movements, and disregarding waving hands, kicking feet in the air, leaning backwards or forwards, etc., Nora moves forty-eight times during the first twelve-minute conversation with Kristine Linde (Taira Court). Compared to Kristine's ten body movements (many of which are initiated by Nora), this shows how agile, nervous and erratic Nora appears to be from the beginning.

29 *Oxford Ibsen*, Vol. V, p. 201.

30 See Pamela Constable and Arturo Valenzuela, *A Nation of Enemies* (New York and London: W.W. Norton & Company, 1991).

31 'The official consensus of the Transition [...] eliminated historical memory from the socio-political consensus, that is, the memory of a past judged inconvenient by the interpretive wars it continues to unleash between truths and unsettled positions in conflict,' Richard, *Cultural Residues*, p. 16.

32 *Oxford Ibsen*, Vol. V, p. 336.

33 Alfredo Castro, personal interview, 10 May 2013.

34 Unless I am misreading the visual signs and the body language, there are hints of a different sexual orientation in Perez's Rank figure. While the other men wear conservative men's clothes, Rank is dressed in black, but with red sneakers and a white belt. When he finally appears in drag, wearing a cute little pink hat, he dresses up as a woman, thereby introducing the figure of the transvestite into the action. His body language throughout is also more 'feminine' than that of the other men on stage, and the private encounters between him and Nora are asexual, intimate but not erotic, as in a friendship between a gay man and a straight woman. I do not think that this is spelled out, but there are invitations to a reading along these lines in the production (and in the contrast to the stiff, almost armoured masculinity of the 2006 production) – a reading that could complicate things further and bring added layers of meaning to the play and Rank's character.

35 Marvin Carlson, 'Ibsen in the Americas', *Ibsen News and Comment: The Journal of The Ibsen Society of America*, Vol. 32 (2012), p. 7. See also Fernanda Carvajal and Camila van Diest, 'Teatro la Maria: Filiaciones inciertas y orquestaciones de la violencia' in Carvajal and van Diest, *Nomadismos y Ensamblajes: Compañías teatrales en Chile 1990–2008* (Santiago: Editorial Cuarto Propio, 2009).

36 Alexandra von Hummel, personal interview, 9 May 2013.

37 Alexandra von Hummel: *Persiguendo a Nora Helmer. Adaptation of 'A Doll's House'* (unpublished script), pp. 6–7.

38 Interview with Alexandra von Hummel, Tamara Acosta (Nora) and Alejandra Oviedo (Kristine Linde). Interestingly, they also claimed that a man would be far less likely to talk to women in this way in public, due to norms of chivalry towards women.

39 Nelly Richard, 'Gender Contortions and Sexual Doubling: Transvestite Parody' in *Masculine/Feminine: Practices of Difference(s)* (Durham: Duke University Press, 2004), p. 43.

40 Senator Adolfo Zaldívar in the leading newspaper *El Mercurio*, August 1995 (quoted from Nelly Richard: *Cultural Residues*, p. 136). The same year, the Chilean Senate majority rejected the policies of the state-funded 'National Women's Service' for 'not being sufficiently categorical in their defence of the family as an institution and as "the basic cell of society", founded "in the monogamous and stable union of a man and a woman in matrimony"', (Richard, *Cultural Residues*, p. 134).

41 Different kinds of music that accompanies the performance much of the time contributes to the post-dramatic effect. This effect is further strengthened in this scene through the discrepancy between the lines uttered by Rank and Linde on the one hand, and the dance on the other.

42 Alexandra von Hummel stated in our conversation that cross-dressing made the male actors look even more virile to her, and that the effect was not to feminise them.

43 Quoted from Richard, *Masculine/Feminine*, pp. 50–51.

44 Marvin Carlson, 'Ibsen in the Americas', p. 9.

45 Nora: 'I'll often think about you and the children [...] May I write to you? [...] I said 'no' [... It would take a] 'a miracle [...] would have to change to the point where ...', *Oxford Ibsen*, Vol. V, p. 286.

46 Nelly Richard: *The Insubordination of Signs* ...

Chapter 3

1 See for instance Julian Petley, *Censorship: A Beginner's Guide* (Oxford: Oneworld Publications, 2009).

2 For a discussion of the history of censorship in British theatre see for example Dominic Shellard, Steve Nicholson and Miriam Handley, *The Lord Chamberlain Regrets ... A History of British Theatre Censorship* (London: The British Library, 2004); and Nicholas de Jongh, *Politics, Prudery and Perversions: The Censoring of the British Stage 1901–1968* (London: Methuen, 2000).

3 Perhaps the clearest example of this strategy in recent history is to be found in apartheid South Africa, where massive censorship generally was put to work in the service of 'public morals'. See J. M. Coetzee, *Giving Offense: Essays on Censorship* (Chicago IL: Chicago University Press, 1996); and Peter D. McDonald, *The Literature Police: Apartheid Censorship and its Cultural Consequences* (Oxford: Oxford University Press, 2009).

4 This is the subject of articles in Caridad Svich (ed.), *Out of Silence: Censorship in Theatre and Performance* (Roskilde: Eyecorner Press, 2012).

5 For an interesting attempt to distinguish between 'Constituent and Regulative Censorships', see Sue Curry Jansen, *Censorship: The Knot That Binds Power and Knowledge* (London: Oxford University Press, 1991).

6 J. M. Coetzee: *Giving Offense*, pp. VII–X.

7 The production was directed by Le Hung and staged at the Youth Theatre, Hanoi. The role of Nora was performed by star Vietnamese actress Lê Khanh, who has featured in many films and is known internationally. I saw the performance in November 2006.

8 See Farindokht Zahedi, *Henrik Ibsen and Iranian Modern Drama. Reception and Influence* (University of Oslo: Unpublished Phd. thesis, 2006).

9 In Zahedi, *Henrik Ibsen*, p. 171, Nejad tells a sinister story from his time in jail: 'One day while I was standing in my cell watching the newcomers, a young man passing my cell saw me through the bars and shouted "Long live Dr Stockmann," after which he was immediately dragged to a cell and beaten by the jailer for his outburst.'

10 Hamid Dabashi, *Close Up. Iranian Cinema, Past, Present and Future* (London: Verso, 2001), pp. 43 and 215.

11 The story is taken from Gholamhossein Sa'edi's *Azadaran-e Bayal* (The Mourners of Bayal, 1964) (Dabashi, *Close Up*, p. 215).

12 Richard Tapper: 'Introduction' in Tapper (ed.), *The New Iranian Cinema. Politics, Representation and Identity* (New York and London: I.B. Tauris, 2002), p. 4.

13 For a full list of prohibitions and an interesting discussion of their effect, see Hamid Reza Sadr, *Iranian Cinema: A Political History* (London and New York: I. B. Tauris, 2006), p. 108ff.

14 Cf. Gönül Dönmez-Colin: *Women, Islam and Cinema* (London: Reaktion Books, 2004).

15 Shahla Mirbakhtyar, *Iranian Cinema and the Islamic Revolution* (Jefferson NC and London: McFarlane and Company Publishers, 2006), p 114.

16 There may be very obvious and specifically local Iranian reasons for the silence about Ibsen in the film, since using Western thinkers, artists or ideas, especially concerning the question of women, have proved to be potentially counterproductive in the local context, because it can very easily be construed as support for Western cultural imperialism. See Nima Naghibi, *Rethinking Global Sisterhood. Western Feminism and Iran* (Minneapolis MN: University of Minnesota Press, 2007), pp. 74–107.

17 Worth special mention in addition to *Sara* are films such as *Banu* (1992), *Pari* (1994), *Leylah* (1997) and *Bemani* (2002).

18 A further significant accusation in Hessam's diatribe against Sara, which departs from what Helmer says, is the implication of adultery when Hessam asks: 'What did he [Goshtasb] get in return to agree to loan you the money?' Sara's angry, despairing outburst, 'Shame on you!' seems to calm his nerves but Sara does not forget the accusation and she hints at it again in the final scene when she talks about how Helmer has disappointed her. This is the only clear hint at sexuality in the film.

19 See Nikki R. Keddie, *Modern Iran: Roots and Results of Revolution* (New Haven CT: Yale University Press, 2006), p. 100: 'in 1936 women were ordered to unveil and dress in Western-style clothing. Some women saw this as equivalent to going out naked and refused to leave their homes, as gendarmes sometimes tore chadors from women on the streets.'

20 See for example Julie Holledge and Joanne Tompkins, *Women's Intercultural Performance* (London: Routledge, 2000), p. 36ff; and Rochelle Wright, 'Ibsen Transcreation in Iran and India', *TijdSchrift voor Skandinavistiek*, Vol. 27, No. 2 (2006).

21 Ziba Mir-Hosseini emphasises from her feminist point of view that what has taken place in Iran since the revolution is not that women have been 'excluded from public life and politics but [that] their participation has actually increased, although in different guises and according to different rules. Paradoxically, the enforcement of *hijab* became a catalyst here: by making public space morally correct in the eyes of traditionalist families, it legitimized women's public presence.' Ziba Mir-Hosseini, *Islam and Gender. The Religious Debate in Contemporary Iran* (Princeton NJ: Princeton University Press, 1999), p. 7.

22 For an account of the complexity of these issues, see Naghibi, *Rethinking Global Sisterhood*, pp. 35–73.

23 'As the history of Western women makes clear, there is no validity to the notion that progress for women can be achieved only by abandoning the ways of a native androcentric culture in favour of those of another culture. It has never been argued, for instance, even by the most ardent nineteenth-century feminist, that European women could liberate themselves from the oppressiveness of Victorian dress ... only by adopting the dress of some other culture. Nor has it ever been argued ... that because male domination and injustice to women have existed throughout the West's recorded history, the only recourse for Western women is to abandon Western culture and find themselves some other culture.' Leila Ahmed, *Women and Gender in Islam: Historical Roots of a Modern Debate* (New Haven CT and London: Yale University Press, 1992), p. 244.

24 'Since women in films have to don the *chador* or other Islamic cover, their portrayal is unrealistic, as they are shown covering themselves from close kin, which in real life they would not do.' Hamid Naficy, 'Islamising Film Culture in Iran: A Post-Khatami Update' in Tapper, *The New Iranian Cinema*, 2002, p. 47. See also Shahla Lahiji, 'Chaste Dolls: Women in Iranian Cinema since 1979', *The New Iranian Cinema*, p. 215ff.

25 For a further reading of this scene, see Holledge and Tompkins, *Women's Intercultural Performance*, p. 40.

26 *Women's Intercultural Performance*, p. 40ff.

27 In his classic production of the play, *Putul Khela*, in Calcutta in 1952, Shombhu Mitra chose to have the 'Nora' character recite Rabindranath Tagore's poem 'Jhulon' ('Swinging') instead of dancing the tarantella.

28 I am grateful to Behzad Ghaderi, former professor at Tehran University, for helping me to understand the significance of the dance and music in the film.

29 This ambiguity is especially conspicuous in Patrick Garland's film with Claire Bloom in the role of Nora, but it is also apparent in Joseph Losey's version with Jane Fonda in the leading role. The problem is to some extent rooted in the nature of the medium. In film close-ups, the camera dwells on the female figure. To put this differently, some film versions of *A Doll's House* make very clear how essential the presence of Helmer and Rank on stage is in Ibsen. Through the introduction of this play-within-the-play, the audience reaction is mirrored on stage. A particular repressive and insensitive view of Nora is called to the audience's attention by being demonstrated on the stage.

30 Cf. Julie Holledge: 'The Global Phenomenon of *A Doll's House*', *Ibsen Studies*, Vol. VIII, No. 1 (2008), p. 21ff.

31 Gayatri Chakravorty Spivak, 'Can the Subaltern Speak?' in Cary Nelson and Lawrence Grossberg (eds), *Marxism and Culture* (Urbana, Chicago IL: University of Illinois Press, 1988), p. 296.

32 Willem Floor, *The History of Theater in Iran* (Washington DC: Mage Publishers, 2005), p. 13.

33 See Hamid Reza Sadr: *Iranian Cinema. A Political History* (London and New York: Tauris, 2006).

34 Mahmood Karimi-Hakak tells the story of his staging of *A Midsummer Night's Dream* in Tehran in 'Exiled to Freedom: A Memoir of Censorship in Iran', *The Drama Review*, Vol. 47, No. 4 (Winter 2003), pp. 17–50. It took him a full five years to get all the necessary permissions, and still the show was closed after four nights and the director prosecuted for 'Raping the Public's Innocence', a charge he escaped by fleeing into exile.

35 Cf. (unknown), 'Iranian "Hedda Gabler" deemed "vulgar, hedonistic"', *Daily Star*, Lebanon, 14 January 2011, http://www.dailystar.com.lb/article. asp?edition_id=10&categ_id=4&article_id=123612#axzz1Es5wxZoC [accessed February 2011]; and Mostagim, R. and Sandels, A., 'IRAN: Police descend on Tehran theater, suspend classic play "Hedda Gabler"', *Los Angeles Times*, 15 January 2011, http://latimesblogs.latimes.com/ babylonbeyond/2011/01/iran-theater-crackdown-ibsen-tehran-censorship. html [accessed February 2011].

36 Cf. *XIX Article 19. Global Campaign for Free Expression. 'Unveiled: Art and Censorship in Iran'*, London, September 2006, p. 28, http://www.article19. org/data/files/pdfs/publications/iran-art-censorship.pdf [accessed March 2011].

37 'In this seemingly neutral activity, the government gave the people what it wanted and it increased its support to cultural activities as well as higher subsidies to facilitate theatre visits. In fact, the subsidies increased by 1000 per cent between 1997 and 2001.' Floor, *The History of Theater in Iran*, 2005, p. 299.

38 I saw this performance during the International Ibsen Festival in Dhaka ('Ibsen through New Eyes') in November 2009.

39 The hijabs do not 'belong' with the otherwise completely Westernized costumes, but they do pertain to the specific circumstances in play here. They are strictly necessary because without them there could be no

performance; the censors would have stopped it immediately. The hijab points in this way to the presence of censorship in the theatre.

40 Nader Borhany Marand, *My Wild Duck*, Fereshteh Ghasempour (trans., unpublished manuscript).

41 4 May 1919 saw massive protests in Beijing against the decisions at the Versailles Peace Conference perceived as favouring Japan and not China, in spite of the fact that China had joined the allies. The May 4th Movement was a progressive, modernising movement that started among students but soon reached further in Chinese society: 'Nationalism, patriotism, progress, science, democracy, and freedom were the goals; imperialism, feudalism, warlordism, autocracy, patriarchy, and blind adherence to tradition were the enemies.' Patricia Buckley Ebrey, *The Cambridge Illustrated History of China* (Cambridge: Cambridge University Press, [1996]); here quoted from the 9th printing, 2007, p. 271.

42 See Elisabeth Eide, *China's Ibsen: From Ibsen to Ibsenism*, Scandinavian Institute of Asian Studies Monograph Series No. 55 (London: Curzon Press, 1987); and He Chengzhou, *Henrik Ibsen and Chinese Modern Drama* (University of Oslo, *Acta Humaniora*, 2002).

43 'Inspired and touched by the students' boldness and despaired by the aftermath that everyone lost their vitality, Lin was hoping to make Hamlet no longer a Renaissance giant, but an ordinary Beijing man in the late twentieth century facing a crucial moment.' Li Ruru, 'Six People in Search of "To be or not to be …"' in Poonam Trivedi and Minamai Ryuta (eds), *Re-playing Shakespeare in Asia* (New York: Routledge, 2010), p. 125.

44 I saw the performance on 6 September 2010 during the International Ibsen Festival at the National Theatre, Oslo.

45 Timothy Cheek, *Living With Reform: China Since 1989* (London and New York: Zed Books, 2006), p. 64.

46 Mao Tse-Tung, 'On the Correct Handling of Contradictions among the People' in *Selected Works of Mao Tse-Tung*, Vol. 5 (Peking: Foreign Languages Press, 1967); reprinted in Mao Tse-Tung, *On Practice and Contradiction*, intro. Slavoj Zizek (London: Verso, 2007), pp. 130–66.

47 Ebrey: *The Cambridge Illustrated History of China*, p. 307.

48 According to Patricia Buckley Ebrey, 'almost three million people were labelled "rightists", which assured that they would no longer have any real influence at work, even if they were allowed to continue in their previous

jobs. Half a million were sent to the countryside to overcome "separation from the masses" through manual labour among them'. *The Cambridge Illustrated History of China*, p. 307.

49 Publisher's note: Mao, *On Practice and Contradiction*, p. 130.

50 For a different take on the performance see Lin Wei-Yu, 'Master in Reflection: An Analysis of Lin Zhaoahua's *The Master Builder*' in Kwok-Kan Tam, Terry Siu-Han Yip and Frode Helland (eds), *Ibsen and the Modern Self* (Hong Kong: Open University of Hong King Press, 2010). Even if Lin Wei-Yu reads the performance as an introspective exploration of Solness's consciousness and self, and explicitly warns against reading it as a 'political statement', he is highly sensitive to the ideologico-political issues at stake in the performance, and he concludes by saying that the exploration of 'the process of introspection is most likely to lead to the emergence of an individual who is capable of independent thought, and thus capable of freeing the self from the governance of popular values and powerful ideologies ... [a] self like this cannot be dominated by a particular ideology to become a supporter of collectivism and patriarchy.' *Ibsen and the Modern Self*, pp. 293–4.

51 Peter Brooks, *Reading for the Plot: Design and Intention in Narrative* (New York: Random House, 1985), p. XI.

52 Derrida develops what he calls the logic of the supplement in his reading of Rousseau in *De la Grammatologie*. Central to his argument is the double character of the supplement, 'The supplement adds itself, it is a surplus, a plenitude enriching another plenitude, the *fullest measure* of presence ... But the supplement supplements. It adds only to replace ... Compensatory and vicarious, the supplement is an adjunct, a subaltern instance which *takes-(the)-place*. As substitute, it is not simply added to the positivity of a presence, it produces no relief, its place is assigned in the structure by the mark of emptiness ... The second signification of the supplement cannot be separated from the first.' Jacques Derrida, *Of Grammatology*, Gayatri Chakravorty Spivak (trans.) (Baltimore: Johns Hopkins University Press, 1976), pp. 144–5.

53 The word 'allegory' has its etymological roots in Greek '*allos* + *agoreuein* (*other* + *speak openly, speak in the assembly or market*)'. Angus Fletcher, *Allegory: The Theory of a Symbolic Mode* (Ithaca NY and London: Cornell University Press, 1993), p. 2.

54 Fletcher, *Allegory*, pp. 22–3.

Chapter 4

1   In fact, China experienced an ecological disaster during the hundred years
    leading up to the revolution in 1949, consisting of deforestation,
    destruction of irrigation and water supplies in combination with floods
    and droughts, further exacerbated by population growth without the 'safety
    valve' of emigration and colonisation that the Western countries had at
    their disposal during the same period. The different forces driving this
    process are discussed in some detail by Mike Davis in his *Late Victorian
    Holocausts* (London: Verso, 2001), where he refers to the calculation that
    China saw 'an absolute decline in irrigated cropland from 21.7 million
    hectares (or 29.4 per cent of the arable) in 1820 to 20 million hectares
    (18.5 per cent) in 1952' (p. 373).

2   See Chapter 3 above, p. 108.

3   See Elisabeth Eide, *Hu Shih and Ibsen. Ibsen's Influence in China 1917–1921
    as Seen through the Eyes of a Prominent Chinese Intellectual* (dissertation),
    University of Oslo, 1973.

4   He, *Henrik Ibsen and Chinese Modern Drama*, p. 11.

5   For a detailed analysis of this first phase in Chinese Ibsen reception, see in
    particular Kwok-Kan Tam, *Ibsen in China: Reception and Influence*, PhD
    thesis, Urbana IL: University of Illinois, 1984; Elisabeth Eide, *China's Ibsen.
    From Ibsen to Ibsenism*, Scandinavian Institute of Asian Studies
    Monograph Series No. 55 (London: Curzon Press, 1987); and He
    Chengzhou, *Henrik Ibsen and Chinese Modern Drama* (Oslo: Acta
    Humaniora, 2002).

6   I have not seen the three productions discussed in this chapter, and the
    goal will naturally not be to give any kind of performance analysis of them.
    As will become clear, the purpose in this chapter lies elsewhere, and I am
    very much aware of the fact that the materials I am analysing are not the
    performances themselves, but traces of them (manuscripts, reviews,
    photos, recordings, interviews with participants, etc.) and relevant
    contextual evidence.

7   Xiaomei Chen, *Occidentalism. A Theory of Counter-Discourse in Post-Mao
    China* (London: Rowman & Littlefield Publishers, 2002).

8   Torbjørn L. Knutsen, Gunnar M. Sørbø and Svein Gjerdåker (eds), *Norges
    Utenrikspolitikk* (Oslo: Cappelen, 1995), pp. 430; and Knut Einar Eriksen

and Helge Ø. Pharo, *Norsk utenrikspolitikks historie*, Vol. 5: *Kald krig og internasjonalisering 1949-1965* (Oslo: Universitetsforlaget, 1997), p. 395.

9 See Tam, *Ibsen in China*, p. 183.

10 See also Chapter 3 above, p. 112f.

11 Mao: 'On the Correct Handling of Contradictions . . .', 2007, p. 150.

12 Letter from Norwegian Embassy in Beijing, 20 October 1955, National Archive (NA), Oslo (UD, B485).

13 'By far the most spectacular contemporary international front organisation is that directed by the World Peace Council, a product of the Partisans of Peace movement [. . .] the World Peace Council purports to be "classless" and non-partisan; it tries to enlist the support of "all men of good will, regardless of race, nationality, political or religious connection." It has occupied a central position in Communist propaganda since 1949 [. . .] since the military strategy of the United States centred around its superiority in atomic weapons, it was to the USSR's advantage to create an atmosphere in which the use of the atomic bomb would be considered morally indefensible,' Bernard S. Morris, 'Communist Front Organisations: Their Nature and Function', *World Politics*, Vol. 9, No. 1 (October 1956), pp. 83-4.

14 'Han syntes ikke han kunne la være å gå, mens de øvrige (vestlige representanter) holdt seg vekk etter samråd med den britiske charge d'affaires som da hadde bestemte instrukser om ikke å møte på tilstelninger som ble arrangert i Fredsrådets navn' (NA, UD, B485).

15 'Det er vel heller grunn til å frykte at Ibsens diktning kan bli utnyttet i propagandaøyemed (f.eks. hans uttalelser mot prøysisk militarisme)' (NA, UD, B1622).

16 NA, B1622 ('arrangementer uten propagandapreg, f.eks. oppførelser av Ibsens skuespill').

17 Attached to the note there is a draft for a secret letter to the Norwegian delegation to NATO in Paris, where the problem is explained, with the concluding request that the delegation should bring the issue up in the Committee for Information and Cultural Exchange, 'so that the countries involved can exchange information about which guidelines they intend to follow' ('for at de interesserte land kan utveksle opplysninger om hvilke retningslinjer de akter å følge'), NA, UD, B1622.

18 NA, B485 ('stille seg reservert overfor eventuelle henvendelser fra kinesiske organisasjoner').

19 Letters/memos from the Norwegian Embassy to the Ministry on
   22 October 1955, 21 February 1956, 19 March 1956 and 22 March 1956.
20 'hadde anledning til å gi sine instruksjoner til ambassaden snarest'
   (NA, B485).
21 'Mr Sheng var klar over at Verdensfredsrådet var litt av en anstøtssten for
   vårt vedkommende, og sa leende at Fredsrådet skulle holdes i bakgrunnen'
   (NA, UD, B485).
22 'Verdensfredsrådet kom ikke inn i bildet og ble ikke nevnt i noen av de
   offisielle taler', report from the Embassy, 2 August (NA, UD, B485).
23 It was an important point for the Chinese to stress that Shaw was Irish, and
   not English – also a political aspect of the event.
24 'den store kulturpersonlighets minne ble feiret uten politisk baktanke'
   (Embassy report, 2 August 1956, NA, B485).
25 NA, B485 ('god propaganda for Norge').
26 Mao Tun, 'Opening Remarks', *Meeting in Commemoration of Great Figures
   of World Culture. George Bernard Shaw – 100th Birth Anniversary – Henrik
   Ibsen – 50th Death Anniversary* (Program) Peking: The Chinese People's
   Association for Cultural Relations with Foreign Countries, 1956, p. 7.
27 Tien Han: 'Let Us Learn from the Great Masters of Realist Drama. In
   Memory of Henrik Ibsen and George Bernard Shaw', Beijing 1956
   (translator and channel of publication unknown; Chinese original printed
   in *Peking Daily*, Beijing, 6–10 July 1956). For a more detailed analysis of
   the celebration of Shaw, and its use for propaganda purposes on this
   occasion, see Wendi Chen, *The Reception of George Bernard Shaw in China,
   1918–1996*, PhD Thesis, University of Minnesota 1999, p. 158ff.
28 Tien, 'Let Us Learn from the Great Masters of Realist Drama', pp. 11–12.
29 Wu Xue, 'Foreword to the Performance', *Ibsen's Nora. Programme Leaflet*,
   Oda Fiskum (trans.), p. 3. Conspicuously enough, Wu did not mention Hu
   Shi, who played an equally important role, not least through his essay on
   'Ibsenism'. However, Hu was never a communist, but supported the
   nationalists, and fled China for Taiwan in 1949 together with the
   Kuomintang.
30 *Ibsen's Nora. Programme Leaflet*, pp. 6–7.
31 In an article in *Beijing Daily* on Friday 27 July 1956, where he recounts
   many of his experiences from his visit to Oslo two months earlier, he
   similarly concludes by stating that Ibsen wanted *A Doll's House* not only to
   be about 'female liberation' but also to speak against 'the irrational and

reactionary legislation and morality of his contemporary society, and [...] against the philistine, self-loving and self-serving viewpoints of the petty bourgeoisie' (Wu: 'Anecdote on Ibsen', Oda Fiskum (trans.).

32 Gerda Ring, 'Speech', in *Meeting in Commemoration of Great Figures of World Culture. George Bernard Shaw – 100th Birth Anniversary – Henrik Ibsen – 50th Death Anniversary* (Program) Peking: The Chinese People's Association for Cultural Relations with Foreign Countries, 1956, p. 28.

33 The role of Nora was performed by Ji Shuping, Helmer by Yu Chun, Rank by Du Peng, Mrs Linde by Bai Ling and Krogstad by Jiang Zhulin.

34 The photo material consists of three large cases/portfolios. They were gifts from the Chinese Youth Art Theatre to Frits von der Lippe, then director at the Riksteateret in Norway. It is now at the National Library in Oslo.

35 This in clear class contrast to the maid, Anne-Marie, who is wearing a plain, grey dress with a white apron and bonnet.

36 This painting is not there in Ibsen's stage directions; it appears on stage in the first performance in Copenhagen, and lives on in the Norwegian tradition of performing the play; see Laura Caretti, 'Ibsen and Raphael' in Astrid Sæther (ed.), *Ibsen and the Arts: Painting-Sculpture-Architecture, Acta Ibseniana*, Vol. 1 (Oslo: Centre for Ibsen Studies, 2002), pp. 81–9; Frode Helland and Julie Holledge, 'A Doll's House as National Tradition: Understanding the Construction of Aesthetic Value' in Kjerstin Aukrust (ed.), *Assigning Cultural Values* (Frankfurt am Main, Peter Lang, 2013), pp. 165–90.

37 See Gerhard Knoop, 'Ibsen minnes i Peking', *Morgenbladet*, 8 August 1956, and '"Et dukkehjem" ble en stor suksess i Peking', *Morgenbladet*, 9 August 1956; and Gerda Ring: 'Dukkehjem og sommer i Kina', *Politiken*, 16 October 1956.

38 *Morgenbladet*, 9 August 1956, 'en norsk stue! [...] som helhet: redelig, ekte og fylt av 80-årenes snusbrune, hjemmekoselige atmosfære.'

39 Cf. Helland and Holledge, 'A Doll's House as National Tradition...'

40 Gerda Ring's understanding of her own role in the preparation of the performance was that she was invited to help 'create a Norwegian atmosphere', and to correct 'mistakes' and 'misunderstandings'. See her account in *Politiken*, 16 October 1956 and the interview in *Verdens Gang*, 6 August 1956 ('Et dukkehjem' ble kinesisk suksess: og Gerda Ring er hjemme igjen').

41 Mao Tse-Tung, *Selected Works* 2007, p. 158.

42 That this is not a contradiction is repeatedly stressed by Chen: 'I emphasize instead the common phenomenon of a co-existing, interrelated and, in many cases, collaborative nature of Chinese occidentalism between various discourses, or official and anti-official discourses' (Chen, *Occidentalism*, p. 6).

43 Wu Xue, 'Some thoughts while staging "Nora"' ('Nora' yen-ch'u so hsiang tao to'), *Literary Gazette* (Wen-i pao), No. 16, 1956. See also Tam, *Ibsen in China*, p. 185.

44 Ring, 'Dukkehjem og sommer i Kina'.

45 For a discussion of the model theatre of the Cultural Revolution, see Xiaomei Chen, *Acting the Right Part. Political Theatre and Popular Drama in Contemporary China* (Honolulu: University of Hawaii Press, 2002).

46 Cf. Chen, *Occidentalism*, and Elisabeth Eide, 'Performances of Ibsen in China after 1949' in Constantine Tung and Colin Mackerras (eds), *Drama in the People's Republic of China* (Albany NY: State University of New York Press, 1987), p. 313ff; and E. Eide, '*Peer Gynt* i Kina, 1983 og en gryende nyfortolkning av Ibsen', *Edda*, Vol. LXIX, No. 3 (1983), pp. 221–6.

47 For a discussion of the position of this theatre during this period see Bettina S. Entell, *Post-Tian'anmen: A New Era in Chinese Theatre. Experimentation during the 1990s at Beijing's China National Experimental Theatre/CNET* (PhD Dissertation, Honolulu: University of Hawaii) 2002.

48 The story about this performance testifies to an equally big change in *Norwegian* policy, since there is no sign of any political uncertainty and anxiousness towards the Chinese in the documents on this production. The end of the Cold War, and above all China's economic growth, had decisively changed the Norwegian perspective.

49 Hence to mount a costly production of an Ibsen play in 1996 almost necessitated sponsorship of some kind, as is explicitly claimed in the application for funding, where Agnethe Haaland and the theatre stressed that, 'The project will be a private production and therefore support will be needed.' (NORAD's archive, letters of 25 and 28 July and 3 August 1997.)

50 Entell records Wu expressing relief at no longer having 'to use hair color or big noses' on stage in productions of foreign plays (Entell, *Post-Tian'anmen*, p. 105).

51 Wu Xiaojiang, 'Universalization, Localization, and Nationalization: Directorial Approaches to Ibsen's Drama on the Chinese Stage' in Pål

Bjørby and Asbjørn Aarseth (eds), *Proceedings. IX International Ibsen Conference, Bergen 5–10 June 2000* (Øvre Erevik: Alheim & Eide Akademisk Forlag, 2001), p. 80.

52 Wu in a newspaper interview with Hans Rossiné: 'Kinesisk Folkefiende til Ibsenfestivalen', *Dagbladet*, 14 April 1996, p. 5.

53 Qiu Xiaolong, *When Red is Black* (New York: Soho Press, 2004), p. 2.

54 '*He Shang* was widely noted even in the West for its positive image of a scientific and modern West, indeed its almost embarrassingly positive evaluation of all things Western' (Chen: Occidentalism p. 24).

55 Joseph Fewsmith, *China since Tiananmen. The Politics of Transition* (Cambridge: Cambridge University Press, 2001), p. 17.

56 Timothy Cheek, *Living with Reform. China Since 1989* (London and New York: Zed Books, 2007), p. 7.

57 'Democracy was only a general term for fairness and equity, not a specific call for a multiparty electoral system', Cheek, *Living with Reform*, p. 7.

58 See Wang Hui, '1989 and Neoliberalism in China', *The End of the Revolution*, 2nd edition, London and New York: Verso, 2011, p. 27ff.

59 Cf. Wang Hui: *China's New Order. Society, Politics, and Economy in Transition* (Cambridge MA: Harvard University Press, 2003) and *The End of the Revolution*.

60 For an extremely well researched overview and analysis of these different trends, see Joseph Fewsmith, *China since Tiananmen*.

61 Cf. Fewsmith, *China since Tiananmen*, p. 159ff and Peter Hays Gries, *China's New Nationalism. Pride, Politics, and Diplomacy* (Berkeley CA: University of California Press, 2005), in particular p. 116ff.

62 See Guangqiu Xu, 'Anti-Western Nationalism in China, 1989–99', *World Affairs*, Vol. 163, No. 4 (Spring 2001), p. 151ff.

63 Cf. Peter Hays Gries, 'A "China Threat"? Power and Passion in Chinese "Face Nationalism"', *World Affairs*, Vol. 162, No. 2 (Fall 1999), p. 65; and Gries, *China's New Nationalism*, 2005, pp. 42, 114 and 147.

64 '*China Can Say No* was an unabashed outpouring of nationalist feeling' (Fewsmith, *China since Tiananmen*, p. 154) that was soon to sell almost 2 million copies. It was soon followed by the sequel *China Can Still Say No* and several publications along the same lines. See also Gries, *China's New Nationalism* and Anne-Marie Brady, *Making the Foreign Serve China*.

Managing Foreigners in the People's Republic (Oxford: Rowman & Littlefield Publishers, 2003), pp. 239–41.

65 'From the 1950s to the 1970s, the number of resident foreigners was small, only a few thousand. However, from 1979 to 1993, the Chinese government's Foreign Experts Bureau records that 350,000 "foreign experts" were invited.' Anne-Marie Brady, 'Treat Insiders and Outsiders Differently: The Use and Control of Foreigners in the PRC', *The China Quarterly*, Vol. 164 (December 2000), p. 946.

66 '[O]ne of the singular features of the Chinese economy is its huge exposure to foreign trade, which accounts for around 75 per cent of GDP, far in excess of other major economies [...] where the figure is 30 per cent or less', Martin Jacques, *When China Rules the World*, 2nd edition (London: Penguin Books, 2012), p. 182.

67 'Chinese nationalism cannot be interpreted in isolation, but must be understood in its international and historical contexts. Moreover, Chinese nationalism is not simply "party propaganda", since ordinary Chinese now play a central role in nationalist politics', Peter Hays Gries, *China's New Nationalism*, pp. 18–19.

68 Claire Conceison, 'International Casting in Chinese Plays: A Tale of Two Cities', *Theatre Journal*, Vol. 53, No. 2 (May 2001), p. 281.

69 The lines are: 'Ever since I followed the King to battles East and West, Year after year, /I have been exposed to the elements and working hard, /I only hate that the immoral Qin causes so much misery for the living beings, / The common people are troubled by constant pain and hardship' (all translations of the script are by Xia Liyang and Xin Hu).

70 Cf. Frank Dikötter, 'Racial Discourse in China: Continuities and Permutations'; and Kai-Wing Chow, 'Imagining Boundaries of Blood: Zhang Bingling and the Invention of the Han "Race" in Modern China' in Frank Dikötter (ed.), *The Construction of Racial Identities in China and Japan* (London: C. Hurst & Co., 1997).

71 Conceison, International Casting in Chinese Plays, p. 290.

72 Wu, 'A Foreign Baby-Doll's House', p. 4; unpublished manuscript (quoted from Conceison, International Casting in Chinese Plays).

73 A further paradox for this reading lies in the fact that the production was funded by Norwegian authorities, and that Wu, then, had obtained foreign funding for a performance designed to discuss or display the problematic

nature of increased influence of foreigners on and in China, venting nationalism through foreign sponsorship.

74 Bettina S. Entell, *Post-Tian'anmen: A New Era in Chinese Theatre*, p. 98.

75 See Jacques, *When China Rules . . .*, p. 609ff; or Brady, *Making the Foreign Serve . . .*, p. 228ff.

76 Rosella Ferrari, *Pop Goes the Avant-Garde. Experimental Theatre in Contemporary China* (London: Seagull Books, 2012), p. 23.

77 Didi Kirsten Tatlow, 'China Opens the Stage Curtains', *New York Times*, 14 December 2011.

78 *Henrik Ibsen – En dannelsesreise i Telemark*, Program booklet, p. 29.

79 'Ibsen2006' was an organisation set-up to co-ordinate and administer the celebration of the Ibsen centenary in 2006, with quite extensive public and private funds at its disposal. For a further discussion of Ibsen 2006, see Chapter 5.

80 Teater Ibsen, 'Forestillinger og publikumsbesøk 2006'.

81 Report to the MFA from Inger Buresund, 16 January 2006.

82 Project description by Un-Magritt Nordseth.

83 The same report from 16 January 2006.

84 Teater Ibsen, 'Forestillinger og publikumsbesøk 2006'.

85 The records seem to indicate that the tickets were not sold; cf. Teater Ibsen, 'Forestillinger og publikumsbesøk 2006'.

86 At the time this meant being in charge of the administration of the International Ibsen Award, the world's biggest award for contemporary theatre artists, and the Ibsen Scholarships given to artistic projects related to Ibsen around the world (see http://www.ibsenawards.com).

87 Sources: Application from Ibsen International by Inger Buresund to the Norwegian Embassy in Beijing, 11 February 2010. Further comments to the application from Ibsen International to the Embassy 16 February 2010, Economic report (Resultatrapport) from accountant Sand Økonomi A/S, 'Report Ibsen in China 2010' from Ibsen International, 4 January 2011.

88 Rustom Bharucha, *Consumed in Singapore. The Intercultural Spectacle of Lear* (Centre for Advanced Studies, National University of Singapore 2000), p. 21.

89 See Jin Xing's *Shanghai Tango: A Memoir* (with Catherine Texier) (London: Atlantic Books, 2007); Erich Follath, 'Ballet, a Sex Change and a Small Revolution: The Odyssey of Jin Xing', *Spiegel Online International*, No. 12

(2006); and Tania Branigan, 'Jin Xing: From Chinese Army Officer to Dancing TV Stardom', *Guardian*, 10 September 2012.

90 Spivak's phrase is: 'White men saving brown women from brown men', Spivak, 'Can the Subaltern Speak?', p. 296.

91 One could say that these difficulties are to a large extent created by the transposition to another genre. The use of techniques from classical ballet, where the male dancers function almost as pure props, there only to lift and hence make the female bodies appear ethereal and weightless, take on other meanings in this production, meanings that tend to work against the proposed message of the performance.

92 The same effect is repeated during the masquerade party, which we see through transparent panes lowered on stage, like a veil, behind which we can see the five Noras dancing a more Chinese-inspired dance (but not from Chinese opera strictly speaking) – pure elegance, in white dresses, visual lure without any sign of desperation or suffering, in other words: commercial spectacle.

93 Bharucha, *The Politics of . . .*, p. 155.

94 Ibsen International: Application to the Norwegian Embassy, 11 February 2010, p. 5.

Chapter 5

1 Immanuel Wallerstein, *European Universalism: the Rhetoric of Power* (New York: New York Press, 2006), Chapter 2.

2 In spite of their differences in policy details and funding, this is the case with prominent institutions such as the British Council, the Alliance Française, the Goethe Institut, or the Chinese Confucius Institutes around the world. They contribute to local culture in many different countries, but are set up to promote the culture and interests (often under the presupposition that this is the same thing) of the donor country.

3 Cf. Frode Helland, 'In – and Out of Place: Three Versions of Ibsen's *The Master Builder*' in Nissar Allana (ed.), *Redefining Inter-Culturalism: A Contemporary Perspective. Delhi Ibsen Festival 2009* (Delhi: The Dramatic Art & Design Academy, 2010).

4 Régis Debray, *Transmitting Culture*, Eric Rauth (trans.) (New York: Columbia University Press, 2000), pp. 10–13.

5 The figures for the different anniversaries are as follows. For 1928 we have registered data on 172 productions, in contrast to the mere 55 in 1925, and the even lower 32 in 1930; in 1956 we have registered 84 productions, but only 39 in 1953, and 50 in 1960; in 1978 there are 94 productions; three years earlier, in 1975, there were 78, and for 1981 we have data on 74 productions; in 2006 the numbers go up to 325, whereas 2003 had 153 productions, and in 2009 it had sunk to 187.

6 The official report from Ibsen 2006 can be downloaded at http://ibsen. nb.no/id/11110863.0. For a thorough and critical review of the Ibsen Year, see Tore Rem, 'Ute av kontroll. Ibsen-året i skyggen av pyramidene', *Samtiden*, No. 1, 2007.

7 Henrik Ibsen, *Peer Gynt. A Dramatic Poem*, John Northam (trans.) (New York: Oxford University Press, 1993), p. 112.

8 Large sections of the following have previously been published in my article 'Empire and Culture in Ibsen. Some notes on the Dangers and Ambiguities of Interculturism', *Ibsen Studies*, Routledge, Taylor & Francis, vol. IX(2).

9 Elisabeth Oxfeldt, *Nordic Orientalism. Paris and the Cosmopolitan Imagination 1800–1900* (Copenhagen: Museum Tusculanum Press, 2005).

10 Cf. Edward Said, *Orientalism. Western Conceptions of the Orient*, reprinted with a new afterword (London and New York: Penguin Books, 1978), p. 38ff.

11 In the draft of this text, however, there was at first no mention of Kaba, but instead of the 'tomb in Medina'. Mohammed was as we know buried in Medina, and the claim that the 'tomb in Medina is empty' is an unequivocal assertion that Peer is Mohammed (or that Anitra thinks so). It is possible, in other words, that Ibsen altered the text at this point to tone down its blasphemic or anti-Islamic impact. Another possible interpretation of this alteration is that it simply shows how Ibsen completely neglected the culturally specific elements to do with religion, and changed them about to suit his own tastes: that the repeated 'Kaba, Kaba' was chosen merely because it sounded oriental and 'Muslim'.

12 For a further discussion of Oxfeldt's work in relation to these questions, see Gisle Selnes, 'Ibsens orientalisme. En hegeliansk historie', *Agora*, Vol. XXV, No. 4 (2007), pp. 5–30; Kari Jegerstedt, 'Anitras etterliv. 'Ibsens kvinner' i en postkolonial kontekst', *Agora*, Vol. XXV, No. 4 (2007), pp. 55–74; and Frode

Helland, 'Empire and Culture in Ibsen. Some Notes on the Dangers and Ambiguities of Interculturalism', *Ibsen Studies*, Vol. IX (2009).

13 Jens Daniel Carolus Lieblein: 'Til Suez' in *Morgenbladet*, 21 October 1869.

14 Henrik Ibsen, *Samlede verker. Hundreårsutgave*, Vol. XV (Oslo: Gyldendal, 1930), pp. 341 and 344–5.

15 Robert McLaren, *Ibsen Comes to Zimbabwe. On the occasion of the 100th Anniversary of Henrik Ibsen's death*, Unpublished report, Harare 2007, p. 2.

16 I have only seen the television version of 'A Journey to Yourself', and my discussion of this production will therefore be more cursory.

17 See http://www.chipawozim.org [accessed May 2013].

18 The Norwegian Embassy in Harare sponsored the production with 200,000 NOK.

19 The production was given 8 million in direct Government funds, and approximately 4 million in private sponsorship. In addition, the Egyptian government sponsored the production with 1 million NOK.

20 The comment from the Egyptian theatre critic Nehad Selaiha tells the story well: 'Given the deplorable quality of the English rendering of the dialogue, flashed on a small screen up front, at floor level, for the benefit of the privileged few in the front seats [...] Since most of the Egyptian audience could not understand Norwegian and were denied access to the wishy-washy translation, one could not help wondering, in view of the fact that nearly half of the bulk of the audience were Norwegians, "for whom the bells were ringing"', *Al-Ahram Weekly* On-line, 1–7 November 2006.

21 Baardson in conversation with Arnhild Skre in *Aftenposten*, 24 September 2006.

22 Ellen Rees, *Ibsen's* Peer Gynt *and the Production of Meaning* (Oslo: Akademika, 2014), *Acta Ibseniana*, Vol. XI, p. 123.

23 This scene opened with the lines from the beginning of the Anitra scene, with the modification that the 'Chorus of Girls' does not sing 'The Prophet has come', but 'Sir Peter has come.'

24 Rustom Bharucha, 'Gundegowda meets Peer Gynt. Intracultural negotiations in theatre' in *The Politics of Cultural Practice. Thinking Through Theatre in an Age of Globalization* (Hanover NH: University Press of New England, 2000) (an earlier slightly different version published in *New Theatre Quarterly*, Vol. XII, No. 46, May 1996, under the title 'Under the Sign of the Onion: Intracultural Negotiations in Theatre').

Coda

1 For a study of the national tradition of performing *A Doll's House*, and the possible influence from the Ibsen festival, see Helland and Holledge, '*A Doll's House as National Tradition . . .*'. See also Keld Hyldig, 'Twenty Years with the International Ibsen Festival', *Ibsen Studies*, Vol. XI, No. 1 (2011).

2 During its twenty-four years of existence, the festival has undergone many shifts and changes, and it has never had a consistent, long-term policy, and it would digress too far to go into the history of these differences. The lack of reliable external funding has also resulted in it shifting in size and proportion of international participation.

3 Most notable among these were the stunning adaptation of *When We Dead Awaken* called 'Ashibagee Esbei' directed by the Manipuri director Rathan Thiyam; Anwer Jafri and Tehrik-E-Niwan's adaptation of *A Doll's House*, from Pakistan, called 'Gurrya Ka Ghar'; and Nader Borhani Marand's version of *The Wild Duck* (discussed in Chapter 3).

4 This production is discussed in more detail in Kamaluddin Nilu's article: 'Democratisation Process in Interculturalism: Staging Ibsen within a Folk Theatrical Form in Bangladesh', *Ibsen Studies*, Vol. XIV, No. 1 (2014), pp. 38–51.

5 Bourdieu, *The Rules of Art*, p. 159ff.

6 For an account of the early years of the company, see Iris Smith Fischer, *Mabou Mines. Making Avant-Garde Theatre in the 1970s* (Ann Arbor MI: University of Michigan Press, 2012).

7 http://www.maboumines.org/productions/mabou-mines-dollhouse

8 Cf. Jacqueline Taucar, 'Playing (with) Gestic Dolls in *Mabou Mines DollHouse*', *Canadian Review of Comparative Literature*, Vol. 38, No. 2 (June 2011), pp. 268–82.

9 Quoted from Amy S. Green, 'Nora's Journey Through a Century of Feminisms to the Postmodern Stage of *Mabou Mines Doll House*' in Sharon Friedman (ed.), *Feminist Theatrical Revisions of Classic Works. Critical Essays* (Jefferson NC: Mcfarland & Company Publishers, 2009), p. 262.

Bibliography

Ahmed, L (1992) *Women and Gender in Islam: Historical Roots of a Modern Debate*, New Haven CT and London: Yale University Press

Bharucha, R (1996) 'Under the Sign of the Onion: Intracultural Negotiations in Theatre', *New Theatre Quarterly*, Vol. XII, No. 46, May 1996

Bharucha, R (2000a) 'Gundegowda meets Peer Gynt. Intracultural negotiations in theatre' in *The Politics of Cultural Practice: Thinking through Theatre in an Age of Globalization*, Hanover NH: University Press of New England

Bharucha, R (2000b) *Consumed in Singapore. The Intercultural Spectacle of Lear*. Singapore: Centre for Advanced Studies, National University of Singapore

Bourdieu, P (1996) *The Rules of Art. Genesis and Structure of the Literary Field*, Susan Emanuel (trans.), Cambridge: Polity Press

Boyle, C M (2000) 'Violence in Memory: Translation, Dramatization and Performance of the Past in Chile' in A B Jones and R Munck (eds), *Cultural Politics in Latin America*, London: Palgrave Macmillan

Boyle, C M (1992) *Chilean Theater, 1973–1985: Marginality, Power, Selfhood*, London and Toronto: Fairleigh Dickinson University Press

Brady, A M (2003) *Making the Foreign Serve China. Managing Foreigners in the People's Republic*, Oxford: Rowman & Littlefield Publishers

Brady, A M (2000) 'Treat Insiders and Outsiders Differently: The Use and Control of Foreigners in the PRC', *The China Quarterly*, Vol. 164

Branigan, T (2012) 'Jin Xing: From Chinese Army Officer to Dancing TV Stardom', *Guardian*, 10 September

Brooks, D (2000) *Bobos in Paradise: The New Upper Class and How They Got There*, New York: Simon and Schuster

Brooks, P (1985) *Reading for the Plot: Design and Intention in Narrative*, New York: Random House

Brynhildsvoll, K and Kittang, A (2004) 'Preface', *Ibsen Studies*, Vol. IV, No. 2

Caretti, L (2002) 'Ibsen and Raphael' in Astrid Sæther (ed.), *Ibsen and the Arts: Painting-Sculpture-Architecture, Acta Ibseniana*, Vol. 1, Oslo: Centre for Ibsen Studies

Carlson M (2012) 'Ibsen in the Americas', *Ibsen News and Comment: The Journal of The Ibsen Society of America*, Vol. 32

Carvajal, F and van Diest, C (2009) 'Teatro la Maria: Filiaciones inciertas y orquestaciones de la violencia' in F Carvajal and C van Diest, *Nomadismos y Ensamblajes: Compañías teatrales en Chile 1990–2008*, Santiago: Editorial Cuarto Propio

Cheek, T (2006) *Living with Reform. China Since 1989*, London and New York: Zed Books

Chen, W (1999) *The Reception of George Bernhard Shaw in China, 1918–1996*, PhD Thesis, University of Minnesota

Chen, X (2002a) *Acting the Right Part. Political Theatre and Popular Drama in Contemporary China*, Honolulu: University of Hawaii Press

Chen, X (2002b) *Occidentalism. A Theory of Counter-Discourse in Post-Mao China*, London: Rowman & Littlefield Publishers

Chow, K W (1997) 'Imagining Boundaries of Blood: Zhang Bingling and the Invention of the Han "Race" in Modern China' in F Dikötter (ed.), *The Construction of Racial Identities in China and Japan*, London: C. Hurst & Co

Chuchryk, P M (1994) 'From Dictatorship to Democracy: The Women's Movement in Chile' in Jane S Jaquette (ed.), *The Women's Movement in Latin America. Participation and Democracy*, Boulder CO: Westview Press

Coetzee, J M (1996) *Giving Offense: Essays on Censorship*, Chicago IL: Chicago University Press

Conceison, C (2001) 'International Casting in Chinese Plays: A Tale of Two Cities', *Theatre Journal*, Vol. 53, No. 2

Constable, P and Valenzuela, A (1991) *A Nation of Enemies*, New York, London: W.W. Norton & Company

Cortés, E and Barrea-Marlys, M (2003) *Encyclopedia of Latin American Theater*, Westport CN: Greenwood Press.

Cozzi, E (1990) 'Political Theatre in Present-day Chile: a Duality of Approaches', *New Theatre Quarterly*, Vol. VI, No. 119

Crouch, C (2004) *Post-Democracy*, Cambridge: Polity Press

Dabashi, H (2001) *Close Up. Iranian Cinema, Past, Present and Future*, London: Verso

Davis, M (2001) *Late Victorian Holocausts*, London: Verso

Debray, R (2000) *Transmitting Culture*, Eric Rauth (trans.), New York: Columbia University Press

de Jongh, N (2000) *Politics, Prudery and Perversions: The Censoring of the British Stage 1901–1968*, London: Methuen

Derrida, J (1976) *Of Grammatology*, G. C. Spivak (trans.), Baltimore MD: Johns Hopkins University Press

Dikötter, F (1997) 'Racial Discourse in China: Continuities and Permutations' in F Dikötter (ed.), *The Construction of Racial Identities in China and Japan*, London: C. Hurst & Co

Dikötter, F (ed.) (1997) *The Construction of Racial Identities in China and Japan*, London: C. Hurst & Co

Dönmez-Colin, G (2004) *Women, Islam and Cinema*, London: Reaktion Books

Dürrschmidt, A (ed.) (2006) *Dem Einzelnen ein Ganzes/A Whole for the Parts, Jan Pappelbaum Bühnen/Stages*, Berlin: Theater der Zeit

Ebrey, P B (2007) *The Cambridge Illustrated History of China*, 9th edition, Cambridge: Cambridge University Press

Eide, E (1973) *Hu Shih and Ibsen. Ibsen's Influence in China 1917–1921 as Seen through the Eyes of a Prominent Chinese Intellectual* (dissertation), Oslo: University of Oslo

Eide, E (1987) *China's Ibsen: From Ibsen to Ibsenism*, Scandinavian Institute of Asian Studies Monograph Series, No. 55, London: Curzon Press

Eide, E (1983) '*Peer Gynt* i Kina, 1983 og en gryende nyfortolkning av Ibsen', *Edda*, Vol. LXIX, No. 3.

Eide, E (1987) 'Performances of Ibsen in China after 1949' in C Tung and C Mackerras (eds), *Drama in the People's Republic of China*, Albany NY: State University of New York Press

Englert, U (2001) *Magus und Rechenmeister: Henrik Ibsens Werk auf den Bühnen des Dritten Reiches*, Tübingen: Francke Verlag

Entell, B S (2002) *Post-Tiananmen: A New Era in Chinese Theatre. Experimentation during the 1990s at Beijing's China National Experimental Theatre/CNET* (PhD dissertation), Honolulu: University of Hawaii

Eriksen, K E and Pharo, H Ø (1997) *Norsk utenrikspolitikks historie*, Vol. 5: *Kald krig og internasjonalisering 1949–1965*, Oslo: Universitetsforlaget

Fabian, J (1983) *Time and the Other. How Anthropology Makes its Object*, New York: Columbia University Press

Farago, J (2013) 'The Debate over Snowden's Asylum in Germany comes to Brooklyn', *New Republic*, 18 November

Ferrari, R (2012) *Pop Goes the Avant-Garde. Experimental Theatre in Contemporary China*, London: Seagull Books

Fewsmith, J (2001) *China since Tiananmen, The Politics of Transition*, Cambridge: Cambridge University Press

Fischer, I S (2012) *Mabou Mines. Making Avant-Garde Theatre in the 1970s*, Ann Arbor MI: University of Michigan Press

Fletcher, A (1993) *Allegory: The Theory of a Symbolic Mode*, Ithaca NY and
    London: Cornell University Press

Floor, W (2005) *The History of Theater in Iran*, Washington DC: Mage Publishers

Follath, E (2006) 'Ballet, a Sex Change and a Small Revolution: The Odyssey of
    Jin Xing', *Spiegel Online International*, No. 12

Foucault, M (1987) *Discipline and Punish*, Alan Sheridan (trans.), London:
    Penguin Books

Frank, A G (1976) *Economic Genocide in Chile: Monetarist Theory versus
    Humanity*, Nottingham UK: Spokesman Books

*George Bernard Shaw – 100th Birth Anniversary – Henrik Ibsen – 50th Death
    Anniversary* (Program) (1956), The Chinese People's Association for
    Cultural Relations with Foreign Countries, Peking

Green, A S (2009) 'Nora's Journey through a Century of Feminisms to the
    Postmodern Stage of *Mabou Mines Doll House*' in Sharon Friedman (ed.),
    Feminist Theatrical Revisions of Classic Works. Critical Essays, Jefferson NC:
    McFarland & Company Publishers

Green, D (2003) *Silent Revolution: The Rise and Crisis of Market Economics in
    Latin America*, New York: Monthly Review Press

Gries, P H (1999) 'A "China Threat"? Power and Passion in Chinese "Face
    Nationalism"', *World Affairs*, Vol. 162, No. 2

Gries, P H (2005) *China's New Nationalism. Pride, Politics, and Diplomacy*,
    Berkeley CA: University of California Press

Guardiola-Rivera, O (2013) *Story of a Death Foretold. The Coup against
    Salvador Allende, 11 September 1973*, London: Bloomsbury

Harvey D (2003) *The New Imperialism*, Oxford, New York: Oxford University Press

He, C (2002) *Henrik Ibsen and Chinese Modern Drama*, University of Oslo,
    Acta Humaniora

Helland, F (2009) 'Empire and Culture in Ibsen. Some Notes on the Dangers
    and Ambiguities of Interculturalism', *Ibsen Studies*, Vol. IX, No. 2

Helland, F (2010) 'In – and Out of Place: Three Versions of Ibsen's *The Master
    Builder*' in N Allana (ed.), *Redefining Inter-Culturalism: A Contemporary
    Perspective, Delhi Ibsen Festival 2009*, Delhi: The Dramatic Art & Design
    Academy

Helland, F and Holledge, J (2013) 'A *Doll's House* as National Tradition:
    Understanding the Construction of Aesthetic Value' in K Aukrust (ed.),
    Assigning Cultural Values, Frankfurt am Main: Peter Lang

Holledge, J and Tompkins, J (2000) *Women's Intercultural Performance*.
    London: Routledge

Holledge, J (2008) 'The Global Phenomenon of *A Doll's House*', *Ibsen Studies*, Vol. VIII, No. 1

Huddle, D L (1997) 'Effects of Neoliberalism on Latin American Development and Poverty: Two Conflicting Views', *Economic Development and Cultural Change*, Vol. 45, No. 4

Hughes, D A (2007) 'Notes on the German Theatre Crisis', *The Drama Review*, Vol. 51, No. 4

Hyldig, K (2011) 'Twenty Years with the International Ibsen Festival', *Ibsen Studies*, Vol. XI, No. 1

Ibsen, H (1993) *Peer Gynt. A Dramatic Poem*, John Northam (trans.), New York: Oxford University Press

Ibsen, H (1972) *The Oxford Ibsen: Brand* and *Peer Gynt*, Vol. III, James Walter McFarlane (ed. and trans.), London: Oxford University Press

Ibsen, H (1961) *The Oxford Ibsen: Pillars of Society, A Doll's House*, Vol. V, James Walter McFarlane (ed. and trans.), London: Oxford University Press

Ibsen, H (1960) *The Oxford Ibsen: An Enemy of the People, The Wild Duck, Rosmersholm*, Vol. VI, James Walter McFarlane (ed. and trans.), London: Oxford University Press

Ibsen, H (1966) *The Oxford Ibsen: The Lady From the Sea, Hedda Gabler, The Master Builder*, Vol. VII, James Walter McFarlane (ed. and trans.), London: Oxford University Press

Ibsen, H (1930) *Samlede verker. Hundreårsutgave*, Vol. XV, Oslo: Gyldendal

Ibsen 2006 The official report from: http://ibsen.nb.no/id/11110863.0 [accessed May 2014]

Invisible Committee, The (2009) *The Coming Insurrection*, Cambridge MA: Semiotext(e), MIT Press

Isherwood, C (2013) 'An Ibsen who Rages over Ritalin and Economic Austerity Plans', *New York Times*, 7 November

Jacques, M (2012) *When China Rules the World*, 2nd edition, London: Penguin Books

Jansen, S C (1991) *Censorship: The Knot That Binds Power and Knowledge*, London: Oxford University Press

Jegerstedt, K (2007) 'Anitras etterliv. "Ibsens kvinner" i en postkolonial kontekst', *Agora*, Vol. XXV, No. 4

Jin, X (2007) *Shanghai Tango: A Memoir* (with Catherine Texier), London: Atlantic Books

Karimi-Hakak, M (2003) 'Exiled to Freedom: A Memoir of Censorship in Iran', *The Drama Review*, Vol. 47, No. 4

Keddie, N R (2006) *Modern Iran: Roots and Results of Revolution*, New Haven CT: Yale University Press

Kirkwood, J (1983) 'Women and Politics in Chile', *International Social Science Journal*, Vol. 35

Klein, N (2007) *The Shock Doctrine: The Rise of Disaster Capitalism*, London: Penguin

Knoop, G (1956) 'Ibsen minnes i Peking', *Morgenbladet*, 8 August

Knoop, G (1980) ' "Et dukkehjem'" ble en stor suksess i Peking', *Morgenbladet*, 9 August

Knutsen, T L, Sørbø, G M and Gjerdåker, S (eds) (1995) *Norges Utenrikspolitikk*, Oslo: Cappelen

Kornbluh, P (2003) *The Pinochet File. A Declassified Dossier on Atrocity and Accountability*, New York: The New Press

Lahiji, S (2002) 'Chaste Dolls: Women in Iranian Cinema since 1979' in R Tapper (ed.), *The New Iranian Cinema: Politics, Representation and Identity*, New York, London: I.B. Tauris

Lieblein, J D C (1869) 'Til Suez', in *Morgenbladet*, 21 October

Lin, W-Y (2010) 'Master in Reflection: An Analysis of Lin Zhaoahua's The Master Builder' in K-K Tam, T S-H Yip and F Helland (eds), *Ibsen and the Modern Self*, Hong Kong: Open University of Hong Kong Press

Mair, P (2013) *Ruling the Void. The Hollowing of Western Democracy*, London: Verso

Mao Tse-Tung (1967) 'On the Correct Handling of Contradictions among the People', in *Selected Works of Mao Tse-Tung*, Vol. 5, Peking: Foreign Languages Press

Mao Tse-Tung (2007) *On Practice and Contradiction*, intro. S. Zizek, London: Verso

Mao Tun (Dun) (1956) 'Opening Remarks', *Meeting in Commemoration of Great Figures of World Culture* (unpublished)

Marand, B N *My Wild Duck*, F. Ghasempour (trans.) (unpublished manuscript)

McDonald, P D (2009) *The Literature Police: Apartheid Censorship and its Cultural Consequences*, Oxford: Oxford University Press

McLaren, R (2007) *Ibsen Comes to Zimbabwe. On the occasion of the 100th Anniversary of Henrik Ibsen's death* (unpublished report), Harare

Miller, A 1979 [1950] *An Enemy of the People: An Adaptation of the Play by Henrik Ibsen*, New York: Penguin Books

Mirbakhtyar, S (2006) *Iranian Cinema and the Islamic Revolution*, Jefferson NC and London: McFarlane and Company Publishers

Mir-Hosseini, Z (1999) *Islam and Gender: The Religious Debate in Contemporary Iran*, Princeton NJ: Princeton University Press

Moretti, F (2013) *The Bourgeois. Between History and Literature*, London: Verso

Morris, B S (1956) 'Communist Front Organizations: Their Nature and Function', *World Politics*, Vol. 9, No. 1

Mostagim, R and Sandels, A (2011) 'IRAN: Police descend on Tehran theater, suspend classic play "Hedda Gabler"', *Los Angeles Times*, 15 January

Naficy, H (2002) 'Islamizing Film Culture in Iran: A Post-Khatami Update' in R Tapper (ed.), *The New Iranian Cinema: Politics, Representation and Identity*, New York and London: I.B. Tauris

Naghibi, N (2007) *Rethinking Global Sisterhood: Western Feminism and Iran*, Minneapolis MN: University of Minnesota Press

Nichols, J and McChesney, R W (2013) *Dollarocracy. How the Money and Media Election Complex is Destroying America*, New York: Nation Books

Nilu, K (2014) 'Democratisation Process in Interculturalism: Staging Ibsen within a Folk Theatrical Form in Bangladesh', *Ibsen Studies*, Vol. XIV, No. 1

Ostermeier, T (1999) 'Ob es so oder so oder anders geht! Ein Gespräch mit den (zukünftigen) Theaterleitern Stefan Bachmann, Mathias Hartmann und Thomas Ostermeier', *Theaterheute: Jahrbuch 1999*, Hannover: Friedrich Verlag

Ostermeier, T (2010) 'Reading and Staging Ibsen', *Ibsen Studies*, Vol. X, No. 2

Ostermeier, T (2013) 'Die Zukunft des Theaters', in *TEXT + KRITIK. Zeitschrift für Literatur. Sonderband*. Munich: Richard Boorberg Verlag

Ostermeier, T, Waltz, S, Sandig, J and Hilje, J, 'Der Auftrag', http://www.schaubuehne.de/uploads/Der-Auftrag.pdf [accessed May 2014].

Oxfeldt, E (2005) *Nordic Orientalism. Paris and the Cosmopolitan Imagination 1800–1900*, Copenhagen: Museum Tusculanum Press

Oxfam, 'A Cautionary Tale. The true cost of austerity and inequality in Europe', http://www.oxfam.org/sites/www.oxfam.org/files/bp174-cautionary-tale-austerity-inequality-europe-120913-en_1.pdf [accessed September 2013].

Petley, J (2009) *Censorship: A Beginner's Guide*, Oxford: Oneworld Publications

Qiu, X (2004) *When Red is Black*, New York: Soho Press

Raab, M (2006) 'In Jedem steckt ein Volksfeind' in F N Mennemeier and B Reitz (eds), *Amüsement und Schrecken*, Tübingen: Francke Verlag

Rees, E (2014) *Ibsen's* Peer Gynt *and the Production of Meaning*, Oslo: Akademika, *Acta Ibseniana*, Vol. XI

Rem, T (2007) 'Ute av kontroll. Ibsen-året i skyggen av pyramidene', *Samtiden*, No. 1

Richard, N (2004) *Cultural Residues: Chile in Transition*, A West-Durán and T Quester (trans.), Minneapolis MN: University of Minnesota Press

Richard, N (2004) *Masculine/Feminine: Practices of Difference(s)*, A A Nelson and S R Tandeciarz (trans.), Durham NC and London: Duke University Press

Richard, N (2004) *The Insubordination of Signs. Political Change, Cultural Transformation, and Poetics of the Crisis*, A A Nelson and S R Tandeciarz (trans.), Durham NC and London: Duke University Press

Ring, G (1956) 'Speech', *Meeting in Commemoration of Great Figures of World Culture. George Bernard Shaw – 100th Birth Anniversary – Henrik Ibsen – 50th Death Anniversary* (Program), The Chinese People's Association for Cultural Relations with Foreign Countries, Peking

Ring, G (1956) 'Dukkehjem og sommer i Kina', *Politiken*, 16 October

Ring, G (1980) ' "Et Dukkehjem" i Peking', *Kunst og Kultur*, Vol. 63, No. 4

Rojo, G (1989) 'Chilean Theatre from 1957 to 1987', *Theatre Journal*, Vol. 41

Rossiné, H (1996) 'Kinesisk Folkefiende til Ibsenfestivalen', *Dagbladet*, 14 April

Sadr, H R (2006) *Iranian Cinema: A Political History*, London and New York: I. B. Tauris

Sage, S F (2006) *Ibsen and Hitler*, New York: Avalon

Said, E (1978) *Orientalism. Western Conceptions of the Orient*, reprinted with a new afterword, London and New York: Penguin Books

Said, E (1994) *Culture and Imperialism*, London: Vintage Books

Schulze, I, 'Sich selbst wieder Ernst nehmen', *Süddeutsche Zeitung*, 12 January 2012 http://ingoschulze.com/text_Sichselbstwieder.html [accessed February 2013].

Selaiha, N (2006) *Al-Ahram Weekly On-line*, 1–7 November

Selnes, G (2007) 'Ibsens orientalisme. En hegeliansk historie', *Agora*, Vol. XXV, No. 4

Shellard, D, Nicholson, S and Handley, M (2004) *The Lord Chamberlain Regrets . . . A History of British Theatre Censorship*, London: The British Library

Skre, A (2006) 'Høyt spill ved Sfinxen', in *Aftenposten*, 24 September

Spencer, C, 'Hedda Gabler: Shocking then, shocking now', *Telegraph*, 29 February 2008: http://www.telegraph.co.uk/culture/theatre/drama/3671492/Hedda-Gabler-Shocking-then-shocking-now.html [accessed 24 January 2014]

Spivak, G C (1988) 'Can the Subaltern Speak?' in C Nelson and L Grossberg (eds), *Marxism and Culture*, Urbana, Chicago IL: University of Illinois Press

Streeck, W (2001) 'The Crises of Democratic Capitalism', *New Left Review*, No. 71, September–October

Svich, C (ed.) (2012) *Out of Silence: Censorship in Theatre and Performance*, Roskilde: Eyecorner Press

Tam, K-K (1984) *Ibsen in China: Reception and Influence*, PhD thesis, Urbana IL, University of Illinois

Tam, K K, Yip, T S and Helland, F (eds) (2010) *Ibsen and the Modern Self*, Hong Kong: Open University of Hong Kong Press

Tatlow, D K (2011) 'China Opens the Stage Curtains', *New York Times*, 14 December

Tapper, R (ed.) (2002) *The New Iranian Cinema: Politics, Representation and Identity*, New York, London: I.B. Tauris

Taucar, J (2011) 'Playing (with) Gestic Dolls in *Mabou Mines Doll House*', *Canadian Review of Comparative Literature*, Vol. 38, No. 2 (June)

Tien Han (1956) 'Let Us Learn from the Great Masters of Realist Drama. In Memory of Henrik Ibsen and George Bernard Shaw' (translator and channel of publication unknown); Chinese original printed in *Peking Daily*, Beijing, 6–10 July

Toledo, A C (2001) *Partizipation von Frauen während der Militärdiktatur in Chile (1973–1990)*, Spektrum Politikwissenschaft, Würtzburg: Ergon Verlag

Trivedi, P and Ryuta, M (eds) (2010) *Re-playing Shakespeare in Asia*, New York: Routledge

Tung, C and Mackerras, C (eds) (1987) *Drama in the People's Republic of China*, Albany NY: State University of New York Press

'Unveiled: Art and Censorship in Iran', *Article XIX: Global Campaign for Freedom of Expression*, London: Media Diversity Institute, September 2006, http://www.article19.org/data/files/pdfs/publications/iran-art-censorship.pdf [accessed September 2014].

United States Senate Report (1975) *Covert Action in Chile 1963–1973*, Washington DC: US Government Printing Office, 18 December

Unknown (2011) 'Iranian "Hedda Gabler" deemed "vulgar, hedonistic"', *Daily Star*, Lebanon, 14 January

von Hummel, A *Persiguendo a Nora Helmer. Adaptation of 'A Doll's House'* (unpublished script).

Wallerstein, I (2006) *European Universalism: the Rhetoric of Power*, New York: New York Press

Wang, H (2003) *China's New Order. Society, Politics, and Economy in Transition*, Cambridge MA: Harvard University Press

Wang, H (2007) *The End of the Revolution: China and the Limits of Modernity*, London: Verso

Wang, H (2011) '1989 and Neoliberalism in China', *The End of the Revolution*, 2nd edition, London and New York: Verso

Watson, I and Epstein, S (1995) 'Theatre after the Dictatorships: Developments in Chile and Argentina', *New Theatre Quarterly*, Vol. XI

Wilkinson, R G and Pickett, K (2009) *The Spirit Level: Why more Equal Societies almost always do Better*. London: Allen Lane

Wright, R (2006) 'Ibsen Transcreations in Iran and India', *TijdSchrift voor Skandinavistiek*, Vol. 27, No. 2

Wu, Xue (1956) 'Some thoughts while staging "Nora" (Nora' yen-ch'u so hsiang tao to)', *Literary Gazette* (Wen-i pao), No. 16

Wu, Xiaojiang (2001) 'Universalization, Localization, and Nationalization: Directorial Approaches to Ibsen's Drama on the Chinese Stage' in Pål Bjørby and Asbjørn Aarseth (eds), *Proceedings. IX International Ibsen Conference, Bergen, 5–10 June 2000*, Øvre Erevik: Alheim & Eide Akademisk Forlag

Xu, G (2001) 'Anti-Western Nationalism in China, 1989–99', *World Affairs*, Vol. 163, No. 4

Zahedi, F (2006) *Henrik Ibsen and Iranian Modern Drama. Reception and Influence*, University of Oslo: Unpublished Phd. thesis

Zizek, S (2010) *Living in the End Times*, London: Verso

Other websites referred to:

http://danielfreitag.com/track/ein-volksfeind-thomas-ostermeier

http://ibsen.nb.no/id/11110863.0

https://ibsenstage.hf.uio.no

http://www.chipawozim.org

http://www.ibsenawards.com

http://www.maboumines.org/productions/mabou-mines-dollhouse

Index